American
Headway

3

THE WORLD'S MOST TRUSTED ENGLISH COURSE

SECOND EDITION

Liz and John Soars

OXFORD

UNIVERSITY PRESS

Scope and Sequence

SKILLS DEVELOPMENT

READING	LISTENING	SPEAKING	WRITING
Worlds apart *Welcome to our world* The lives of two families from different parts of the world (jigsaw) p. 6	**A world in one family** Ana from Spain and her son, Xavier, talk about living in the U.S. p. 8	**A class survey** Lifestyles p. 5 **Exchanging information** Comparing two families from different parts of the world p. 6 **What do you think?** Discussing the pros and cons of bringing up a family in another country p. 8 **Role play** Acting out everyday situations p. 9	**An informal letter** Correcting mistakes (1) Finding and correcting mistakes in a sample letter *I do mistakes WW* **Writing a letter to a friend, correcting each others' letters** p. 99
Charles, Prince of Wales *The life of a hardworking future king* – the private and public man p. 14	**Who earns how much?** How much do different jobs pay? p. 13 **Spoken English – giving opinions** *I guess … I'd say …* *I think so, too. Actually …* p. 13	**Talking about you** How often do you do things? p. 11 **Project** Interviewing someone about his/her job p. 12 **Discussion** Which job deserves most money? p. 13 The role of monarchy p. 15 **Exchanging information** Talking about your free time activities p. 16	**Letters and e-mails** Differences in formal and informal writing Beginnings and endings of letters and e-mails *I am writing in response …* *Give my regards to Robert.* **E-mailing an old friend with news** p. 100
A Shakespearean Tragedy *Romeo and Juliet* The love story in cartoons p. 22	**The first time I fell in love** Three people talk about their experiences of early love p. 24 **Dictation** Transcribing a summary of an interview p. 20	**A Shakespearean Tragedy** Retelling the story of Romeo and Juliet from pictures p. 22 **What do you think?** Shakespeare and his plays p. 22 Falling in love – Who do we fall in love with? Which couples are well-suited? p. 24	**Telling a story (1)** Two stories: "The farmer and his sons" "The Emperor and his daughters" Linking ideas *as soon as* *However* **Writing a folk tale or fairy tale** p. 101
Kids then and now *Kids who have it all* Bringing up kids in the 1970s and now p. 30	**Rules for life** Three people talk about their personal philosophies p. 29 **Spoken English – have got to** *I've got to go now. Bye!* p. 29 **Song** *I Believe* by Ian Dury p. 29	**Discussion** Laws in the U.S. and your country p. 28 What's important to you in life? p. 29 **What do you think?** Bringing up children Household rules p. 30	**A biography** Mother Teresa of Calcutta Combining sentences *Her father, who was Albanian, died, leaving her mother to bring up the family.* **Researching facts about a famous person and writing a biography** p. 102
Life fifty years from now *Life in 2060* An international group of scientists make their predictions p. 38	**World weather warnings** Five weather forecasts from around the world p. 36 **Rocket man** Steve Bennett, scientist and space traveler p. 37 **Spoken English – pretty** *The weather was pretty bad.* p. 37	**Discussion** Talking about changes in the environment p. 35 **What do you think?** Space tourism p. 37 Predictions about the future p. 38 **Role play** Making arrangements to meet p. 41	**Writing for talking** – my cause for concern A speech by a teenager about the influence of video games on children *The thing I'm concerned about …* *Let me explain why.* **Writing a talk about an issue that concerns you** p. 103
The heart of the home *My Kitchen* Three women's kitchens in three different countries (jigsaw) p. 46	**My closest relative** Five people talk about who they feel closest to in their family p. 48 **Spoken English – adding emphasis** *My father I don't get along with.* *What I like about her is …* *The thing I love about him is …* p. 48	**Project** Your most treasured possession p. 45 **Talking about you** Your kitchen p. 46 Discussion **First-born/second-born children** Who do you feel closest to in your family? p. 48	**Describing a place** – a description of a room **Relative pronouns** *who / that / which* **Participles** *I spend hours listening to music.* **Writing about your favorite room** p. 104

1 A world of difference

STARTER

1 Each question has one word missing. Write it in.

1. Where do you come from?
2. When and where you born?
3. You live in a house or an apartment?
4. Why you studying English?
5. Which foreign countries have you been?
6. What you do last night?
7. What are you going do after this class?

2 Ask and answer the questions with a partner.

> Where do you come from?

> Mexico.

3 Tell the class about your partner.

Susana comes from Mexico. She's studying English because...

I DIDN'T KNOW THAT!
Tenses and auxiliary verbs

1 Answer the questions in the *One World Quiz*. Discuss your answers with a partner.

2 **CD1 2** Listen and check your answers. Make notes about the extra information you hear for each one. Discuss this as a class.

> **GRAMMAR SPOT**
>
> **1** Read the questions in the quiz again. Identify the tense in each one. Which two are passive?
>
> **2** Answer these questions. Give examples from the quiz.
>
> Which tenses use the auxiliary verbs *do/does/did* to form questions and negatives?
>
> Which tenses use the verb *to be* (*is/are/was/were*)? Which use *have/has*?
>
> ▶▶ **Grammar Reference 1.1–1.5 p. 129**

Write your own quiz

3 Work in two groups.

- Do some research and write six questions about the world, past and present.
- Ask and answer the questions with the other group. Which group is the winner?

ONE WORLD QUIZ

1 In which country **do** men and women **live** the longest?

a Japan   b Germany   c The U.S.

2 In which year **did** the world population **reach** 6 billion?

a 1989   b 1999   c 2005

3 If you **are standing** on the equator, how many hours of daylight do you have?

a 12   b 16   c 24

4 Where **does** most of the world's oil **come** from?

a Russia   b Saudi Arabia   c Venezuela

5 Which of the seven wonders of the world **is** still **standing**?

a The Lighthouse of Alexandria
b The pyramids of Egypt
c The Colossus of Rhodes

6 Why **didn't** dinosaurs **attack** humans?

a Because they were vegetarian.
b Because they became extinct before humans were on the earth.
c Because they didn't run fast enough.

7 Where **was** the Titanic **sailing** to when it sank?

a Southampton   b Rio de Janeiro   c New York

8 How long **has** Hawaii **been** a U.S. state?

a since 1952   b since 1959   c since 1963

9 How many people **have won** the Nobel Peace prize since it started in 1901?

a 26   b 58   c 94

10 How long **have** people **been using** the Internet?

a since 1969   b since 1976   c since 1984

11 Which language **is spoken** by the most people in the world?

a Spanish   b Chinese   c English

12 In which country **were** women first **given** the vote?

a Canada   b Paraguay
c New Zealand

PRACTICE

You're so wrong!

1 Correct the information in the sentences.

1. The Pope lives in Montreal.
   He doesn't live in Montreal! He lives in Rome.
2. Shakespeare didn't write poems.
   You're wrong! He wrote hundreds of poems.
3. Vegetarians eat meat.
4. The Internet doesn't provide much information.
5. The world is getting colder.
6. John F. Kennedy was traveling by plane when he was killed.
7. Brazil has never won the World Cup.
8. The 2008 Olympics were held in Tokyo.

2 **CD1 3** Listen and check. Notice the stress and intonation. Practice making the corrections with a partner.

's = is or has?

3 Is *'s* in these sentences the auxiliary *is* or *has*?

1. Who's making that noise?   **is**
2. She's done really well.   *has*
3. My sister's a teacher.   *is*
4. Who's been to Thailand?   *has*
5. He's leaving early.   *is*
X 6. What's produced in your country?   *has*   *is*

4 **CD1 4** Listen to some more sentences with *'s*. After each one say if it is *is* or *has*.

Talking about you

5 Complete the questions with the correct auxiliary verb and name the tense.

1. What time _do_ you usually get up on weekends?
2. What time _did_ you get up this morning?
3. How long _does_ it usually take you to get from home to school?
4. Who _is_ sitting next to you? What _is_ he/she wearing?
5. How long _have_ you known the teacher?
6. What _were_ you doing when your teacher came into the room?
7. What _do_ (not) you like doing in English class?
8. Which school subjects _did_ (not) you like when you were younger?
9. Which other foreign languages _have_ you studied?
10. What presents _were_ you given on your last birthday?

Ask and answer the questions with a partner.

MAKING CONVERSATION
Short answers

1 **CD1** **5** Ruth is picking up her children, Nick and Lily, from school. Listen and complete the conversation. Which child is more polite? In what way?

Ruth So kids, _did_ you have a good day at school?

Nick No.

Lily Yes, I _did_. We _were_ practicing for the school concert.

Ruth Oh, wonderful! _Do_ you have a lot of homework?

Lily Ugh! Yes, I _do_. I have Geography, Spanish, and Math! _Do_ you have a lot, Nick?

Nick Yeah.

Ruth Nick, _did_ you remember to bring your soccer uniform?

Nick Um …

Lily No, he _didn't_. He forgot it again.

Ruth Oh, Nick, you know we need to wash it. _Are_ you playing soccer tomorrow?

Nick No.

Ruth Lily, _do_ you need *your* uniform tomorrow?

Lily Yes, I _do_. I have a softball game after school. We're playing our rival team. _near future_

Ruth _Did_ they beat you last time?

Lily Yes, they _did_. But we'll beat them tomorrow.

Nick No, you _won't_! Your team's terrible.

Ruth OK, that's enough, children. Put on your seatbelts! Let's go!

SPOKEN ENGLISH Sounding polite

1 In English conversation it can sound impolite to reply with just *yes* or *no*. We use short answers with auxiliaries.

> "Did you have a good day?" "Yes, I did/No, I didn't."

2 It also helps if you add some more information.

> "Do you have a lot of homework?" "Yes, I do. I have Geography, Spanish, and Math."

3 Reply to these questions. Use short answers and add some information.
  1. Did you have a good day?
  2. Do you like pizza?
  3. Did you enjoy the movie?
  4. Has it stopped raining?

▶▶ **Grammar Reference 1.6 p. 129**

---

2 Rewrite Nick's lines in Exercise 1 to make him sound more polite.
   CD1 **6** Listen and compare the conversations.

3 Work in groups of three. Look at CD1 5 and CD1 6 on page 114. Practice them, sounding polite and impolite.

PRACTICE

1 Match a line in **A** with a short answer in **B** and a line in **C**.

A	B	C
1. Did you hear that noise?	No, I haven't.	They didn't have my size.
2. Are you doing anything tonight?	No, I'm not.	I think it was thunder.
3. Have you seen my cell phone anywhere?	Yes, it is.	Thank goodness!
4. Did you get those shoes you liked?	Yes, I did.	Do you want to come over?
5. Is it time for a break?	No, I didn't.	Did you lose it again?

CD1 7 Listen and check. Practice with a partner.
Pay attention to stress and intonation.

A class survey

Find out about the students in your class.

2 Read the class survey and answer the questions about you.
Add two more questions.

3 Work with a partner. Ask and answer the questions in the
survey. Give short answers in your replies and add some
information.

> Are you interested in any sports?

> Yes, I am. I often go skiing in the
> winter and I like playing tennis.

4 Tell the class about your partner.

> Milo's interested in two sports—skiing and tennis. He often ...

5 What can you say about your class?

> Nearly everyone is interested in at least one sport. Most of
> the boys love football. Some of us like skiing.

Check it

6 There is one mistake in each sentence. Find it and correct it.
1. Rae comes from Canada and he speak French and English.
2. Which subjects Susan is studying in school?
3. "Do you like football?" "Yes, I like."
4. Did you watched the game last night?
5. What does your parents do on the weekend?
6. I think is going to rain.
7. What was you talking to the teacher about?
8. I don't think John's arrive yet.

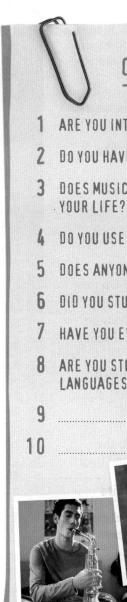

CLASS SURVEY
----

1 ARE YOU INTERESTED IN ANY SPORTS?

2 DO YOU HAVE A PET?

3 DOES MUSIC PLAY AN IMPORTANT PART IN
  YOUR LIFE?

4 DO YOU USE THE INTERNET MUCH?

5 DOES ANYONE IN YOUR FAMILY SPEAK ENGLISH?

6 DID YOU STUDY ENGLISH IN ELEMENTARY SCHOOL?

7 HAVE YOU EVER BEEN TO THE U.S.?

8 ARE YOU STUDYING ANY OTHER FOREIGN
  LANGUAGES?

9 _____

10 _____

READING AND SPEAKING
Worlds apart

1 Discuss these questions about your family.
- Who is in your immediate family?
- Name some of your extended family.
- Who are you close to?
- Who do you live with now?
- Who did you grow up with?

2 Read the PROFILES of two families from very different parts of the world. Who is in the family? Where do they come from? What do you know about their countries?

3 Divide into two groups.

> **Group A** Read about the **Kamau family** from Kenya.
>
> **Group B** Read about the **Qu family** from China.

4 In your groups answer these questions about the Kamaus or the Qus.

1. Where do they live? What are their homes like?
2. How long have they lived there?
3. What jobs do the parents do? Do they earn much money?
4. What do they spend their money on?
5. What do you learn about the children? What do they do?
6. How long have the parents known each other?
7. What do you learn about other members of the family?
8. What hopes and ambitions do the parents have for themselves and their children?

5 Work with a partner from the other group. Compare and swap information about the families and their mottos.

1. What similarities and differences can you find?
2. How have their lives changed over the years?
3. What regrets or worries do they have now?

WELCOME TO

The Kamaus from KENYA

PROFILE

FATHER: Boniface Kigotho Kamau, 35
MOTHER: Pauline Wanjiku, approximately 29 (exact age unknown)
DAUGHTER: Joyce Muthoni, 8
DAUGHTER: Sharon Wanjiru, 16 months

Boniface and his wife, Pauline, live in Ongata Rongai, a small town near the capital, Nairobi. They have two daughters: Joyce, who is in her third year of school, and 16-month-old Sharon.

Their home is a two-bedroom apartment, one of 20 in a single-story block. Boniface works as a taxi driver at the international airport in Nairobi. Each morning he leaves home at 4:30 A.M. in his white Toyota—cracked windshield, 200,000 miles on the speedometer—and is back by 10 P.M. On a good day he finds two clients. In a typical month he takes home about $215.

"It's a hard job, but I like it," he says. "I meet new people, so I get some experience of the world—even though I have never been outside Kenya."

Pauline is a dressmaker but isn't working right now. She stays at home to take care of the kids. The weekend is often the only time Boniface sees Joyce and Sharon. Boniface and Pauline met in 1994: "We liked each other immediately," says Boniface. "I didn't want a woman from the city, so when I learned that Pauline was from the country, I was pleased."

They married in 1995, and at first they lived in a slum. They often didn't have a lot to eat, just sukuma wiki (a green vegetable). Then, in 1996, Boniface won $90 in a bicycle race. The money helped them move to a better area and paid for driving lessons so that Boniface could become a taxi driver.

His salary doesn't go far. Rent is $45 a month, and he gives the same amount to his parents, who don't work. Also, as the most successful of six brothers and sisters, Boniface is expected to help their families, too. He says, "I am always so stressed about money." Joyce's school fees cost another $40 a month.

"We are trying to give our children the best education," says Pauline, who, like her husband, never finished school. "Joyce wants to be a doctor."

Next year, Sharon is going to preschool, so Pauline will have more time to start her own dressmaking business. By then, the family might have a new home. "This apartment is not a good place to raise a family," says Boniface. "The bathrooms are communal—one for every four families." Boniface plans to build a three-bedroom house in the suburbs of Nairobi.

THE FAMILY IS HAPPIEST WHEN they have some spare money: Boniface takes them to see the wild animals at Nairobi National Park.

FAMILY MOTTO Try to do your best at all times.

OUR WORLD

The Qus from Beijing, CHINA

FATHER: Qu Wansheng, 44
MOTHER: Liu Guifang, 43
DAUGHTER: Chen, 17
GRANDFATHER: (Qu's father) Huanjun, 84

Qu and Liu have known each other since childhood. The most noticeable change in China since then is the size of families. Qu was the youngest of six. Liu grew up as one of five children. But they have only one daughter.

Qu and Liu are happy to have a girl. Like most parents in China, they put the needs of their only child, Chen, first. She is applying to study at the prestigious Beijing University. Qu, a propaganda officer at the municipal services bureau, and Liu, who works at the No. 3 computer factory, are saving every last yuan for their daughter's education.

The family has lived in their house in central Beijing for 70 years. It is in one of the capital's ancient Hutong alleyways. These areas are known for their close-knit families and warm hospitality. The elderly sit outside and chat. People wander to the stores in their pajamas. It is a way of life cherished by Qu, but he can see that this relaxed routine is increasingly out of step with a nation experiencing one of the most amazingly quick changes in human history.

"We are not in a hurry to get rich," says Qu. "I don't want to rush around trying to make money—I am not a machine. I put my family first."

Tens of thousands of alleyways have been knocked down in the past few years, and their house is said to be next for demolition. And when the old communities go, the traditional family structure, in which children take care of their elderly parents at home, goes, too.

But for now, the Qus keep the old ways. The grandfather, Qu Huanjun, 84 and frail, is the center of the family. "My father lives here, so this is the headquarters of the family," says his son. "My brothers and their families come to visit most weekends. We are very close."

They are sad that their daughter has grown up alone because she has no brothers or sisters. "Our daughter is lonely," says Liu. "I always wanted to have two children."

Qu and Liu are proud of their daughter. Chen is bright and well-balanced. She wants to study archaeology. "College will cost a great deal of money," says her father. "So we try to live frugally and save for our daughter."

THE FAMILY IS HAPPIEST WHEN they are all together in the evening.
FAMILY MOTTO Save money, live simply, care for your friends, tell the truth.

Vocabulary work

6 Find the six highlighted words in your text. Work out the meanings from the contexts.

Match the words to the meanings in the chart.

The Kamaus
1. someone who makes clothes
2. with only one floor
3. an area of old houses in bad condition
4. shared by a group of people
5. broken
6. worried

The Qus
1. loved and treasured
2. weak and unhealthy
3. narrow lanes between buildings
4. knocking down buildings
5. close and caring
6. economically

7 Work with a partner from the other group. Teach them your words.

What do you think?

- In what ways are these families typical of their country?
- What is a typical family in your country? Is there such a thing?
- Is your family typical? Why/Why not?

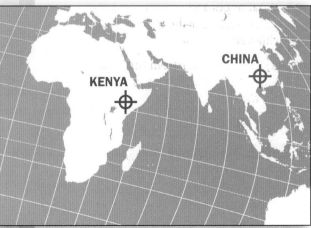

LISTENING AND SPEAKING

A world in one family

1 Do you know anyone who has married someone of another nationality? Do they have any children? Tell the class.

2 Look at the photo of the family. There are *three* nationalities in the family. How can this be?

Xavier   Ana   Teo   James

3 **CD1 8** Listen to Xavier talking about his family. Read and answer the questions. <u>Underline</u> any you cannot answer.

1. What nationality are Xavier and his parents, Ana and Teo? Which city do they live in?
2. How did Xavier's parents meet? Give details. Why did they decide to live in the U.S.?
3. When and why did Xavier first notice his nationality?
4. Why weren't Xavier and James bilingual as children?
5. How many times has Xavier been to Spain? How old was he? How many times has James been?
6. What contact does Xavier have with his father's family? How long did Xavier and his family stay in Peru every summer? *2-3 weeks*
7. What is Xavier studying? What is James going to study?
8. What is Xavier hoping to do in the future? Where is he planning to live?
9. What is James doing right now? What's he going to do?
10. What does Ana think are the pros and cons of bringing up a family in another country? *good bad*

4 **CD1 9** Now listen to Xavier's mother, Ana. Answer the questions that you <u>underlined</u> in Exercise 3.

What do you think?

- What are the pros and cons of bringing up a family in another country? Make two lists.

  + You get the best from two cultures   *– You don't feel completely at home in either of them*

- Discuss your lists as a class.

VOCABULARY

What's in a word?

These exercises will help you to think about how you learn vocabulary.

Meaning

1 These sentences all contain the nonsense word *uggy*. Is *uggy* used as a **verb**, an **adjective**, a **noun**, or an **adverb**?

frail 1. My grandmother's very old and *uggy* now so she can't get out much. *(adj)*

cherish 2. She gave me my grandfather's gold watch. I'll *uggy* it forever. *(v)*

slums 3. The poor people lived crowded together in *uggies* in the old part of the city. *(n)*

4. They can't afford to buy meat and fish. They live very *uggily* on rice and potatoes. *frugally (adv)*

Can you guess what *uggy* means in the four sentences?

Which real English word goes into each sentence?

- cherish   • frail   • slums   • frugally

Pronunciation

2 Say these words aloud. <u>Underline</u> the word with the different vowel sound.

1. /oʊ/ or /ʌ/   rose goes does toes
2. /i/ or /eɪ/   meat beat great street   *greet*
3. /eɪ/ or /ɛ/   paid made played said
4. /ʌ/ or /oʊ/   done phone son won   *sun one*

CD1 10 Listen and check.

▶▶ **Phonetic symbols p. 155**

3 Say these words aloud. Which syllable is stressed?

mother   enjoy   apartment   holiday   **population**

CD1 11 Listen and check.

Word formation

4 Complete the word *act* in the sentences using the suffixes from the box.

-ress   -ion   -ing   ~~-ive~~   -ivities

1. My grandfather is 84, but he's still very act *ive* .
2. My sister's an act *ress* . She's often on TV.
3. Act_____ is not always a well-paid job.
4. This is not a time to do nothing. It is a time for act_____.
5. We do a lot of act_____ in class to learn English.

Words that go together

5 Match a word in **A** with a line in **B**.

A	B
cosmopolitan	carelessly
well-paid	city
close-knit	in love
drive	a race
fall	family
win	job

Keeping vocabulary records

6 Discuss how you can keep vocabulary records.

- Do you have a special notebook or do you record your vocabulary electronically?
- Do you write a sentence with the new word?
- Do you write the translation? What about pronunciation?

📌 My notes

records /ˈrɛkərdz/ *noun*
a written note of something
- *I keep vocabulary records.*

record /rɪˈkɔrd/ *verb*
to write down or keep information electronically
- *I record my vocabulary electronically.*

▶▶ **WRITING** AN INFORMAL LETTER *p. 99*

EVERYDAY ENGLISH
Everyday situations

1 Work with a partner. Where could you hear the following lines of conversation? Who is talking to who?

1. I need to make an appointment. It's pretty urgent. I've lost a filling.
2. A medium latte and a muffin, please.
3. I can't make the meeting. I'm <u>stuck</u> in traffic.
4. Can you put in your PIN number and press "Enter"?
5. Bottled or <u>tap</u>? And do you want ice and lemon in it? *beer*
6. I don't think you've met Greg. He's joining us from our New York office.
7. How many bags are you checking in?
8. The elevator's on your right. Would you like someone to help you with your luggage?
9. Please hold. Your call is important to us. All our operators are busy at the moment, but one of them will be with you shortly *(music)* …
10. There are still tickets for the 5:45 performance, but the 8:45 performance is sold out, I'm afraid.

2 Match a line from Exercise 1 with a reply.

a. ☑7 Just the one.
b. ☑3 Don't worry. We'll start without you and brief you later.
c. ☑6 Hello. Good to meet you. I've heard a lot about you.
d. ☑8 No, thank you. I'll manage.
e. ☑10 That's fine. We'll have two, please, one adult, one child.
f. ☑2 For here or to go?
g. ☑4 Oh, no! I can't remember my number for this card. Oh, what is it?
h. ☑9 If I have to listen to that again, I'll go crazy!
i. ☑5 Bottled, please. Ice but no lemon.
j. ☑1 We have a cancellation this afternoon. 2:45, if that's OK?

CD1 12 Listen and check. How does each conversation end?

3 Listen again. Pay attention to the stress and intonation. Practice some of the conversations with your partner.

Role play

4 Work with a partner. Turn to page 143 and act out the situations.
CD1 13 Listen and compare.

2 The work week

Blue Monday, how I hate Blue Monday

STARTER **CD1 14** Listen to the song called **"Blue Monday."**
- What is the singer's favorite day of the week? *sunday morning*
- What's wrong with the other days? *busy*
- Which days are OK?

MY FAVORITE DAY OF THE WEEK
Present tenses – states and activities

1 Look at the photos.
What do the people do? What are they doing?
In pairs, ask and answer questions.

What does Vicky do?	*She's a student.*
What's she doing?	*She's doing her homework.*

2 **CD1 15** Listen to them talking about their favorite day of the week. What is it? Why?

Vicky's favorite day of the week is . . . because she . . .

3 Listen again and complete the sentences.

1. I _____ with my parents during the semester.
2. I _____ day today.
3. ... it _____ work at all. Time _____ by.
4. The restaurant _____ redecorated right now ...
5. I _____ because it's challenging, but I _____ surfing.
6. The boards _____ here in the U.S.
7. We never _____ on weekends or holidays ...
8. Now we're harvesting, so we _____ at all.

What else can you remember about each person?

Vicky likes being with her friends all the time.

4 Work with a partner. What is your favorite and least favorite day of the week? Why?

Vicky

Terry

Dave

Jenny and Mike

GRAMMAR SPOT

1 What are the tenses in these sentences? Why are they used?

I **have** two classes on Monday.
I'**m having** a bad day today.

Find more examples, active and passive, in CD1 15 on p. 115.

2 Which of these verb forms is right? Why is the other wrong?

I like		I know	
I'm liking	my job.	I'm knowing	we're very lucky.

Some verbs are rarely used in Continuous tenses. These are called stative verbs. Underline the five stative verbs in the box.

no-ing

| love | understand | work | want | enjoy | cost | need | learn |

3 Adverbs of frequency (*always*, *never*) answer the question *How often?* Find examples in CD1 15 on p. 115.

▶▶ **Grammar Reference 2.1–2.4 pp. 130–1**

PRACTICE

Questions and answers

1 Read about Dave, the police officer from page 10. Which question goes with which paragraph?

How often do you go surfing?   **What do you think of your job?**

~~What's your background?~~   **Do you have a business?**

Why do you like surfing?   **What hours do you work?**

What is your favorite day of the week?

CD1 16 Listen and check.

2 Complete the questions about Dave. Then ask and answer them with a partner.

Where does he live?   *In Los Angeles, California.*

1. Where . . . he live?
2. . . . he married?
3. Why . . . morning shift?
4. How many hours . . . ?
5. What . . . like about his job?
6. What . . . think . . . while . . . surfing?
7. Where . . . next month?
8. . . . business doing well?
9. What . . . on Sunday evenings?

CD1 17 Listen and check.

TALKING ABOUT YOU

3 Make sentences about *you* using the prompts in the box.

I visit friends as often as I can.

. . . as often as I can.	Sometimes I . . .
. . . eight hours a day.	. . . one night a week.
. . . when I'm on vacation.	. . . twice a year.
. . . on Sunday.	I hardly ever . . .
I always . . .	. . . whenever I'm not working.

4 Talk to a partner about you. Tell the class about your partner.

Dave Telford police officer and surfer

1   What's your background?

I'm 35, and I'm single. I live in Los Angeles, California. I'm a police officer. I've been in the police force for over ten years. I love my job, but my passion is surfing.

2   What hours do you work?

I work different shifts. The morning shift starts at 5:00, and I can't stand that because I have to get up at 4:30. My favorite shift is 2:00 in the afternoon until midnight because I get home about 12:30. What's good is that I work ten hours a day for four days, then have three days off.

3   What do you think of your job?

My job is extremely busy and very hard. But I like it because it's challenging, and I never know what's going to happen. I like working in a team. We look after each other and work together.

4   Why do you like surfing?

My work is very stressful, so I surf to get away from it all. It's just me and the sea, and my mind switches off. I concentrate so hard on what I'm doing that I don't think about anything else.

5   How often do you go surfing?

I go surfing whenever I'm not working. Sometimes I'm on the beach before 7:00 in the morning. I go all over the world surfing. Next month I'm going to Costa Rica, and in the fall I'm going to Thailand.

6   Do you have a business?

I have a surfing school. I teach all ages, from kids to seniors. The business is doing well. I'm also opening two shops that sell surfboards. The boards are made here in the U.S.

7   What is your favorite day of the week?

I like Sundays best of all. I work as a lifeguard all day, then around 6:00 me and my friends barbecue some burgers and relax. Awesome! I've been all around the world, but when I look around me, I think there's nowhere else I'd rather be.

Simple and continuous

1 **CD1 18** Listen to two people talking about who's who in "The Office." What are their names? What are their jobs?

d	Simon	**Accountant**
b	Edward	*Human Resources (HR) Manager*
c	Anna	Managing Director (MD)
a	Jenny	**Personal Assistant (PA)**
e	Matthew	Information Technology (IT) Manager
a	Christina	*Sales Director*

2 What are the people doing? What are they wearing?

Simon's sitting at the head of the table reading something. He's wearing a sweater.

CD1 18 Listen again. What comment is made about each person?

Simon shouts a lot, but he listens, too.

3 Match a job from Exercise 1 with a job description and a current project.

The MD is responsible for running the whole company. Currently, he is ...

reservation

Job description	Current project
is responsible for running the whole company	*software*
	buying new hardware
makes appointments and arrangements	*making bookings for a conference*
	visiting new customers in China
negotiates prices and contracts	recruiting new staff
runs an IT support team	*discussing plans and targets with the Board*
is in charge of budget and cash flow	preparing a financial report
deals with employees	

profit (income)

4 Work with a partner. Read the conversation aloud.

A What's your job?
B I'm a Human Resources Manager.
A So what do you do exactly?
B I deal with employees and their training.
A And what are you working on right now?
B I'm recruiting and interviewing. We're trying to find new staff for our office in Tokyo.

5 Make similar conversations using the jobs in Exercise 1. Choose another job, for example, film director, journalist ...

PROJECT

Interview someone you know about his/her job. Tell the class about this person.

I talked to ..., who's a ... He ..., and he starts work at ... He has to ... He likes his job because ... On his days off he ...

THE OFFICE

STATE AND ACTIVITY VERBS

6 Are these sentences right (✓) or wrong (✗)? Correct the wrong sentences.

1. I'm not wanting an ice cream. ✗
2. Are you understanding what I'm saying? ✗
3. I'm enjoying the class. It's great. ✓
4. I'm thinking you're really nice. ✗
5. What are you thinking about? ✓
6. I'm not believing you. You're telling lies. ✗
7. I'm knowing you're not agreeing with me. ✗
8. She's having a lot of money. ✗

ACTIVE AND PASSIVE

7 Read the statistics. Choose the correct form, active or passive. Do any of the statistics surprise you?

STATISTICS ABOUT JOBS AND MONEY IN THE U.S.

1 Nearly half the population (155m) **involve / are involved** in some form of employment.

2 More than 1.8 million people **employed / are employed** by the government.

3 The average worker **pays / is paid** $42,000 a year.

4 The average single worker **pays / is paid** 23.6% of his salary in taxes.

5 Women **earn / are earned** on average 12% less than men for full-time work.

6 Children **give / are given** on average $10 a week allowance money.

7 The average person **spends / is spent** $70 per week on transportation.

8 The average household **owns / are owned** two cars.

▶▶ **Grammar Reference 2.5–2.6 p. 131**

8 Put the verbs in the present passive, simple or continuous.

1. "Can I help you?" "I**'m being helped** (help), thank you."
2. A lot of manufactured goods _are made_ (make) in Asia.
3. "Why are you taking the bus?" "My car is _being serviced_ (service)."
4. A large percentage of the food we buy _is imported_ (import).
5. The banking industry in the U.S. _is situated_ (situate) in New York.
6. _Is_ the tip _included_ (include) in the bill?
7. The hotel is closed while the bedrooms _are being remodel_ (remodel).
8. Basketball players _are paid_ (pay) far too much money.

LISTENING AND SPEAKING
Who earns how much?

1 Work with a partner. Look at the chart. Discuss which job you think goes with which salary.

Who earns how much in the U.S.? *

$30,000 $200,000   **$1 million**

$140,000   **$25,000**

Doctor   Basketball player
Senior Director   Nurse
Teacher   Supermarket cashier
Police officer   Pilot
Lawyer   Farmer

$20,000 $65,000

$40,000   **$750,000**

$48,000

* The average annual salary is $42,000.

2 You are going to hear two people discussing the chart. **CD1 19** Listen to **Part 1**. Answer the questions.

1. Which jobs do they discuss? Which salaries do they agree on?
2. Complete the sentences.
   They think a doctor earns either $_____ or $_____.
   They think either a _____ or a _____ earns $750,000.
   They think a _____ earns about $65,000.
3. What comment do they make about … ?
   • doctors   • basketball players   • senior directors   • pilots

3 **CD1 20** Listen to **Part 2**. Answer the questions.

1. Who do they think are the lowest earners?
2. How much do they think farmers earn?
3. Do they agree about a teacher's and a police officer's salary?
4. What is the woman's final point?

SPOKEN ENGLISH Giving opinions

1 Notice the ways of expressing an opinion.
   I guess …   I'd say …   I suppose …
   Find three more in CD1 19 and CD1 20 on p. 116.

2 Are these ways of agreeing or disagreeing?
   I think so, too.   Definitely.   I know what you mean, but …
   I'm not so sure.   Actually, …   Absolutely.

3 What do we mean when we say … ?
   Could be.   Maybe, maybe not.   Possibly.

4 Discuss the salary chart again using some of these expressions.

---

4 Work in small groups. Turn to page 143. Which salaries do you think are unfair? Are any surprising?

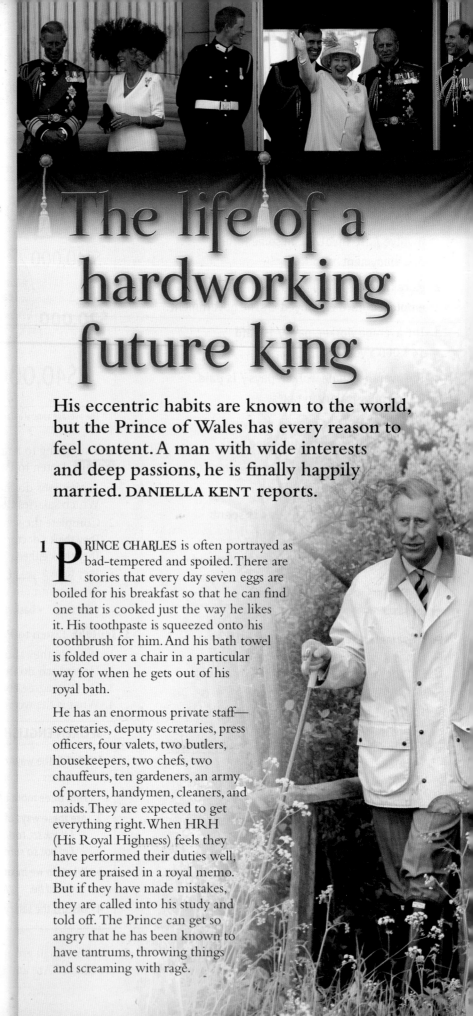

READING AND SPEAKING
Charles, Prince of Wales

1 Do you know the names of the people on the balcony? What is the relationship between them?

2 Work with a partner. Write down what you know about Prince Charles. Compare your ideas as a class.

He's about 60.
He's heir to the British throne.

3 What do you think occupies most of his time? Write a number from 0–5 next to each activity with 0 = not at all and 5 = a lot.

____ earning a living
____ hunting
____ entertaining
____ traveling
____ skiing
____ performing royal duties
____ being with his family

4 Read the article. Answer the questions after each part.

Part 1
1. What gives you the impression that Charles is extremely wealthy?
2. What happens to his staff if they do well? What happens if they don't?

Part 2
3. What is the routine when he entertains?
4. What is the private side of Prince Charles?

Part 3
5. What are some of his public duties?
6. What good deeds does he do?

Part 4
7. "Prince Charles has everything." What does he have? What doesn't he have?
8. What is Duchy Originals? What is happening to it? What does it sell?
9. In what different ways is Charles referred to?
   future King   Prince of Wales . . .

The life of a hardworking future king

His eccentric habits are known to the world, but the Prince of Wales has every reason to feel content. A man with wide interests and deep passions, he is finally happily married. DANIELLA KENT reports.

1 PRINCE CHARLES is often portrayed as bad-tempered and spoiled. There are stories that every day seven eggs are boiled for his breakfast so that he can find one that is cooked just the way he likes it. His toothpaste is squeezed onto his toothbrush for him. And his bath towel is folded over a chair in a particular way for when he gets out of his royal bath.

He has an enormous private staff—secretaries, deputy secretaries, press officers, four valets, two butlers, housekeepers, two chefs, two chauffeurs, ten gardeners, an army of porters, handymen, cleaners, and maids. They are expected to get everything right. When HRH (His Royal Highness) feels they have performed their duties well, they are praised in a royal memo. But if they have made mistakes, they are called into his study and told off. The Prince can get so angry that he has been known to have tantrums, throwing things and screaming with rage.

The private and public man

2 Charles is eccentric, and he admits it. He talks to trees and plants. He wants to save wildlife but enjoys hunting, shooting, and fishing. He dresses for dinner, even if he's eating alone. He's a great socializer. Poets, artists, writers, broadcasters, politicians, actors, and singers all eat at his table. Arriving at Highgrove, his family home, on a Saturday afternoon, guests are entertained in the height of luxury. They are then sent on their way before lunch on Sunday, having been shown around his beautifully-kept gardens.

The Prince also entertains extravagantly at Sandringham, one of the Queen's homes, at least twice a year. There are picnic lunches on the beach, expeditions to local churches, and lavish dinners with organic food. Conversation is lively, but the heir to the throne has to be careful what he says, because he knows only too well that anything he says in private may be repeated in public.

The future monarch that we don't see is a man of great humor who cares passionately about the state of the British nation and is devoted to his two children, William and Harry. He is madly in love with "his darling wife," which is how he refers to Camilla in public.

A dutiful life

3 Together Charles and Camilla perform royal duties, both at home and abroad. He attends over 500 public engagements a year. He visits hospitals, youth groups, performing artists, charities, and business conferences. He hosts receptions to welcome visiting heads of state and VIPs. He travels abroad extensively, as an ambassador to the United Kingdom, representing trade and industry. He works hard to promote greater understanding between different religions. He is also President of the Prince's Charities, which are active in promoting education, business, the environment, the arts, and opportunities for young people. The group raises over £110 million annually.

Camilla shares Charles's passion for hunting and also his interest in conservation of towns and countryside. The one thing she leaves to Charles is skiing. She prefers to stay at home when he makes his annual trip to Klosters in Switzerland.

Everything except the top job

4 Since his second marriage, Prince Charles has everything he wants, except, as his first wife Diana (who was killed in a car accident in 1997) used to call it, "the top job." Yet despite not being on the throne, he has worked hard to accomplish so much. He is concerned about the state of the country he loves and is frustrated that governments do little to tackle those problems about which he feels so strongly.

The Prince of Wales has his own food company, Duchy Originals. It originally sold cookies, but it is now expanding to become one of Britain's best-known and most successful organic brands, with over 200 different products, including food, drinks, and hair and body care products.

Charles, well-intentioned, hardworking, conservative, and old-fashioned, continues to do his duty as he sees it. But he is no longer alone. One day he will be King, and his darling Camilla will be at his side.

5 Now that you have read the article, have you changed your mind about any of your answers in Exercise 3?

VOCABULARY WORK

Which of these adjectives are positive and which are negative?

hardworking – positive

hardworking	bad-tempered
spoiled	eccentric	old-fashioned
sociable	cautious	passionate
frustrated	successful	well-intentioned

Give an example of Charles's life or behavior that illustrates each adjective.

hardworking – He performs a lot of royal duties and does charity work.

DISCUSSION

- What do you know about the attitude of the British people to their royal family?
- What countries do you know that have a royal family? Are the members of the family popular? What do they do?

VOCABULARY AND SPEAKING
Free time activities

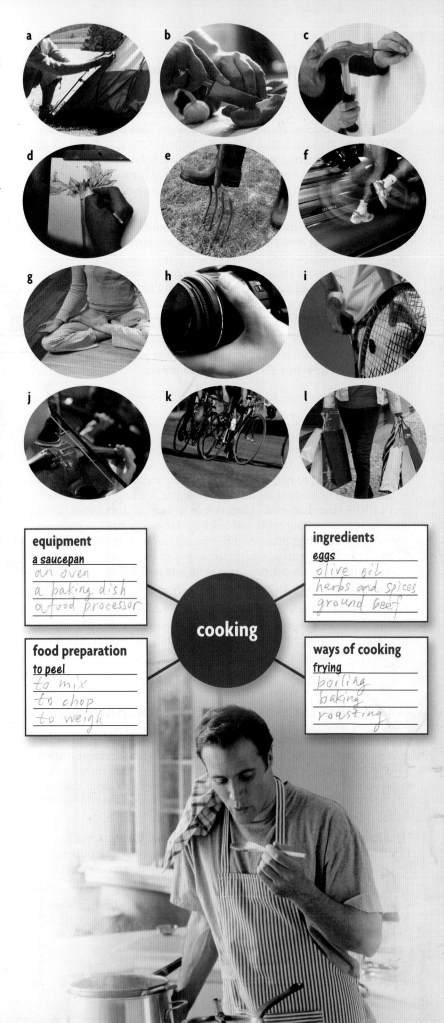

1 What do you do when you aren't working?
Make a list of what you do in your free time.

   go on the Internet   *play golf*   *go for a run*

   Who do you do it with? Where? Tell the class.

2 What activities can you see in the photos?
Which of them …?

   • do you do alone, or with another person
   • do you do at home, or in a special place
   • needs special clothes or equipment

3 Which of these things go with the activities?

a drill	a recipe
planting *=gardening*	serving an ace
sales	a sleeping bag
a racket	a screwdriver
a concert	a bargain
zoom *in (out)*	staying fit
sweating	meditating
wearing a helmet	a flashlight
sketching *—drawing*	weeding

4 Complete the diagram about cooking with
words from the box.

boiling	to chop
to mix	a baking dish
herbs and spices	ground beef
an oven	baking
roasting	a food processor
olive oil	to weigh

5 Choose an activity that you are interested
in. Draw a similar diagram and choose the
categories. Fill it in.

6 **CD1 21** Listen to John talking about his
hobby. Make notes under these headings.

   • Favorite hobby
   • Where and when he does it
   • Clothes and equipment
   • What he likes about it
   • The best part

7 Work in small groups. Use the headings
from Exercise 6 and your diagram to talk
about what you like doing in your free time.

equipment
a saucepan
an oven
a baking dish
a food processor

ingredients
eggs
olive oil
herbs and spices
ground beef

cooking

food preparation
to peel
to mix
to chop
to weigh

ways of cooking
frying
boiling
baking
roasting

EVERYDAY ENGLISH
Making small talk

1   When do we make small talk? Who with? What about?

2   **CD1 22**   Read and listen to the conversation between Ann and Joaquim. Where are they? What is Joaquim doing there?

Ann	So, what do you think of Chicago, Joaquim?
Joaquim	*really interesting/great city/beautiful buildings/people so friendly* **It's really interesting. Chicago's such a great city. There are some beautiful buildings, and the people are so friendly!**
Ann	Yes, they are! When did you get here?
Joaquim	*... ago/flight from Miami/a bit late/didn't matter*
Ann	Oh, good. Where are you staying in Chicago?
Joaquim	*... Avenue Hotel/convenient for the office/room not very big/OK*
Ann	That's too bad! Don't worry. Where are you from?
Joaquim	*Brazil/born in São Paulo/live in a suburb of Rio de Janeiro/pretty/sea*
Ann	Really? It sounds beautiful. Your English is very good. Where did you learn it?
Joaquim	*... very kind/a lot of mistakes/school for years/been to the U.S. many times*
Ann	Oh, have you? How interesting! And what are you doing here in Chicago, Joaquim?
Joaquim	*... attending a conference/here for five days/home on the 17th*
Ann	Oh, so soon! And have you managed to get around our city yet?
Joaquim	*... not seen very much/a walk along the lakefront path/taken a boat tour from the Navy Pier/not seen the John Hancock Observatory yet*
Ann	Well, I hope you enjoy it. Don't work too hard!
Joaquim	*... try to enjoy myself/bye/nice to talk*

3   What information does Joaquim add to keep the conversation going? How does Ann show she's interested? Find examples.

4   Work with a partner. Use the prompts to practice the conversation.
CD1 22   Listen again. How well did you do?

SPOKEN ENGLISH   Softening a negative comment

1   In conversation, we sometimes don't want to sound too negative. We soften negative comments.

We were late landing.	*We were **a bit** late landing.*
My room is tiny.	*My room **isn't very big**, but it's OK.*

2   Make these comments softer. Use the words in parentheses.

1. It's expensive. *(bit)*
2. It's hard. *(quite)*
3. It's cold. *(warm)*
4. They're rude. *(friendly)*
5. I earn very little. *(much)*
6. There's nothing to do. *(very much)*

---

5   **CD1 23**   Listen to the questions and answer them. Make a comment and add some information. Add a question if you can.

> **Who do you work for?**

> **Siemens. I've been with them for four years. They're a good company. How about you?**

CD1 24   Listen and compare.

6   You are abroad on a business trip. Invent a name and a background for yourself.

You are at a social event. Stand up and socialize! Ask and answer questions.

▶▶   **WRITING** LETTERS AND E-MAILS *p. 100*

3 Good times, bad times

STARTER Play the *Fortunately, Unfortunately* game as a class.

Start: I woke up very early this morning.

Student A   Fortunately, it was a beautiful day.
Student B   Unfortunately, I had to go to school.

VINCENT VAN GOGH

Past tenses and *used to*

1 Look at the pictures by the painter Vincent Van Gogh. What do you know about him? Was he happy? Was he successful?

2 Read the notes below about Vincent Van Gogh. Complete the questions about his life.

The Red Vineyard was sold for 400 francs in 1890.

Vincent Van Gogh

1853–1890

Vincent Van Gogh was born in 1853. When he was a young man he worked in London and Paris, but he was fired.

He tried to commit suicide.

In Paris, Vincent met many famous artists while he was .

In 1888 he moved to Arles in the south of France. Another famous painter came to live with him. He was an old friend.

One evening Van Gogh left the house carrying a 🔖 . He cut off part of his ear.

After this, he moved into an asylum. Many of his most famous paintings were completed here.

In 1890, while he was 🔖 , he shot himself in the chest. Two days later he died. He was buried.

When he died, he had no money.

1. Where **was he born**?
2. What . . . job?
3. Why . . . ?
4. Why . . . ?
5. Which . . . ?
6. What . . . when he met them?
7. Who . . . ?
8. Where . . . first meet?
9. What . . . ?
10. Why . . . ?

11. Which . . . ?
12. What . . . doing . . . ?
13. Why . . . ?
14. Where . . . ?
15. Why didn't . . . ?

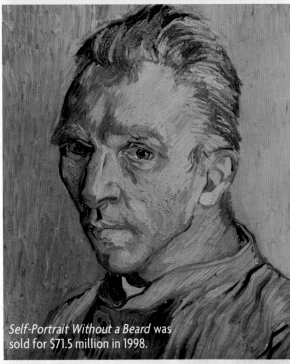

Self-Portrait Without a Beard was sold for $71.5 million in 1998.

Irises was sold for $53.9 million in 1987.

CD1 25 Listen and check the questions.

3 Read the complete text about Vincent Van Gogh. With a partner ask and answer the questions from Exercise 2.

CD1 26 Listen and check.

Vincent

Vincent Van Gogh, the genius unrecognized in his own lifetime

Vincent Van Gogh was born in Brabant in the Netherlands in 1853. As a young man he worked as an art dealer in London and Paris. He was fired from this job because he had argued with customers about art.

In 1881 he tried to commit suicide. He was depressed because he had fallen in love with his cousin, but she had rejected him.

In 1886 he went to Paris to study art, and it was while he was studying that he met Degas, Pissarro, Seurat, Toulouse-Lautrec, Monet, and Renoir.

After two years in Paris, Van Gogh went to live in Arles in the south of France. His friend and fellow painter, Gauguin, who he had met in Paris, came to join him. The two men settled down in Arles, but there was a lot of tension between them. They used to quarrel fiercely, mainly about the nature of art.

One evening in December 1888, Van Gogh left the house carrying a razor blade. He'd been arguing with Gauguin again and was very distressed. He cut off part of his ear.

After this, he moved voluntarily into an asylum for the insane at St-Rémy-de-Provence. He used to wake up at six in the morning and go out to paint. It was here, in the last two years of his life, that many of his most famous paintings were completed. These included *Starry Night*, *Irises*, and *Self-Portrait Without a Beard*.

In 1890 he left the warm south and moved to Auvers-sur-Oise. Here he continued working despite his growing depression. It was while he was painting outside that Vincent shot himself in the chest. Two days later, he died. He was buried in the cemetery in Auvers.

When Van Gogh died, he had no money because he'd only sold one of his paintings, *The Red Vineyard*, in his entire life. His sister-in-law took his collection to Holland, where his work was published. He was instantly recognized as a genius.

GRAMMAR SPOT

1 In these sentences, which verb form is . . . ?
Past Simple   Past Continuous   Past Simple passive

> He **worked** as an art dealer.
> He **was fired**.
> He **was studying** art.

Find more examples of the three verb forms in the text.

2 In this sentence, what happened first?

> He **was fired** because he **had argued** with customers.

had argued is an example of the Past Perfect tense. How is this tense formed? Find more examples in the text.

3 Look at the sentence.

> Vincent **used to** wake up at six.

Do you think this happened once or many times? Find another example of *used to* in the text.

▶▶ **Grammar Reference 3.1–3.7 pp. 131–3**

Pronunciation

4 **CD1 27** Listen and repeat the weak forms and contracted forms.

/wʌz/	/wʌz/
What was he doing?	**He was studying.**
/wɪ/	/hɪd/
They were working ...	**He'd had an argument.**
/ðeɪd/	/hɪd bɪn/
They'd met in Paris.	**He'd been arguing.**

5 Write the verbs from the box in the chart according to the pronunciation of *-ed*.

| ~~worked~~ tried rejected |
| completed continued died |
| published recognized moved |

/t/	/d/	/ɪd/
worked published	tried continued died moved recognized	completed rejected

CD1 28 Listen and check.

PRACTICE

I didn't do much

1 **CD1 29** Listen to four people saying what they did last night. Who said these lines? Write a number from 1–4.

3 ___ I went out to eat with a couple of friends.
4 ___ We talked for a while.
1 ___ I didn't do much.
2 ___ I got home about nine.
1 ___ I had an early night.
3 ___ I didn't get home until about midnight.
4 ___ I did some stuff on the computer.
3 ___ It was a very late night for me!

2 What did *you* do last night? Discuss in small groups.

Discussing grammar

3 Compare the use of tenses in these sentences. Say which tense is used and why.

1. It | *rained* all day yesterday.
   | *was raining* when I woke up.

2. I *wore* a suit for my interview.
   She looked great. She *was wearing* a black top and new jeans.

3. "What *were* you *doing* when you lost your phone?"
   "Shopping."
   "What *did* you *do* when you lost your phone?"
   "Bought a new one."

4. When Bill arrived, | we *were having* lunch.
   | we *had* lunch.
   | we'd *had* lunch.

5. I got to the theater. The movie | *started.*
   | *had started.*

6. When I was a kid I *used to play* football with my dad.
   I *played* football with my kids last Saturday.

A newspaper story

4 Read the newspaper article. Put the verbs in parentheses in the correct past tense, active or passive.
   CD1 30 Listen and check.

5 **CD1 31** Listen to a radio news item on the subject of the same accident. What do you learn that wasn't in the newspaper article?

SMASH!
Clumsy visitor destroys priceless vases   By Tom Ball

A CLUMSY visitor to a local museum has destroyed a set of priceless 300-year-old Chinese vases after slipping on the stairs.

The three vases, which (1)_____ (produce) during the Qing dynasty in the 17th century, (2)_____ (stand) on the windowsill at the City Museum for forty years. Last Thursday they (3)_____ (smash) into a million pieces. The vases, which (4)_____ (donate) in 1948, (5)_____ (be) the museum's best known pieces.

The museum (6)_____ (decide) not to identify the man who (7)_____ (cause) the disaster. "It was a most unfortunate and regrettable accident," museum director Duncan Robinson said, "but we are glad that the visitor (8)_____ seriously _____ (not injure)."

The photograph (9)_____ (take) by another visitor, Steve Baxter. "We (10)_____ (watch) the man fall as if in slow motion. He (11)_____ (fly) through the air. The vases (12)_____ (explode) as though they (13)_____ (hit) by a bomb. The man (14)_____ (sit) there stunned in the middle of a pile of porcelain when the staff (15)_____ (arrive)."

The museum declined to say what the vases were worth.

VOCABULARY
Spelling and pronunciation

1 **CD1 32** Listen and repeat these words. What do they tell you about English spelling and pronunciation?

good /gʊd/ food /fud/ blood /blʌd/
road /roʊd/ rode /roʊd/ rowed /roʊd/

Words that sound the same

2 **CD1 33** Listen and write the words you hear. What do they have in common? Compare with a partner. Did you write the same words?

3 Read these words aloud. Write another word with the same pronunciation.

1. male **mail**
2. blew _blue_
3. piece _peace_
4. where _wear_
5. sun _son_
6. week _weak_
7. hole _whole_
8. pair _pare_
9. allowed _aloud_
10. weight _wait_

4 Write the correct spelling of the words in phonemic script.

1. /pis/ **Peace** is the opposite of /wɔr/ _War_.
2. I'm not /əlaʊd/ _allowed_ to /wɛr/ _wear_ make-up.
3. I'd like a /pɛr/ _pair_ of /blu/ _blue_ jeans, please.
4. I /wɔr/ _wore_ the same socks for a /hoʊl/ _whole_ /wik/ _week_.
5. I had to /weɪt/ _wait_ in the rain and I caught the /flu/ _flu_.

Spelling

5 Read these words aloud. Which two words rhyme?

1. (love)   move   (glove)
2. some   home   come
3. dear   fear   pear
4. lost   most   post
5. meat   cheat   great
6. boot   shoot   foot
7. eight   weight   height
8. blood   wood   flood
9. flower   power   lower

CD1 34 Listen and check.

6 These words have the same vowel sound but different spellings. Spell the words.

/u/ t _oo_ th   tr _u_ th   j _ui_ ce   thr _ew_
/ɔ/ c _augh_ t   d _aw_ n   w _a_ r   fl _aw_ (less)
/ər/ _ear_ th   w _or_ ld   b _ur_ n   f _ur_ /fir
/ɛr/ t _ear_   f _air_ /fare   squ _are_   th _ere_ /their

Lost sounds

7 In some words we lose sounds.

chocolate   /tʃɑklət/ has two syllables, not three.
comfortable   /kʌmftəbl/ has three syllables, not four.

Read these words aloud. Cross out the lost sounds.

different   several (3)
(2) business   restaurant (3)
(2) marriage   interesting (3)
(3) vegetable   temperature (3)

CD1 35 Listen and check.

8 Some words have silent letters. Cross out the silent letters in these pairs of words.

1. foreign   sign
2. climb   bomb
3. neighbor   weigh
4. honest   hour
5. knee   knock
6. psychology   psychiatrist

CD1 36 Listen and check.

The mailman brought the male.

READING
A Shakespearean tragedy

1 What do you know about William Shakespeare?

2 Look at the list of characters in the story of *Romeo and Juliet*. What do you know about the story? How did people at that time decide who to marry? Who made the decision?

3 Read 1–5 in the story. Answer the questions.
1. Why did the Montagues and the Capulets hate each other?
2. Why wasn't it a good idea for Romeo to go to the Capulets' party?
3. What happened when Romeo and Juliet first met?
4. "Wherefore art thou Romeo?" (= *Why are you Romeo?*) Why was Juliet upset about Romeo's name?
5. How long had they known each other when they decided to get married?
6. Why did Friar Laurence agree to marry them?
7. Why did Romeo try to stop the fight?

4 Read 6–9 in the story. Answer the questions.
1. Who did Juliet go to for help?
2. What was the Friar's plan?
3. Which part of the plan worked?
4. What went wrong with the plan?
5. Why did Romeo kill himself?
6. Why did Juliet kill herself?
7. How did their families feel at the end?

5 CD1 37 Listen to actors speaking Shakespeare's lines, and follow them in the story. Read the lines in more modern English on page 144.

6 Retell the story using the pictures.

What do you think?

- Whose fault was the tragedy?
- In the play, Romeo and Juliet fall in love at first sight. Do you think this is too soon to fall in love?
- Shakespeare wrote comedies, tragedies, and history plays. What titles do you know? Do you know any of the stories?

▶▶ **WRITING** TELLING A STORY (1) *p. 101*

Romeo

The Montagues

Lord Montague — *Romeo, son of Montague* — *Mercutio, Romeo's best friend*

> Peace! I hate the word As I hate hell, all Montagues and thee!

I Many years ago, in the ancient Italian city of Verona, there were two very rich but warring families, the Montagues and the Capulets. They had hated each other for so long that no one could remember how the feud had started. Fights often used to break out in the streets.

> My heart's dear love is set on the fair daughter of rich Capulet.

> ...This alliance may so happy prove, to turn your households' rancour to pure love.

4 The next morning, Romeo raced to Friar Laurence and begged him to marry them. The Friar agreed, hoping this would unite the families. That afternoon, Juliet joined Romeo, and they were wed. They parted, but planned to meet again that night.

> O hateful day! Never was seen so black a day as this. O woeful day! ...

> Romeo, Romeo, Romeo! Here's drink – I drink to thee.

7 Juliet returned home and took the drug. The next day, everyone thought she was dead. She was carried to the family tomb, from where, according to the Friar's plan, Romeo would rescue her.

AND Juliet by William Shakespeare

Benvolio,
Romeo's cousin

Friar Laurence,
a priest

The Prince

Paris, a nobleman
suitor of Juliet

Juliet's nurse

Tybalt, Juliet's
cousin

Juliet, daughter
of Capulet

Lord Capulet

The Capulets

Did my heart love till now? For I ne'er saw true beauty till this night.

My only love sprung from my only hate, . . .

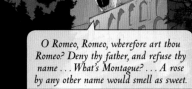

O Romeo, Romeo, wherefore art thou Romeo? Deny thy father, and refuse thy name . . . What's Montague? . . . A rose by any other name would smell as sweet.

2 Lord Capulet was planning a celebration for his daughter, Juliet. Romeo, Lord Montague's son, went to the party uninvited. He saw Juliet and fell instantly in love! They touched hands. They talked. Only then did they discover their families were enemies!

3 That night, Juliet stood on her balcony and declared her love for Romeo. Romeo had climbed up a wall and was listening. They swore eternal love to each other, and promised to marry in secret the next day.

Thou wretched boy . . . shalt with him hence.

Now, Tybalt, . . . Mercutio's soul is . . . above our heads, either thou or I, or both, must go with him.

Take thou this vial, . . . and this liquor drink . . . no pulse . . . no breath shall testify thou livest . . . two and forty hours . . .

Give me! . . . Love give me strength.

5 Returning to Verona, Romeo found Benvolio and Mercutio being attacked by Tybalt. Romeo tried to stop the fight. He failed, and Mercutio was killed. Romeo had to take revenge! He fought Tybalt and killed him. The Prince, hearing of the deaths, banished Romeo from Verona.

6 More disaster was to come. Juliet's father had decided she should marry a nobleman, Paris. How could she tell her father she had already married Romeo? Juliet ran to Friar Laurence for help. The Friar gave her a sleeping potion to make her appear dead. The Friar would tell Romeo to arrive as she was waking up. They could then escape together.

Eyes, look your last. Arms, take your last embrace . . . Here's to my love! O true Apothecary, thy drugs are quick. Thus with a kiss I die.

What's here? A cup closed in my true love's hand? Poison, I see . . . I will kiss thy lips . . . some poison doth hang on them to make me die . . . Thy lips are warm! Oh, happy dagger! Let me die!

For never was a story of more woe than this of Juliet and her Romeo.

8 But Romeo never received the Friar's letter. Thinking that his beloved Juliet had died, he bought poison and went to the tomb. He kissed her and drank the poison. Juliet woke up to see Romeo lying dead beside her. She wept and kissed him, hoping that the poison would kill her, too. Finally, she took his dagger and stabbed herself.

9 The families of the Montagues and the Capulets arrived at the tragic scene. They were overwhelmed with grief, and horrified at the pain that their families' hatred had caused. Thus they buried their feud, along with their precious children, Romeo and his sweet Juliet.

LISTENING AND SPEAKING
The first time I fell in love

1 What do you think these quotations mean?

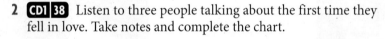

"People ask what love is. If you have to ask, you don't know."

"Love is a kind of madness."

"Love is blind."

"When you're in love, 1 + 1 = everything, and 2 − 1 = nothing."

"Love is what is left when being in love has burned away."

"Love is the most beautiful of dreams and the worst of nightmares."

2 **CD1 38** Listen to three people talking about the first time they fell in love. Take notes and complete the chart.

	Sarah	Tommy	James
1. How old was he/she?	13	9	21
2. Who did he/she fall in love with?	Max (boy)	Clara (girl)	Ruth (girl)
3. Was it a pleasant experience?	Yes	No	Yes
4. Was the love reciprocated?	No, he didn't have the passion	No, she didn't know he love her	Yes she felt the same
5. How did it end?	he went back to his friends	she thought she was too young	They got married and four kids

3 In groups, compare your answers. Listen again to check.

4 What are some of the effects of being in love that the people describe?
"He made me go all weak at the knees."

What do you think?

- Who do we fall in love with? Someone like ourselves, or someone different? Do opposites attract?

- "The course of true love never did run smooth." (Shakespeare – *A Midsummer Night's Dream*) Think of couples, perhaps famous, perhaps not, who didn't have or haven't had an easy romance. What happened to them?

- What couples do you know who are well-suited? Why do they go well together?

Sarah

Tommy

James

EVERYDAY ENGLISH
Giving opinions

1 **CD1 39** Read and listen to the conversation. What is it about? Which two people agree with each other?

A So, what do you think of Meg's new boyfriend? He's really great, isn't he?

B Definitely! I think he's absolutely wonderful!

A Mmm. Me too. I just love the stories he tells.

B So do I. He's very funny. I really like his sense of humor.

A They get along so well, don't they?

C Well, maybe. He's very nice, but I don't think that he's the one for her.

B That's not true! They absolutely adore each other!

C Mmm. I'm not so sure.

B Come on! You're just jealous. You've always liked her.

C Actually, that's not true at all. But I really like her sister.

In groups of three, practice the conversation.

2 Listen again to the conversation. Answer the questions.

1. **A** and **B** agree with each other. What are their actual words?

2. **A** uses two question tags. Practice them.

He's really great, isn't he?
They get along so well, don't they?

Is **A** *really* asking for information, or does she just want the others to agree with her?

3 Complete these question tags.

1. We had a great time in Thailand, **didn't we** ?
2. The weather was great, *wasn't it* ?
3. The French really love their food, *don't they* ?
4. It's a lovely day today, *isn't it* ?
5. Karen and Tom are a really nice couple, *aren't they* ?
6. Tom earns so much money, *doesn't he* ?
7. They want to get married, *don't they* ?

CD1 40 Listen and check.

SPOKEN ENGLISH Making an opinion stronger

1 Adverbs like *very, really, just,* and *absolutely* help make an opinion stronger.

It's good. → It's **very** good. → It's **really** good.
It's bad! → It's **just** awful! → It's **absolutely** awful!

2 We can use an adverb to qualify an adjective or a verb.

He's **really great**, isn't he?
I **really don't like** his sense of humor.

Find more examples in the conversation in Exercise 1.

---

4 Work in pairs to make these opinions stronger. Use a wide voice range to sound enthusiastic.

1. She's very nice. **She's absolutely wonderful!**
2. The movie was good. *just great*
3. The hotel's all right. *really fabulous*
4. I like dark chocolate. *absolutely adore*
5. I like Peter. *really love*
6. The book wasn't very good. *absolutely awful*
7. I don't like noisy restaurants. *just can't stand*

CD1 41 Listen and repeat.

5 Write down some opinions on …

- the last movie you saw
- something in today's news
- the weather
- the clothes that someone is wearing today
- what a celebrity is currently doing
- a show on TV

6 In pairs, ask for and give opinions.

I saw that new movie last week.

Oh! What did you think of it?

Great! I really enjoyed it. The acting was just amazing!

4 Getting it right

● **Grammar:** Modal and related verbs
● **Vocabulary:** Phrasal verbs (1)
Everyday English: Polite requests and offers

STARTER Look at the sentences. Say them aloud as a class.

You	can must should have to	go.

1. Say the negative.

2. Say the question.

3. Say the 3rd person singular with *he.*

4. Which verb is different in form?

MODERN DILEMMAS
should/must/have to/be allowed to

1 Work in groups. *The Times* newspaper has a section called *Modern morals* where readers help other readers with problems. Read the problems in *Readers ask*. What advice would you give? Use these phrases:

I think they should …   I don't think she should …   He must …

2 Read the lines from *Readers reply* on page 27. Which lines do you think go with which problems?
Read the full replies on page 145. Do you agree with the advice?

3 Look again at *Readers ask* 1–7. Find the questions used to *ask for* advice. Find the verbs used in *Readers reply* a–g to *give* advice.

Modern morals

Readers ask

1 How should I deal with my difficult and disagreeable neighbor? He is in the habit of dumping his garden waste along the public sidewalk between our two houses.
Jim T. via e-mail

2 Is it OK to greet people you don't know with a "How are you?" In California (my home) it's considered friendly, but here in New York some people react with a cold look. Should I be less friendly in my greetings?
Erica Fleckberg, New York

3 My new PC automatically picks up wireless networks to gain access to the Internet. This includes the one belonging to my neighbor. Is it right for me to use it?
Richard Dalton, via e-mail

4 My stepfather's driver's license was suspended for six months for speeding, but we have learned that he still drives over the speed limit all the time. Should we keep quiet or inform the police?
Stella Milne, Connecticut

5 I am a medical student. After I graduate in June, I have one month before my first job starts. My fiancée says that I am not allowed to claim unemployment benefits for this month. I disagree, because I'll be unemployed. The benefits are for all those who are out of work, isn't it? What do you think?
J. R. Collin, via e-mail

6 Is it wrong for me to record CDs borrowed from my local library? I am not denying anyone the money, as I wouldn't buy the CD anyway.
Pete Rodriguez, via e-mail

7 Is it ever permissible to lie to children? I lied to my two-year-old granddaughter to remove her from a fairground ride without a tantrum. I said: "You must get off now because the man is going to get his dinner." She got down without a fuss. But I'm worried that if she remembers this, she won't trust me in the future.
Barbara Hope, Philadelphia

GRAMMAR SPOT

1 These sentences give advice. Which is the stronger advice?

You **should** check online.
You **must** tell your neighbor.

2 Which sentences express permission? Which express obligation?

| I | can
am allowed to
must
have to | go. |

3 Complete the sentences with *have to*, *don't have to,* or *shouldn't*.

Children _____ go to school.

You _____ ride your bike on the sidewalk.

People over 65 _____ go to work.

4 The past of these sentences is the same. What is it?

I must go.   I have to go.

▶▶ **Grammar Reference 4.1–4.5 pp. 133–4**

Readers reply

a You must call "Crimestoppers" and report him. You don't have to give your name.

b I think you are allowed other benefits. You should check online.

c You don't have to be like New Yorkers just because you're in New York.

d You have to act with self-control. I don't think you should confront him.

e It's not only wrong, it's illegal. You are not allowed to do this.

f Not only should you lie sometimes, you often have to.

g You must tell your neighbor this. It's the only right thing to do.

PRACTICE

Discussing grammar

1 Choose the correct verb to complete the sentences.

1. I don't get along with my boss. Do you think I *should / must* look for another job?
2. We're throwing Tom a surprise birthday party. You *shouldn't / can't* tell him about it.
3. Please, Dad, *can / must* I go to Tom's party? It'll be great.
4. You *should / have to* drive on the left in England.
5. Do you *must / have to* wear a uniform in your job?
6. Are you *can / allowed* to take cell phones to school?
7. I *must / had to* go to bed early when I was a child.
8. You *shouldn't / don't have to* go to the U.S. to learn English, but it's a good idea.

CD1 42 Listen and check.

Giving advice

2 **CD1 43** Listen to the three conversations. After each one discuss these questions.

1. What is the problem?
2. What is the advice?
3. Do you agree with it? Give *your* advice if it's different.

3 Listen again and complete the lines with the exact words.

1. I don't know if I _____ go or not.
2. They told her she _____ to have friends over while they were away.
3. Oh, come on! You _____ come. It's a party.
4. Look. You _____ tell your mom and dad.
5. You're _____ to eat in the store.
6. Do you think I _____ tell her to stop?
7. No, no, you _____ say anything.
8. I _____ to say something.
9. I _____ go to the store for my dad.
10. I think he _____ pay the fine.

Practice the conversations in **CD1 43** on page 118.

Rules present

1 Work with a partner. Read these American laws. Compare them with laws in your country. Are they the same?

In the U.S. ...
1. You can get married when you're 18.
2. In most states, you can't drive a car until you are 16.
3. You must be at least 18 to vote.
4. You have to wear a seat belt in the front seat of a car.
5. In some states, you can't use a cell phone while driving.
6. Young people don't have to do military service.
7. In many states, children aren't allowed to ride a bicycle without a helmet.
8. Children at most private schools have to wear uniforms.

2 What other laws are there in your country? Think of places such as roads, parks, government buildings, libraries, and schools. Tell the class.

Rules past

3 Read "American Education 1840–1918." Use what you find out to choose the correct verb form in the statements.

1. Before 1840, children *had to/didn't have to* go to school.
2. By 1870 people *had to/didn't have to* pay to go to school.
3. By 1900, many children *had to/weren't allowed to* go to school until they were 14.
4. By 1918, most children *weren't allowed to/ didn't have to* leave school until they were 16.

4 Look at "One-room Schools." Which of the rules do you think were true? Discuss with a partner. Complete the rules with *had to/didn't have to/ weren't allowed to*.

American Education 1840–1918

Nineteenth century American education is often called "The Common School Period." It was during this time that education became available to "common" people. In the 1840s, school attendance became compulsory for elementary-age children, aged 5–12. By 1870, every state provided free elementary education. By 1900, 31 states required children aged 8–14 to attend school. As a result, 72% of American children attended school by 1910—half of them in one-room schoolhouses. By 1918, most states passed laws making education compulsory until age 16.

One-room Schools

1 Students of all ages ___had to___ share one teacher and one classroom.
2 The youngest children ___had to___ sit in front, close to the teacher.
3 Boys and girls ___weren't allowed to___ sit together.
4 Teachers ___were allowed to___ hit their students.
5 Students ___didn't have to___ do very much homework.
6 Students ___have to___ take an oral test at the end of the school day.
7 Children ___didn't have to___ go to school all year round.
8 Teachers ___had to___ live with local families.

LISTENING AND SPEAKING
Rules for life

1 **CD1 44** Listen to three people talking about their rules for life and make notes after each one.

Millie, 15

_____
_____
_____

Richard, 33

_____
_____
_____

Frank, 65

_____
_____
_____

2 Discuss their ideas. Are they optimists or pessimists? Do you agree or disagree?

SPOKEN ENGLISH *have got to*

1 *Have got to* means the same as *have to* but is used more in spoken English. In American English *have got to* is an intensive form of *have to*. It's often reduced to *gotta* when we speak. Look at these examples from CD1 46 .

> *You've got to give meaning to your life by what you do.*
> *You've got to look for the good in people.*

2 Complete the conversations with *'ve got to/'s got to*.

1. "Isn't your mom away this week?"
   "Yeah, so Dad _*'s got to*_ do all the cooking."

2. "Where's my briefcase? I _____ go to work."
   "It's where you left it. In the hallway."

3. "Mom, why can't I go out now?"
   "You _____ clean up your room first."

4. "Won't you be late for work?"
   "Oh, no! Look at the time. I _____ go now. Bye!"

   CD1 45 Listen and check. What extra information do you hear in the answers? Practice the conversations.

▶▶ **Grammar Reference 4.2 p. 133**

Song – "I Believe"

3 Look at the photo and read about Ian Dury. Who was he?

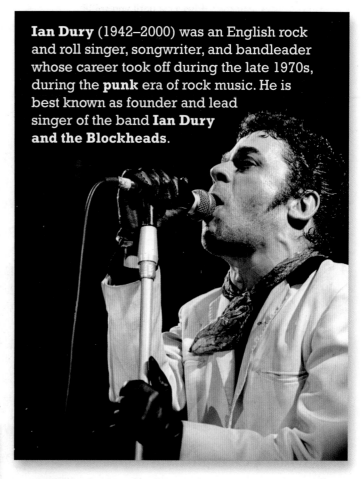

Ian Dury (1942–2000) was an English rock and roll singer, songwriter, and bandleader whose career took off during the late 1970s, during the **punk** era of rock music. He is best known as founder and lead singer of the band **Ian Dury and the Blockheads.**

4 **CD1 46** Listen to the song called "I Believe." It expresses Ian's philosophy on life. Is he an optimist or a pessimist?

5 Work with a partner. Turn to page 146. Read the song. Discuss which words best complete the lines.

6 **CD1 46** Listen again and check your answers. Which of the things in 1–8 does he believe in?

1. Recycling trash.
2. Healthy outdoor activities.
3. Having a lot to eat and drink.
4. Being truthful and kind.
5. Having strong opinions about everything.
6. Good manners.
7. Putting yourself first.
8. Peace, not war, is possible.

7 Which of the things in Exercise 6 are important to you? Discuss as a class.

▶▶ **WRITING** A BIOGRAPHY *p. 102*

READING AND SPEAKING
Kids then and now

1 Close your eyes and imagine your bedroom when you were 10. What was in it? Were there many electronic items? Tell the class about your room.

2 Read the introduction to the newspaper article on page 31. Answer the questions.

1. What did a child's bedroom use to be like?
2. Why is the bedroom of today's child like a space station?
3. Why is it sometimes the most expensive room in the house?
4. What question is asked at the end of the introduction? What is your opinion?

3 The main part of the article describes a modern-day family in an experiment done by a TV company. Look at the photo and the heading. Who are the people? What do you think the experiment was?

4 Here are some words from the article. Use them to predict each paragraph. Check new words in a dictionary.

> **Paragraph 1:**
> 21st century family   Jon made a fortune
> large house   huge bedrooms   hi-tech toys

> **Paragraph 2:**
> Jon's childhood   small apartment
> mother died   five kids   share household chores

> **Paragraph 3:**
> back to the 70s   house stripped of all gadgets
> wash own clothes   battered old van $65 a week

> **Paragraph 4:**
> temper tantrums   Hannah's wardrobe emptied
> Josh – piano, no TV

> **Paragraph 5:**
> learned to appreciate small treats
> baked cookies   started to save

5 Read paragraphs 1–5 quickly. Were your ideas correct?

6 Read to the end of the article. Answer the questions.

1. How did Jon make a fortune?
2. How was Jon's childhood different from his children's?
3. In what ways was his father strict?
4. How did the TV company transform their lives?
5. What did Hannah and Josh have to do that they didn't have to do before?
6. How did the kids react to the changes at first? How did their attitude change?
7. How did the kids make extra money?
8. What is Jon's advice to other parents?

Vocabulary work

Read the sentences below. Find the phrasal verbs in the text which mean the same as the words in **bold**.

1. Electronic items **increase** the value of the rooms.
2. The father, Jon, **founded** his own business.
3. He was one of five children **raised** by his father, when his mother died.
4. Josh had to **stop** watching his widescreen television and **start** taking piano lessons.
5. They enjoyed the meals they'd **cooked** themselves.
6. We shouldn't **surrender** to our kids' demands.

What do you think?

Discuss in groups.

- Do you think a lot of children are spoiled these days?
- What household rules do you think are a good idea for families?

  You must always make your bed.
  Everyone has to help at meal times.

Write a list of rules and read them to the class.

Kids who have it all

GO BACK JUST THIRTY YEARS and look inside a child's bedroom. What do you see? Some books, a few dolls or toy cars, some stuffed animals, and perhaps a desk. Look inside the bedroom of today's kids and it's a 21st century space station.

Computers and other hi-tech toys can make a youngster's bedroom the most expensive room in the house. But it's not only electronic items that push up the value. Today's children also have sports equipment, designer clothes, and accessories such as sunglasses, watches, and jewelry. Do they have everything and appreciate nothing? A TV channel tried an experiment. TANYA BOWERS REPORTS

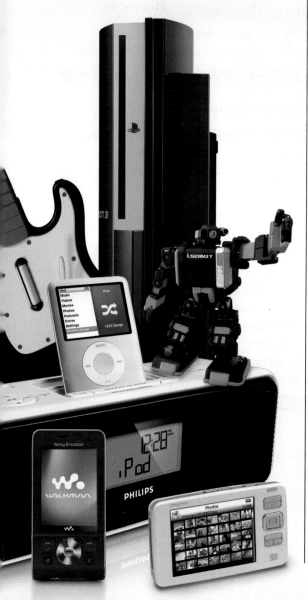

Back to the 1970s

1 The popular reality TV show "It's Your Life" transported a typical 21st century family back in time to the 1970s. The Gregory family lives in a large house in New Jersey. Fifteen years ago the father, Jon, set up his own business and made a fortune. The children, Hannah, 12, and Josh, 10, have huge bedrooms full of expensive hi-tech toys and clothes. They don't have to help at all with the running of the house.

2 This is all very different from Jon's childhood in the 70s. He grew up in a small apartment in Newark, one of five children brought up by their father after his mother died. Discipline, order, and thrift ruled his life. "We ate what we were given. We walked to school and we had to share all the household chores. We had to do what we were told. Dad was very strict."

3 The TV show transformed the Gregorys' house and their lives. For two weeks the family had to go back to the 70s and live Jon's childhood. The house was stripped of all modern gadgets and equipment. Hannah and Josh had to wash and iron their own clothes, do the dishes, and help clean the bathroom. The family car was traded in for a battered, old VW van, and they had to live on just $65 a week.

4 At first there were temper tantrums as the children tried to adjust. Hannah couldn't believe that she wasn't allowed to buy hair mousse and was horrified to find her closet emptied, leaving her with jeans, two shirts, and a formal dress. Josh had to give up watching his widescreen television and take up the piano. They didn't have to walk to school but were filled with embarrassment when their dad drove them to the school in their "new" van.

5 However, gradually Hannah and Josh learned to appreciate small treats. They enjoyed eating the meals they'd put together themselves. They made some extra money by selling cookies they'd baked to their neighbors. They started to save rather than spend and understand the value of a $150 pair of sneakers.

What should today's parents do?

It's difficult to get things right as a parent. Jon says: "We shouldn't give in to our kids' demands. There's no feeling like getting something you've worked really hard for." Hannah now has $50 in the bank, all earned by doing extra jobs around the house. She has learned some valuable lessons about life and she doesn't buy hair mousse anymore!

VOCABULARY AND SPEAKING
Phrasal verbs (1)

Literal or idiomatic meanings?

1 Look at the cartoons. Which two meanings of *take off* are idiomatic? Which is literal?

a *His business has really taken off.*

b *She took her boots off.*

c *The flight to Singapore took off on time.*

2 In these groups of sentences which two phrasal verbs are idiomatic? Which is literal?

1. a. He *brought up* five children on his own.
   b. The porter will *bring* your bags *up* to your room.
   c. She *brought up* the subject of money.
2. a. Do you think you'll *get through* your final exam?
   b. I tried to call you but I couldn't *get through*.
   c. His van couldn't *get through* that narrow gate.
3. a. The water was *cut off* because she didn't pay the bill.
   b. Hello, hello? I can't hear you. I think we've been *cut off*.
   c. She *cut off* a big piece of meat and gave it to the dog.
4. a. Her health has really *picked up* since she moved to a sunny climate.
   b. Can you *pick up* my pen for me? It's under your chair.
   c. I *picked up* some Spanish when I was traveling in Peru.

Separable or inseparable?

3 These sentences all contain **separable** phrasal verbs. Replace the words in *italics* with a pronoun.

1. He turned on *the light.*   **He turned it on.**
2. She's taken off *her boots.*   **She's taken them off.**
3. He took up *golf* when he retired.
4. We picked up *Spanish* very quickly.
5. I looked up *the words* in my dictionary.
6. They brought up *five children* really well.
7. I've given up *sweets* at last.

4 These sentences all contain **inseparable** phrasal verbs. Replace the words in *italics* with a pronoun.

1. She takes after *her father.*   **She takes after him.**
2. Nearly everyone got through *the exam.*
3. We looked after *their cats.*
4. He gets along with *his sister.*
5. I'm looking for *my glasses.*
6. They're looking forward to *the vacation.*
7. We couldn't put up with *the noise* any longer.

Talking about you

5 Complete the phrasal verbs in the questions with **one** of the words in the box. Then ask and answer the questions with a partner.

with	up	to	after

1. Who do you take _____ in your family?
2. Do you get along _____ both your parents?
3. Have you recently taken _____ any new sports or hobbies?
4. Do you often look _____ words in your dictionary?
5. Are you looking forward _____ going on vacation soon?
6. Do you pick _____ foreign languages easily?
7. Do you have any bad habits that you want to give _____ ?

CD1 47 Listen and compare your answers.

EVERYDAY ENGLISH
Polite requests and offers

1 Match a line in **A** with a line in **B**. Who is talking to who? Where are the conversations taking place?

A	B
1. ___ I'll give you a ride into town, if you like.	a. Diet or regular?
2. ___ It's a present. Do you think you could gift wrap it for me?	b. Go ahead. It's very stuffy in here.
3. ___ Pump number 5. And could you give me a token for the car wash?	c. One moment. I'll have to look it up.
4. ___ Two large Cokes, please.	d. I'm sorry, it's not working today.
5. ___ Could you show me how you did that?	e. Oh, sorry, I didn't realize that you couldn't get through.
6. ___ Would you mind moving your car?	f. Yes, of course. I'll just take the tag off.
7. ___ Would you mind if I opened the window?	g. That would be great. Could you drop me at the library?
8. ___ Can you tell me the code for Tokyo, please?	h. Certainly. Just go to "System Preferences" and click on "Displays."

CD1 48 Listen and check your answers.

Music *of* English 🎵

English voice range is very wide, especially in polite requests.

1 **CD1 49** Listen and repeat.

Could you show me how you did that?

Would you mind moving your car?

2 **CD1 48** Listen again to the lines in Exercise 1. Practice the conversations.

▶▶ Grammar Reference 4.6–4.7 p. 134

---

2 **CD1 50** Listen to four more conversations. What is each one about?

1. _____ 3. _____

2. _____ 4. _____

3 Listen again. What are the exact words of the request or offer? Try to remember the conversations with your partner.

Role play

Work with a partner. Choose a situation and act it out in front of the class.

In a restaurant	In a clothing store	At home
Student A you are a vegetarian customer	**Student A** you want to buy a sweater	**Student A** you are having a party
Student B you are a waiter	**Student B** you are the sales assistant	**Student B** you are a friend, offer to help
table by the window	help	come over and help
menu	sweater in the window	buy drinks, etc. on your way
ready to order	only color	while preparing food
vegetarian	try on – my size	decorate the room, blow up balloons
eat fish	really suits	set up the music system
dessert	on sale	choose some CDs
coffee	70% discount	doorbell! – let the guests in
the check	bargain – take it	

STARTER Scientists predict that global warming will
change our world forever. Look at the photos.
What do you think will happen?

I think/don't think that ... will ...

THINGS OUR GRANDCHILDREN MAY NEVER SEE
Making predictions

1 CD2 2 Hannah and Dan are expecting their first baby. They're looking at the
photos in the newspaper. Listen to their conversation. Answer the questions.

1. What is Hannah worried about?
2. Why is Dan surprised?
3. What do the scientists say about the future?
4. What examples of global warming does Hannah mention?
5. How does Dan try to reassure Hannah? What does he say?

2 Listen again and complete the lines with the *exact* words from the conversation.

1. What _____ the world _____ like when he or she grows up?
2. Don't they make you worry about what _____ happen in the future?
3. Of course, things _____ change a lot in the next hundred years, ...
4. No one says it _____ get warmer or it _____ get warmer anymore.
5. Scientists say that it definitely _____ warmer.
6. They say temperatures _____ rise by up to 39°F.
7. You _____ a baby soon.
8. We _____ do our part.
9. OK, but maybe it _____ help. It _____ too late already.

What do you think will happen?

3 Work in groups. Ask questions about the future with *Do you think ... will ...?* Answer with *may, might, could,* or *will.*

1. the earth/continue to get warmer?

> Do you think the earth will continue to get warmer?

> Yes, it will, definitely.

> I'm not so sure. It might.

> I don't think it will.

2. all the ice/melt at the Poles?
3. polar bears/become extinct?
4. more people/travel by train?
5. air travel/banned to reduce CO_2 emissions?
6. new sources of energy/found?
7. there/be more droughts or floods in the world?
8. lifestyles/have to change?

CD2 3 Listen and compare your ideas.

PRACTICE

Discussing grammar

1 Work with a partner. Decide which is the correct verb form.

1. **A** Have you decided about your vacation yet?
   B No, not yet. We've never been to Costa Rica so we *will / might* go there.

2. **A** *Will you / Are you going to* take an umbrella?
   B No, I'm not. The forecast says it*'ll / might* be fine all day.

3. **A** Why are you making a list?
   B Because *I'll go / I'm going* shopping. Is there anything you want?

4. **A** Would you like to go out to dinner tonight?
   B Sorry, *I'll work / I'm working* late. How about tomorrow night? *I'll call / I'm calling* you.

5. **A** What *are you doing / will you do* Saturday night?
   B I'm not sure yet. I *will / may* go to a friend's or she *will / may* come here.

6. **A** Are you enjoying your job more now?
   B No, I'm not. *I'm going to / I will* look for another one.

7. **A** Your team's no good! It's 2–0 Brazil!
   B Come on. It's only half-time. I think they *are going to / could* still win.

8. **A** You *won't pass / aren't passing* your exams next month if you go out every night.
   B I know, *I might / I'll* study harder. I promise.

CD2 4 Listen and check. Practice the conversations, paying attention to stress and intonation.

GRAMMAR SPOT

1 Which predictions are most sure? Which are less sure?

It **might/may/could** change.
It **is going to/will** change.

2 Which *two* answers to the question are correct? Which is not? Why?

"Can you come on Sunday?"

| Sorry, I can't. | I'm seeing
I'm going to see
I'll see | my grandmother. |

3 Which of these future forms expresses ...?

• an intention   • a prediction   • an arrangement

Our love **will last** forever.
I'm going to start exercising next week.
We**'re meeting** James at 11:00 in the conference room.

▶▶ **Grammar Reference 5.1–5.3 p. 135**

World weather warnings

2 What are these extreme types of weather?

thunderstorms   floods   hurricane   heatwave   snowstorms

3 **CD2 5** Listen to five short weather forecasts from around the world. Number the countries in the order you hear them.

The U.S.		Thailand	1	Mexico		South Africa		Canada	
heatwave		*heatwave*		*hurricane*		*snowstorms*		*hurricane* *thunderstorms*	

4 Listen again to the forecasts. Make notes about the weather in each country.

5 Work with a partner. Use your notes to describe the weather in each country. What's the weather forecast for where *you* are for the next few days?

I think / don't think . . .

6 Make sentences with *I think . . . will* and the prompts in **A**. Match them with a sentence in **B**.

I think it'll be a cold night tonight. Wear warm clothes if you go out.

A	B
1. it/a cold night tonight	___ But we'd better get moving.
2. I/get a new computer	1 Wear warm clothes if you go out.
3. I/take a cooking class	___ I want a laptop this time.
4. you/like the movie	___ You have all the right qualifications.
5. we/get to the airport in time	___ It's a great story and really well cast.*ed*
6. you/get the job	___ I can't even boil an egg.

CD2 6 Listen and check. Practice the lines.

7 Make sentences with *I don't think . . . will* and the words in **A** in Exercise 6. Match them with a sentence in **C**.

I don't think it'll be a cold night tonight. You won't need to take a jacket.

C
___ There's too much traffic.
___ I'll get lessons from my mom.
___ It may seem old-fashioned to you but it's OK for me.
1 You won't need to take a jacket.
___ You're too young and you have no experience.
___ It's not really your kind of thing.

CD2 7 Listen and check. Practice the lines and continue some of them.

Talking about you

8 Make true sentences about *you*. Say them aloud in small groups.

1. I/go for coffee after class
2. I/go shopping this afternoon
3. I/eat out tonight
4. our teacher/tell us that our English/improving
5. it/rain tomorrow
6. my grandchildren/go on vacation on the moon

> I might go for a coffee.

> I think/don't think I'll go for coffee.

LISTENING AND SPEAKING
Rocket man

1 Look at the pictures. Which rockets do you recognize?

2 Read about Steve Bennett. Who is he? What was his dream? How is it coming true? What do you understand by *space tourism*?

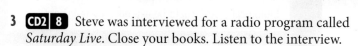

Rocket Man
Steve Bennett

As a little boy, like lots of little boys, Steve Bennett dreamed of becoming a spaceman, but unlike most little boys, Steve's dream is coming true. Steve is a leading rocket scientist and he's now building his own rocket. In a few years he's going to travel into space with two other passengers. He believes the age of mass space tourism is on the horizon.

3 **CD2 8** Steve was interviewed for a radio program called *Saturday Live*. Close your books. Listen to the interview.

- What's your impression of Steve? Would you describe him as "a realist" or "a dreamer"? Professional or amateur?
- Would you like to travel with him into space?

4 Work with a partner. Read the questions below. Which can you answer?

1. Why is Steve so sure space tourism will happen? Why are Richard Branson and Jeff Bezos called "big names"?
2. In what way does he compare space travel with the Internet?
3. How will the passengers be like the early American astronauts? What are they *not* going to do?
4. What influenced Steve as a small child? Why is his rocket called *Thunderstar*? What was he not allowed to watch?
5. What was his parents' attitude about space travel?
6. Why does he think it is necessary for humans to be in space?
7. Why is skydiving good training for space tourists?
8. How much has the couple paid?
9. What does Steve think about every day?

CD2 8 Listen again and check your ideas.

What do you think?

- Is space tourism a good idea?
- Is space travel important to the world? Why/Why not?
- Should the money be spent on other things? Give examples.

SPOKEN ENGLISH   *pretty*

1 Look at how Steve uses *pretty* in the interview.
  *I kept it **pretty** quiet . . .*
  *That's **pretty** much where the human race needs to be.*

2 The adverb *pretty* is often used in informal, spoken English. It means "not a lot" but "more than a little."
  *She's **pretty** nice.*
  *The weather was **pretty** bad.*

3 Work with a partner. Ask the questions and reply including *pretty* in the answer.
  1. A Did your team win?
     B No, but they did well.
  2. A You haven't lost your cell phone again!
     B No, no. I'm sure it's in my bag somewhere.
  3. A Do you enjoy skiing?
     B I do, but I'm hopeless at it.
  4. A What do you think of my English?
     B I think it's good.
  CD2 9 Listen and check. Practice again.

▶▶ **WRITING** WRITING FOR TALKING **CD2 10** *p. 103*

READING AND SPEAKING
Life fifty years from now

1 The future is difficult to predict. What things in our lives today do you think scientists fifty years ago did NOT predict?

2 Look at the text "Life in 2060." Read the introduction and paragraph headings 1–7 only. What do *you* predict about the topics?

3 Which sentences a–g do you think go with which topic?

  a. Lost limbs will regrow, hearts will regenerate.

  b. This knowledge will help reduce suicide rates, one of the major causes of death worldwide.

  c. ... the most sensational discovery ever, that is, confirmation that life really does exist on Mars.

  d. It is now routine to extend the lives of laboratory animals by 40%.

  e. ... your fridge will "know" when you are low on milk or any other item, ...

  f. Soon their existence will be no more controversial than the existence of other galaxies 100 years ago.

  g. It could cause a global revulsion against eating meat ...

4 Read the article and put sentences a–g in the right place.

5 Are these statements true (✓) or false (✗)?

  1. Women will be able to give birth at the age of 100.

  2. It will be possible to replace all the parts of the body.

  3. Animal parts will be used for human organ transplants.

  4. Scientists think that computers won't ever do the work of the human brain.

  5. Scientists believe that if we can talk to animals, we won't want to eat them.

  6. Alien life has already been found on Mars.

  7. There could be an infinite number of other universes.

  8. The walls in your house will change color to suit your mood.

  9. Your armchair will help you do your housework.

  10. Pills will replace food.

What do you think?

- Read the article again and <u>underline</u> the predictions that most surprise you.
  Which do you believe will definitely happen?
  Which might happen?
  Which do you believe won't happen?

- What predictions can you make? Choose from these topics:

transportation	jobs	television	communication
the home	food	clothes	sports

Life in

An international group of forty scientists have made some very surprising predictions about the future. They say that in the next fifty years the way we live will change beyond our wildest dreams. Here are some of their predictions. You may find some of them surprising.
BEA ROSENTHAL reports.

1 Life expectancy

Within 50 years, living to 100 while still enjoying active, healthy lives will be the norm. Professor Richard Miller of the University of Michigan says: "☐ We will be able to do the same for humans." So with regular injections, centenarians will be as vigorous as today's sixty-year-olds. Women will be able to give birth well into old age; their biological clocks could be extended by ten years.

2 Growing body parts

Professor Ellen Heber-Katz says: "People will take for granted that injured or diseased organs can be repaired in much the same way as we fix a car. ☐ Damaged parts will be replaced. Within 50 years whole-body replacement will be routine." But doctors will need huge supplies of organs for transplant. Where will they come from? Scientists say these could be grown inside animals from human cells.

3 Understanding the brain

We don't yet know how the brain gives us our awareness of being alive. "But," says Professor Susan Greenfield of Oxford University, "in 50 years we may have a clearer idea of how the brain generates consciousness." Studies of the brain and the nature of consciousness will bring much greater understanding of disorders such as schizophrenia and depression. ☐ Other scientists go further than Professor Greenfield. They believe that by 2060 computers will develop their own consciousness and emotions. Human beings may eventually be replaced by computers in some areas of life.

2060

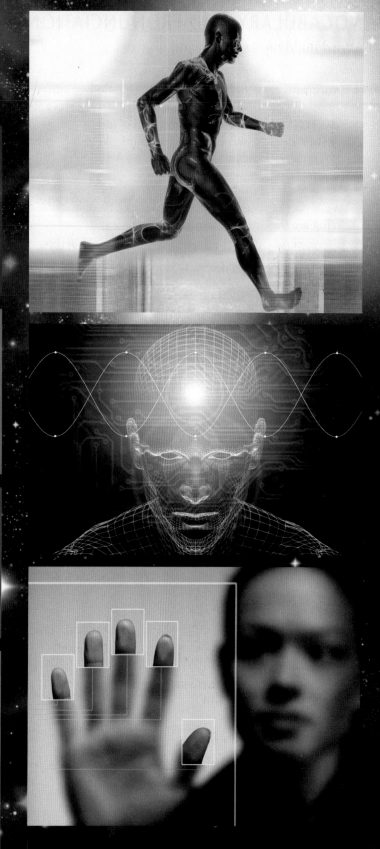

4 Understanding animals

Thanks to a device which can "read" emotions, feelings, and thoughts, we will be able to "talk" to animals. The story of Dr. Dolittle* will be fact, not fiction. "This could first work with primates, then mammals, then other vertebrates, including fish," says Professor Daniel Pauly from Canada. " [_____] , so we might all become vegetarian."

* fictional character for children

5 Discovering aliens

A number of scientists predict that the biggest breakthrough in the next 50 years will be the discovery of extraterrestrial beings. Dr. Chris McKay of NASA says: "We may find evidence of alien life frozen in the ancient permafrost on Mars." Scientists hope that the current interest in space missions to this planet means that there is every chance of making [_____] Dr. McKay also believes that evidence of alien life forms may even be found here on Earth.

6 Parallel universes

Advances in quantum physics will prove that there are parallel universes. In fact there may be an infinite number of them. These universes will contain space, time, and some of them may even contain you in a slightly different form. For years parallel universes only existed in the works of science fiction, but now Professor Max Tegmark says: "[_____]."

7 Our homes

What might our houses be like in the second half of the 21st century? This is Professor Greenfield's prediction:

As you enter the living room, sensors will detect your presence and the walls will start to glow. Talk to the walls and, activated by your voice, they will change to a color of your choice, "pink" to "green" to "blue," whatever suits your mood.

Sink into your glowing cyber-armchair, relax in the knowledge that the house computer will perform all your everyday household tasks. The voice system in the chair will address you by name and advise a change in position that will be better for your spine.

In the kitchen, [_____] and it will automatically send orders to the supermarket. However, it is in the kitchen where "new" meets "old." Food remains in its old-fashioned form. Pills, so confidently predicted in the 20th-century to replace food, exist, but nobody wants them. There is too much pleasure in cooking, chewing, and tasting all kinds of food.

Finally

Predicting the future has occupied mankind for generations. However predictions have not always been correct. The huge influence of many of today's technical marvels, such as the Internet or cell phones, was never predicted.

VOCABULARY AND PRONUNCIATION
Word building – suffixes and prefixes

1 Work with a partner. Look at the information on suffixes.

> **SUFFIXES** are used to form different parts of speech.
> What endings do you notice on these words?
> What part of speech are they?
>
> act   act**ion**   act**ive**   active**ly**

What part of speech are the words in the box?
What are the different word endings?

prediction	colorful	excitement	suitable
shorten	confidently	creative	business
automatically	imagination	qualify	careless

2 Look at the information on prefixes.

> **PREFIXES** are used to change the meaning of words. Look at these words with prefixes.
>
> **pre**dict   **re**grow   **extra**terrestrial   **dis**order
>
> Which means . . . ?
>
> *before   outside   again*
>
> Which is a negative prefix?

Choose a prefix from the box to make the words mean the opposite.

un-   in-   im-   il-   dis-   ir-

1. possible   **impossible**   5. appear
2. patient   6. regular
3. lucky   7. formal
4. legal   8. conscious

3 Work in two groups. Make new words with the base words using the suffixes and/or the prefixes. Which group can make the most words?

PREFIX	BASE WORD	SUFFIX
un- im- **re-** dis- **mis-** in-	agree arrange conscious expense happy help kind polite react success understand use	**-ness** -ment -ion **-ful** **-less** **-able** -ive

4 Complete the sentences with a word from Exercise 3.

1. Carlos and Diana don't get along at all. They dis_____ about everything.
2. Money does not always lead to h_____ness.
3. My aunt says today's kids are all rude and im_____.
4. Thanks for your advice, it was really h_____ful. I really appreciate your k_____ness.
5. My dad is u_____less at fixing his computer. I always have to help him.
6. Please don't mis_____ me. I didn't mean to be un_____. I'm really sorry.
7. Timmy fell off his bike and hit his head. He was un_____ for a few hours.
8. What was your wife's re_____ion when she heard you'd won the lottery?

CD2 11 Listen and check.

Changing word stress

5 In some words the stressed syllable changes in the different forms. Read aloud these pairs of words.

'athlete ath'letic	pre'fer 'preference
i'magine imagi'nation	em'ployer emplo'yee

CD2 12 Listen and check. Practice again.

6 **CD2 13** Listen to four short conversations. Write down the pairs of words with stress changes. Practice the conversations.

1. _____   _____
2. _____   _____
3. _____   _____
4. _____   _____

EVERYDAY ENGLISH
Arranging to meet

1 **CD2 14** Listen to two friends, Gary and Mike, arranging to meet over the weekend. Complete the calendars.

Gary

22 FRIDAY
Morning
Afternoon
Evening

23 SATURDAY
Morning
Afternoon *meet appointment med*
Evening

24 SUNDAY
Morning *take 9:5 train*

Mike

22 Friday
Morning
Afternoon *finish work early*
Evening *gam class*

23 Saturday
Morning *hair cut*
Afternoon *s. stand lunch*
Evening *g. to a theat*

24 Sunday
Morning *10:30 breakfast*

Why is it difficult to find a time? Where and when do they finally agree to meet?

Making suggestions

2 **CD2 14** Listen again to the conversation. Complete the suggestions with the exact words Gary and Mike say.

1. I was __wondering__ if we __could__ meet.
2. I __could__ meet you in the afternoon.
3. What ____ Saturday afternoon?
4. Is Saturday evening __any good__?
5. Why __don't__ we meet at the station?
6. __Let's__ meet there for breakfast.
7. __How__ about ten o'clock?
8. Can you __make__ it 10:30?

Music of English ♪♫

1 **CD2 15** Listen and repeat the suggestions in Exercise 2. Pay attention to the stress and intonation.

2 Work with a partner. Take turns reading aloud the suggestions and answering with a suitable reply from below.

> *I'd love to – but …*
> *I'm afraid that's no good …*
> *Um, let me see.*
> *I can't, I have an appointment with …*
> *Sorry, the evening's out for me.*
> *Sounds good to me.*
> *Fine. 10:30 it is.*

Role play

3 It is Saturday morning. You want to meet a friend over the weekend. Fill in your calendar. What are you doing this weekend? When are you free?

23 Saturday	
Morning	
Afternoon	
Evening	
24 Sunday	
Morning	
Afternoon	
Evening	

4 Find a partner. Make suggestions and arrange to meet.

Are you doing anything on Saturday morning?

I'm afraid I'm going …

What about the afternoon?

Let me see …

I was wondering if you'd like to …

When you have finished, tell the class when and where you're meeting.

We're meeting on Saturday afternoon. We're going …

6 What matters to me

Grammar: Information questions
Vocabulary: Adjectives and adverbs
Everyday English: In a department store

STARTER

1 Think of someone in the room. Don't say who it is.
The other students must ask questions to find out who it is.

Is it a male or a female?   *What color is her hair?*

Does she have blue eyes?   *What kind of clothes does she wear?*

2 Do the same about someone famous.

DESCRIPTIONS
Information questions

1 Match a question with an answer.

DESCRIBING PEOPLE	
1. _e_ What's she like?	a. She's in her twenties.
2. ___ What does she look like?	b. She likes snowboarding.
3. ___ What does she like doing?	c. Five foot eight.
4. ___ How tall is she?	d. She's tall and pretty.
5. ___ What color are her eyes?	e. She's really nice. Very easygoing.
6. ___ How old is she?	f. She's fine.
7. ___ What kind of clothes does she wear?	g. Blue.
8. ___ What's her hair like?	h. It's sort of long, blond, and straight.
9. ___ How is she?	i. Not formal. Casual. She has a lot of style.

CD2 16 Listen and check. Work with a partner. Practice the questions and answers. Cover one column, then the other.

2 Ask and answer the questions about a relative.

> **What's your brother like?**

> He's a great guy, very kind. You'd like him.

You can use the ideas in the box to help.

a lot of fun	a bit quiet	very sociable	good-looking
pretty dark	attractive	medium height	about six feet
in his mid-twenties	straight	short	curly

3 Underline the correct answer.

DESCRIBING PLACES

1. **What's your apartment like?**
   It's modern, but it's cozy. / I like it.
2. **How big is it?**
   Yes, it is pretty big. / About 850 square feet.
3. **How many rooms are there?**
   There's a lot of room. / There are three rooms.
4. **What size is the kitchen?**
   It's square. / Nine feet by eight.
5. **Which floor is it on?**
   Wooden. / The fourth.
6. **Which part of town is it in?**
   It's south of the river. / I get the number 79 bus.
7. **How far is it to the stores?**
   Just five minutes. / It takes half an hour.

CD2 17 Listen and check. With your partner, practice the questions and answers.

4 Ask and answer questions about where you live. You can use the ideas in the box to help.

on an old block   noisy   has a view of . . .
a terrace where we can sit outside
first floor   enormous   tiny

> What's your apartment like?

> It's a bit small, but it's comfortable.

5 Look at the questions for describing things. Put a word from the box into each question.

much   How   brand   of   long   for   size

DESCRIBING THINGS

1. What _____ is it? *Sony.*
2. How _____ does it weigh? *3 pounds.*
3. What's it made _____? *Carbon and titanium.*
4. What's this button _____? *It turns it on.*
5. _____ big is the screen? *13.2 inches.*
6. How _____ is the battery life? *Eight hours.*
7. What _____ is the hard disk? *80 gigabytes.*

CD2 18 Listen and check. With your partner, practice the questions and answers.

6 Ask and answer similar questions about your laptop/ cell phone/camera/MP3 player.

> What brand is it?

> It's a Dell.

GRAMMAR SPOT

1. *What* and *which* can be followed by a noun.
   What color/**Which** floor . . . ?
   Find examples on these pages.
2. *How* can be followed by an adjective or an adverb.
   How tall/far . . . ?
   Find examples.
3. Match a question and an answer.

What's she like?	Very well, thanks.
How is she?	Very nice and pretty.

▶▶ **Grammar Reference 6.1–6.2 p. 136**

PRACTICE

Getting information

Ask questions for these situations.

1. Do you have whole wheat bread?
   White bread?
   What kind of bread do you have?
2. Would you like vanilla ice cream?
   Strawberry? Chocolate?
3. Do we go left or right at the traffic lights?
   Or straight?
4. Is your camera a Canon? A Samsung?
   An Olympus?
5. Do you like pasta? Hamburgers? Spicy food?
6. Is that your sister's top you're wearing?
   Suzie's? Or your own?
7. Does it take 30 minutes to get to the airport?
   An hour?
8. Is your house half a mile from the beach?
   One mile?
9. Do you go to the movies once a week?
   Every other day?
10. Do two of you want coffee? Four of you?
    All of you?
11. Do you wear size eight shoes? Nine? Ten?

CD2 19 Listen and compare.

VOCABULARY
Adjectives

1 Work in pairs. Look at advertisements 1–3. Which advertisement is for …?

a date   something to eat   a vacation destination

2 Find some adjectives in the ads.

❶ Mamma Mia

Mamma Mia pasta sauces. From much-loved Bolognese to our latest garlic and basil. Made from the finest organic ingredients in the old-fashioned way.

**So tempting!
Just like homemade.
You'll be amazed!**

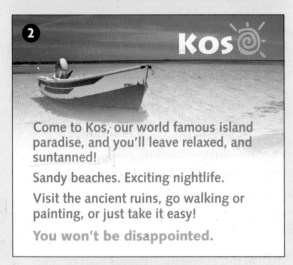

❷ Kos

Come to Kos, our world famous island paradise, and you'll leave relaxed, and suntanned!

Sandy beaches. Exciting nightlife.

Visit the ancient ruins, go walking or painting, or just take it easy!

You won't be disappointed.

❸ LOVE, MAYBE?

Pretty, slim, blue-eyed lady, 35, tired of living alone, seeks tall, dark, handsome, easygoing, charming M with great sense of humor, 30–40, for fun and long-lasting friendship. And possibly more! Box 349056

-ed and -ing adjectives

3 How do these words end in the advertisements?

amaz-   relax-   excit-   disappoint-   tir-   charm-

Complete the sentences with one of these adjectives ending in -ed or -ing.

1. Having a massage is very **relaxing** .
2. I was _____ when they offered me the job. I was sure I'd blown the interview.
3. Our vacation was _____ . It rained every day.
4. I was so _____ on my wedding day, I couldn't eat.
5. The trip was very _____ . I was exhausted.
6. He says such nice things. He is _____ . He makes you feel so special.

Adjectives and nouns that go together

4 Some adjectives and nouns often go together.

sandy beach   *ancient ruins*

Match an adjective and a noun. Sometimes there is more than one possibility.

adjective	noun
fresh latest pretty	friend fruit clothes
clear fast crowded	fashions hair job
casual close handsome	restaurant food woman
straight cozy challenging	man room sky

CD2 20 Listen and check.

Compound adjectives

5 Find some compound adjectives in the ads.

much-loved   *old-fashioned*

Match a word from **A** and **B** to make compound adjectives.

A	B
well (×2) full long good second eye brand	new dressed hand behaved time looking catching term

Think of a noun that goes with each adjective. What's the opposite?

full-time job   *part-time job*

6 Test each other on the compound adjectives in Exercise 5.

Another word for handsome.
good-looking

What kind of job is it if you work forty hours a week?
full-time

Adverbs

1 Look at advertisements 4–6. Which ad is for …?

a pain killer   a watch   a house to rent

2 Find adverbs that end in -ly in advertisements 4 and 5.

simply   beautifully

Find some adverbs that don't end in -ly in advertisement 6.

just   too

4

LOG FIRES IN THE CATSKILLS

$1,250 pw

Live simply in this beautifully restored 19th century country cottage. Sit peacefully in front of the fire. Situated in a charming town, sleeps 6, fully equipped.

andycurran@fastnetus.com

5

You don't actually own one of our handmade instruments. You merely look after it for the next generation.

Probably the best investment you'll ever make.

6 Painful headaches that just won't go? Backache, too?

Relieve aches and pains fast with Cuprodil! Cuprodil goes straight to the pain.

You'll soon feel good again!

✧ CUPRODIL

Adverbs and verbs that go together

3 Some verbs and adverbs often go together.

drive carefully   walk slowly   explain clearly

Match a verb and an adverb. Sometimes there is more than one possibility.

verb	adverb
wait sit behave shine fight leave whisper die rain act speak breathe	badly peacefully heavily quickly patiently fluently suddenly deeply brightly comfortably softly bravely

4 Act out some of the verbs and adverbs in front of the class.

> You're driving carefully!

> You're waiting patiently!

Adverbs that don't end in -ly

5 Complete the sentences with an adverb from the box.

again	fast	hard	loud	wrong
even	right	straight	together	almost

1. Peter and I lived _together_ in college.
2. He's a good student. He tries _hard_.
3. "Where's the town hall?" "Go _straight_ ahead."
4. Say that _again_. I didn't hear you.
5. Don't talk so _loud_! Everyone can hear you.
6. Why do you drive so _fast_? Slow down!
7. His wife's name is Mariana, not Maria! Get it _right_.
8. The vacation was a disaster. Everything went _wrong_.
9. This room is cool, _even_ in summer.
10. "Are you ready?" "_Almost_. Give me another five minutes."

CD2 21 Listen and check.

Project – My most treasured possession

1 **CD2 22** Listen to three people describing what they'd save if their home was on fire. What is it? Why would they save it?

2 What is *your* most treasured possession? Prepare to talk about it.

I couldn't live without my …
It's important to me because …
It was given to me by …
I've had it for …
It reminds me of …

READING AND SPEAKING
The heart of the home

1 Close your eyes and think of your kitchen at home.
- Who's in it?
- What's happening?
- What are they doing?
- What can you smell?

2 Read the introduction to *My Kitchen* at the top of page 47. Do you agree that the kitchen is the heart of the home? Is it where *your* family gets together?

3 Work in three groups.

Group A   Read about **Santina**, from Italy.
Group B   Read about **Elizabeth**, from the United States.
Group C   Read about **Lakshmamma**, from India.

Answer the questions.

1. What does she do?
2. What does her husband do?
3. Where does she live?
4. What's her house like?
5. How does she feel about her kitchen?
6. Is her life easy or difficult?
7. What does her family eat?
8. Does she seem to be happy?
9. What do you think she worries about?

4 Find a partner from the other groups.
Compare and swap information.

5 Which person is most likely to say …?

1. *"I can never decide where to go swimming."*
2. *"We have found you a very nice girl. Why won't you marry her?"*
3. *"If anyone wants me, I'm weeding and watering."*
4. *"I'm too busy to cook today."*
5. *"I live my life in tune with nature."*
6. *"I'd love to have a new kitchen."*

What do you think?

In your opinion, who …?
- is the wealthiest materially
- is the happiest spiritually
- is the most creative cook
- has the hardest life

Give reasons for your answers.

Speaking

1. What food do you most associate with home? Is there a particular day of the week or time of year when you eat it?
2. Talk about your kitchen. Answer questions 1–12 from the text.

▶▶ **WRITING** DESCRIBING A PLACE *p. 104*

My Kitchen

Italy

Homemaker Santina Corvaglia, 61, lives in an old two bedroom farmhouse in southeast Italy with her husband, Carlo, 56, who's a mechanic. They have a 31-year-old daughter, Francesca.

1.   **Q How much is your house worth?**
     A About $80,000.

2.   **Q What is your kitchen like?**
     A It's not very big. It's my little corner of the house. It's where I belong, and where I'm happiest.

3.   **Q How big is it?**
     A 129 sq. ft.

4.   **Q What's your favorite thing?**
     A My cabinets full of different Italian herbs.

5.   **Q How much time do you spend in the kitchen?**
     A About four hours every day. And the same in the garden.

6.   **Q How many meals do you cook a day?**
     A Three. For the three of us, and whoever comes by—friends, relatives. My family is the most important thing to me. I want grandchildren!

7.   **Q What's in your fridge and cabinets?**
     A Vegetables, water, milk, eggs, cheese, ham, sausages, lemonade, butter, pasta, canned tomatoes, beans, honey, and homemade jam.

8.   **Q What would make your life easier in the kitchen?**
     A Nothing. I have all I need.

9.   **Q Who helps you?**
     A My daughter helps sometimes. My husband wouldn't dream of it, and I wouldn't want him to.

10. **Q How often do you sit down and eat together as a family?**
     A Twice a day.

11. **Q How much do you spend on groceries every week?**
     A I grow my own vegetables, and we have chickens and rabbits, so I only spend about $50 a week. But there is a drought this year.

12. **Q What can you see from your kitchen windows?**
     A My garden, my orchard, and my olive trees.

The kitchen is the **heart of the home**. It's where the family gets together for the important things in life—food, conversation, and celebration. Three women from around the world invite us into their kitchens. PENNY ROGERS reports.

California, U.S.

Elizabeth Anne Hogan, 45, is a lifestyle coach living in a 16-room house on the beach in California. It has six bathrooms, five bedrooms, and a swimming pool. Her husband, Mike, 47, is a businessman. They have two children: Hailey, 14, and Hanna, 9.

1. **Q How much is your house worth?**
   A About $800,000.

2. **Q What is your kitchen like?**
   A The kitchen is futuristic. I don't know how everything works, so it's all a bit "alien" to me.

3. **Q How big is it?**
   A 200 sq. ft.

4. **Q What's your favorite thing?**
   A The two ovens, but they take up too much space.

5. **Q How much time do you spend in the kitchen?**
   A About seven to eight hours a day. But not cooking. It's the room we live in.

6. **Q How many meals do you cook a day?**
   A Two to three, if you count cereal and bagels. But only one, if you mean actually doing things with real food.

7. **Q What's in your fridge and cabinets?**
   A Fruit, vegetables, chips, milk, yogurt, takeout, cheeses, and cereal. A lot of takeout food. And dog food.

8. **Q What would make your life easier in the kitchen?**
   A A chef. We do everything for the kids ourselves. No nannies, housekeepers, or cooks for them.

9. **Q Who helps you?**
   A My husband and kids take food out of takeout containers and put it on plates. Does that count as helping?

10. **Q How often do you sit down and eat together as a family?**
    A Every morning and evening.

11. **Q How much do you spend on groceries every week?**
    A $200. Everything is low-fat and organic, pre-packed and prepared. It's all delivered.

12. **Q What can you see from your kitchen windows?**
    A A panoramic, 180-degree view of the Pacific Ocean.

India

Lakshmamma, 50, is a homemaker living in a three-roomed mud hut near Bangalore. Her husband, Adaviyappa, 55, works on a cattle farm. They have two sons, Gangaraju, 30, and Ravi, 25, who both live at home.

1. **Q How much is your house worth?**
   A To rebuild it would cost about $2,000.

2. **Q What is your kitchen like?**
   A It's small and dark. I dislike just about everything about it. It's so old.

3. **Q How big is it?**
   A 54 sq. ft.

4. **Q What's your favorite thing?**
   A The stone where I grind my spices.

5. **Q How much time do you spend in the kitchen?**
   A Six to seven hours a day—sometimes more. I'm always cooking or washing.

6. **Q How many meals do you cook a day?**
   A Two or three.

7. **Q What's in your fridge and cabinets?**
   A We don't have a fridge. On shelves I have lentils, rice, spices such as chilies, turmeric powder, some vegetables, and salt.

8. **Q What would make your life easier in the kitchen?**
   A Running water. A daughter-in-law would be good as well! But God has given me life and I am grateful.

9. **Q Who helps you?**
   A My sons help when they have time. My husband doesn't help.

10. **Q How often do you sit down and eat together as a family?**
    A Men eat before women in our community. We don't eat together.

11. **Q How much do you spend on groceries every week?**
    A $15. Sometimes less. It depends how much money we have.

12. **Q What can you see from your kitchen windows?**
    A Not much! I have no windows in my kitchen.

LISTENING AND SPEAKING
My closest relative

1 Discuss the statements in small groups. Are they true for your family?

- Mothers feel closer to their sons.
  Fathers feel closer to their daughters.
- The first-born child is ambitious, responsible, dominant, and insecure.
  The second child is free, independent, creative, and easygoing.
  The last-born child is the baby—spoiled, happy, confident, and secure.

2 **CD2 23** Listen to five people talking about who they feel closest to in their family. Complete the chart.

	Jen	Brett	Julia	Susan	Chris
I feel closest to . . .	my mother	grandmother	father	sister	twin brother
He/she is easy to talk to.	✓	✓	✓		
We do things together.	✓	✓	✓		✓
We have a similar character.	✓	✓	✓		
I like the way he/she thinks.	✓	✓	✓		
We are different.				✓	✓

3 Who said these expressions? What do you understand by them?

1. *"We have our ups and downs, of course ..."* Jen
2. *"We don't really see eye to eye on anything."* Brett
3. *"In many ways she drives me crazy."* Susan
4. *"We're like oil and water."* Chris
5. *"They fight like cats and dogs."* Chris

SPOKEN ENGLISH Adding emphasis

1 We can change the order of words in a sentence to add emphasis. What is the more usual word order for these sentences?

1. *She's very open, my mother.* My mother is very open
2. *My father I don't really get along with.* I don't really get along with my father
3. *My mother I hardly ever see.* I hardly ever see my mother
4. *He's pretty cool, my dad.* My dad is pretty cool
5. *Me, I'm a lot quieter.*

2 Notice how these sentences add emphasis.

> ***What I like about her is** her attitude.*
> ***What I like about him is that** he's interesting and interested.*
> ***The thing I love about her is the way** everyone knows her.*

3 What could people say about . . .?

1. Joe: his sense of humor
     the way he makes everyone laugh
2. Tina: her kindness
     the way she makes everyone feel good
3. Beth: her attitude to life
     the fact she doesn't care what other people think

Discussion

- Work in pairs. Discuss who you feel closest to in your family, and why.
- Work in groups of four. Who has a similar family relationship to yours?
- Discuss as a class. Which family member are most people closest to?

EVERYDAY ENGLISH

In a department store

1 What are the big department stores in your town? What are they famous for? Do you like shopping in them?

2 Look at the board showing where the various departments are in a store.

Where would you find ...?

- a tie
  in menswear, on the first floor
- a wallet *2 Leath*
- earrings *1 Je*
- a saucepan *B k*
- a hairdryer *B E*
- shower gel *1*
- a doll *4 T*
- a DVD player *4 T*
- women's boots *2 L*
- the ladies' room *3 R*
- a birthday card *1*
- a shaving mirror *3*
- lipstick *1*
- a vase *B C*
- sneakers *4 S*
- a sofa *3 F*
- sheets *3 Li*
- a suitcase *2 L*
- a pair of tights *2*
- a light snack *3 T*

Store Guide

4 Fourth Floor
Toys and Babywear
Hair Salon
TV, Audio, and Phones
Sports

3 Third Floor
Furniture
Linens
Bathroom Accessories
The Terrace Cafeteria 🍴
Restrooms 🚻
Baby Facilities 🚼

2 Second Floor
Ladies' Fashions
Lingerie
Leather goods
Luggage

1 First Floor
Menswear
Stationery
Toiletries
Jewelry
Cosmetics

B Basement
Kitchenware
China and Glassware
Electrical Appliances

3 In which department could you see these signs?

4 Hair Salon
a. Cut and blow dry $50
Highlights from $70

b. Kitchenware
b. Buy two coffee mugs, get one free!

2 Luggage
c. Travel in style— matching bags for long weekend breaks or short vacations

1 Menswear
d. Half price! Final clearance on men's sweaters before the spring!

3 The Terrace Cafeteria
e. CUSTOMERS ARE REMINDED THAT ONLY FOOD AND DRINK PURCHASED ON THESE PREMISES MAY BE CONSUMED HERE

1 Stationery
f. Back to school! Beat the rush. Get your pens, paper, and folders NOW!

Premises

4 Which of these two signs ...?
- is telling you how to take things back
- is inviting you to save as you spend

Open a loyalty card today and you will receive a 10% discount on all your purchases.

If goods are returned in their original packaging with a receipt within 28 days we will offer an exchange or refund.

5 **CD2 24** Listen to some conversations in a department store. Which department are they in? What are they trying to buy?

6 Listen again and complete the lines.
1. **A** *What size* do you wear? *4 S*
   B Nine. That's 41, isn't it?
   A *I think you'll find* 43 would be more comfortable, sir.
2. **B** I'm afraid *that all we have* . We're *sold out* that size. *S*
   A Will you *be getting* any more *in* ?
   B We should *be getting delivery* by the end of the week.
3. **A** Do you have *any sofas like this* in stock *4 to 8 weeks* ? *3 F*
   B No, we don't. They all *have to be ordered* .
4. **A** Would you like me *to gift wrap it* ?
   B Ooh, *that would be great* ! Thank you so much! *1 S*
5. **A** It *doest fit me* . It's too tight.
   B Too bad. It *really suits* . What's *it made* of? *1 M*
   A Cashmere. It's so soft!
6. **A** Keep your *receipt* . That's your warranty. *3, 4 S*
   B *How long* is the *warranty* for?
   A For a year.

With a partner, practice the conversations.

7 Practice having conversations in other departments. Act them out in front of the class.

7 Passions and fashions

Grammar: Present perfect – simple, continuous, passive

Vocabulary: Things I'm passionate about

Everyday English: Making the right noises

STARTER Talk about three things you have NEVER done.

I've NEVER been to a baseball game.
  Me neither. I hate baseball.
I've NEVER had a pet.
  I have. I've had two dogs and a cat.
I've NEVER read a Harry Potter book.
  Really? I've read them all.

300 MILLION BOOKS SOLD!

Present Perfect – simple, continuous, passive

1 Look at the book titles. Have you read any of them or seen the movies? Do you know anything about the author, J.K. Rowling?

Harry Potter and the Sorcerer's Stone (1997)
Harry Potter and the Chamber of Secrets (1998)
Harry Potter and the Prisoner of Azkaban (1999)
Harry Potter and the Goblet of Fire (2000)
Harry Potter and the Order of the Phoenix (2003)
Harry Potter and the Half-blood Prince (2005)
Harry Potter and the Deathly Hallows (2007)

2 Complete the questions about J.K. Rowling. Use *did*, *was*, *has*, or *have*.

1. Where and when __was__ she born?
2. When __did__ she write her first story? What __was__ it about?
3. What __was__ she doing when she had the idea for Harry Potter?
4. Where __did__ she teach English?
5. When __was__ the first Harry Potter book published?
6. How long __has__ she been writing the books?
7. How many __has__ she written?
8. How many children __has__ she had?
9. How many books __have__ been sold?
10. Which books __have__ been made into movies?
11. How much money __has__ she made?
12. How many authors __have__ become billionaires?

3 **CD2 25** Read and listen about J.K. Rowling. What does J.K. stand for?

4 Work with a partner. Ask and answer the questions in Exercise 2.
 CD2 26 Listen and check.

J.K. Rowling
Author and billionaire

THE EARLY YEARS

Joanne Kathleen Rowling, author of the best-selling Harry Potter series of books, was born in 1965, near Bristol, England. Her birthday, July 31, is the same as her famous hero, Harry Potter.

School days

Joanne did well in school. Her favorite subjects were English and foreign languages, and she studied French in school. She graduated in 1986 and over the next few years had a variety of jobs. However, her passion was writing. She had written her first story, "Rabbit," about a rabbit with measles, at age six.

Harry Potter is born

She started writing the first Harry Potter book in 1990. The idea for Harry—a lonely 11-year-old orphan who is actually a wizard—came to Rowling while she was traveling by train between Manchester and London. Although she left England a short time after that to teach English in Portugal, she continued to write Harry's story.

She returned to Britain in 1993 and settled in Scotland. It was a difficult time—she was out of work and depressed—but finally completed her first book, *Harry Potter and the Sorcerer's Stone*. It was published in Britain in 1997 and quickly became a hit with both children and adults.

J.K. ROWLING TODAY

JKR has been writing Harry Potter books for nearly 20 years. She writes in longhand, and each book takes one year to complete. She has now completed the series of seven Harry Potter books. The last book, *Harry Potter and the Deathly Hallows*, came out in July 2007. Her books have won numerous awards including Children's Book of the Year.

She married Dr. Neil Murray in 2001. She has had three children: a boy, David, and two girls, Mackenzie and Jessica.

Fans all over the world

The books have been translated into over 60 languages, and over 300 million copies have been sold worldwide. The first six books have been made into movies. She has become the highest-earning woman in Britain, richer than the Queen! She has made over £600 million, more than one billion dollars. This makes her the first person ever to have become a billionaire from writing books.

GRAMMAR SPOT

1 Name the three tenses. Why are they used?

> She **lives** in Scotland.
> She **lived** in Portugal for three years.
> She's **lived** in Scotland since 1993.
> She's **lived** in England, Portugal, and Scotland.

2 Which question asks about the activity? Which asks about the quantity?

> How long **has** she **been writing** Harry Potter books?
> How many **has** she **written**?

3 These sentences sound unnatural in the active. Make them passive. Find them in the text.

> People have translated her books into 60 languages.
> People have sold 300 million copies of her books.
> People have made six of the books into movies.

▶▶ **Grammar Reference 7.1–7.6 pp. 136–8**

5 **CD2 27** Jack, aged 10, is a big fan of the Harry Potter books. Listen and complete the questions he was asked. What are his answers?

1. How long _have you been_ a fan of the books?
2. How many of the books _have you_ ? _read ?_
3. Which _did you_ like best?
4. _Have you seen_ any of the Harry Potter movies? _And did you_ like them all?
5. Do you have any idea how many Harry Potter books _have been sold_ in the world?
6. What _do you know_ about the author?
7. _Have_ a lot of your friends _read_ the books?
8. I know that in addition to Harry Potter you have another passion. How long _have you been_ soccer? _playing_
9. What would you rather do this afternoon? Read Harry Potter or play soccer? _you know the answer._

6 What books and movies are you a fan of? Talk to a partner. Ask and answer similar questions to Exercise 5. Tell the class.

PRACTICE

DISCUSSING GRAMMAR

Work with a partner.

1 Look at the pairs of sentences. Which tenses are used? Why? Discuss the differences in meaning.

1. I lived in Seoul for two years.
   I've lived in Seoul for two years.
2. I work for an international company.
   I've worked for them since 2006.
3. How long have you been working in Tokyo?
   How many countries have you worked in?
4. Have you ever met anyone famous?
   Did you meet anyone famous at the party?
5. I've already finished.
   I haven't finished yet.
6. Who's been eating my chocolates?
   Who's eaten my chocolates?
7. The President was shot in 1963.
   Have you heard? The President's been shot.
8. How long are you here for?
   How long have you been here for?

2 Underline the correct verb form.

1. His plane *took off / has taken off* a few minutes ago.
2. The president *has resigned / has been resigned* and a new president *has elected / has been elected*.
3. I *work / 've been working* in Dubai since last March. When *did you arrive / have you arrived*?
4. How many e-mails *have you sent / have you been sending*?
5. What *did you do / have you been doing* in the bathroom? You *were / 've been* in there for ages.
6. A huge snowstorm *has hit / has been hit* New York.

CD2 28 Listen and check.

3 Where can the words in the box go in these sentences? Sometimes several words are possible.

just	yet	already	ever	never

1. I've read that book.
2. I've been reading an interesting book.
3. Has it been made into a movie?
4. He's learned to drive.
5. The game hasn't finished.
6. Have you been to Argentina?

Compare answers with the class.

CALVIN KLEIN

4 Calvin Klein is a famous fashion designer. He has had a very interesting life so far. Look quickly through the chart of events in his life. What different things has he designed?

Age	Life event
0	Born on **November 19, 1942**, in the Bronx, New York
14	Developed a passion for fashion and drawing
18	Graduated from the **High School of Art and Design**
20	Studied at Manhattan's Fashion Institute of Technology where he met first wife, **Jayne Centre**
22	Married Jayne in **September 1964**
26	Launched his own clothing company with childhood friend Barry Schwartz. Daughter, **Marci, born**
28	Started designing **sportswear**
30	Introduced his trademark Calvin Klein **jeans**
31	Won the **Coty Award**—the youngest designer ever to win it. He won this three times from **1973–1975**.
32	Divorced Jayne
40	Started selling his own **CK brand underwear**
40–44	Won **Fashion Designers of America award** three times
44	Remarried—**Kelly Rector**, a wealthy New York socialite and photographer
45	Started making his own **perfumes**, called *Obsession* and *Eternity*. His most recent perfume, *Euphoria*, was introduced in **2007**.
50–now	Works with Kate Moss. Designs for Julia Roberts, Gwyneth Paltrow, and Helen Hunt
51	Won **America's Best Designer award** in **1993**. Divorced Kelly
55	Launched his own CK brand **cosmetics** and **makeup**
Now	He's still designing. His company makes $6 billion every year.

a passion for fashion

5 Study the chart with a partner. Ask and answer these questions about Calvin Klein's life.

1. How long has Calvin Klein been interested in fashion?
   Since he was about 14.

2. What different kinds of clothes has he designed in his career?

3. How many times has he been married and divorced?

4. How many children does he have?

5. How many awards has he won?

6. How long has he been making his own perfumes? What are they called?

7. Which famous people has he worked with and designed for?

8. How long has he been selling cosmetics?

CD2 29 Listen and check your answers. What extra information do you learn about Calvin Klein's life?

Time expressions

6 Complete the sentences with phrases from the box.

while he was studying at the Fashion Institute 2	four years after he got married 4
when he was 14 1	since the 1970s 7
in 1972 3	Between 1982 and 1986 8
for ten years 5	until he was 44 6

1. His interest in fashion began _when he was 14_.
2. He met his first wife, Jayne, _while he was studying at the Fashion Institute_.
3. The first Calvin Klein jeans were introduced _in 1972_.
4. His daughter was born _four years after he got married_.
5. His marriage to Jayne lasted _for ten years_.
6. He didn't marry again _until he was 44_.
7. He's been designing sportswear _since the 1970s_.
8. _Between 1982 and 1986_ he won the same award three times.

Role play

Imagine you are a journalist. You are going to interview Calvin Klein about his life. Write questions to ask him with your partner. Then roleplay the interview.

Interviewer	*Where were you born?*
CK	*In New York. In the Bronx.*
Interviewer	*Have you always been interested in fashion?*
CK	*Yes, I have. Well, most of my life, since I was 14.*

▶▶ **WRITING** DESCRIBING A PERSON *p. 105*

Have you ever ...?

7 Work with a partner. Choose from the list below and have conversations.

> **Have you ever bought a pair of designer jeans?**
>> **No, I haven't. I can't afford them.**
>> **Yes, I have. I'm wearing them now.**
>> **Where did you buy them?**

- buy/a pair of designer jeans?
- read/a book in English?
- run/marathon?
- make/a cake?
- meet/someone on the Internet?
- sleep/in a tent?
- lose/your cell phone?
- go/formal party?
- ride/a motorcycle?
- win/a competition?
- write/a love letter?
- be/given a present you didn't like?

Tell the class about your partner.

Maria's never bought a pair of designer jeans because ...

SPOKEN ENGLISH *How long ...?*

1 Read the two conversations. What are the two questions with *How long*?

1. **A** *How long are you here for?*
   B *Just three days. I arrived yesterday and I leave tomorrow.*

2. **A** *How long have you been here?*
   B *I've been here a week already. I arrived last Saturday.*

Which question refers to past up to the present?
Which question refers to a period around now (past and future)?

2 What is the correct question for these answers?

1. Four more days. We came two days ago.
2. Since Monday.
3. Until Friday. We're leaving Friday morning.
4. Over half an hour! Where have you been?
5. We're staying a month altogether.

CD2 30 Listen and check. Practice with a partner.

READING AND SPEAKING
Soccer – a global passion

1 Soccer—do you love it or hate it? Why? Have a class vote. How many famous soccer players can you name? What teams do they play for?

2 Whether you love it or hate it, soccer is difficult to ignore. Read only the **introduction** and the **final part** of "The Beautiful Game."

1. What statistics are given? Do any of them surprise you?
2. How did soccer become known as "the beautiful game"?
3. In what ways is soccer a "simple" game?
4. Which famous players are mentioned? What do they have in common?

3 Read "How soccer began." Answer the questions.

1. What was *tsu chu*?
2. Which nationalities were the first to play a kind of soccer? When?
3. What images do you have of "mob soccer"? Describe a game.
4. How was the game played at English public schools?
5. What caused chaos when the boys tried to play soccer in college?
6. How did the idea of half-time start?
7. Why is London important to soccer?
8. What was the "sticking point"? Which game was also born? Why?

4 Read "Soccer around the world."

1. Complete the sentences with the name of the continent.

   a. _____ has become more enthusiastic about soccer since the 2006 World Cup.
   b. _____ has the wealthiest soccer teams in the world.
   c. Not all countries in _____ have a passion for soccer.
   d. _____ and _____ often lose their most talented players to rich European teams.
   e. In _____ soccer has become more popular with girls than boys.

2. Which continents are most/least enthusiastic about soccer?
3. Why do some continents often lose players to European teams?
4. How and where has the World Cup increased interest in soccer?

What do you think?

- Soccer "has totally changed the worlds of sports, media, and leisure." What does this mean?
- Does soccer unite or divide the world? How?
- Why are some teams so famous worldwide? Which players are superstars today?
- Do you agree with the conclusion about why soccer has become a global passion?

The

Over the last hundred years, the game of soccer has totally changed the worlds of sports, media, and leisure. Soccer is played worldwide by more than 1.5 million teams and 300,000 clubs. An amazing eight out of ten people in the world watch the World Cup. It is, as the great Brazilian soccer player Pelé described it, "the beautiful game." *Andrew Hunt reports.*

How soccer began

As far back as 2500 BCE the Chinese played a kicking game called *tsu chu*. Similar games were played by the Romans and North American Indians. In England in medieval times "mob soccer" was wildly popular. In 1583, Philip Stubbs said of soccer players:

"sometimes their necks are broken, sometimes their backs, sometimes their legs, sometimes their arms."

By the mid-19th century, with the help of English public schools, the game had become less violent. Each school had different rules for playing the game. Problems arose when boys from the different schools went to the Universities of Oxford and Cambridge and wanted to continue playing. This is from the description of a match played in Cambridge in 1848:

"… The result was chaos, as every man played the rules he had been accustomed to at his school."

It became common to play half a match by one side's rules, the second half by the other's. That's how half-time came about. However, this was not good enough for the university men. They decided to sort out the rules once and for all.

On Monday, October 26, 1863, they met in London. By the end of the day they had formed the Soccer Association, and a *Book of Laws* was on its way. The sticking point was whether a player could pick up the ball and run with it or not, and this was not decided until December 8. From this decision the games of both soccer and rugby were born.

Beautiful Game

Soccer around the world

Europe is home to the world's richest professional teams: Manchester United, AC Milan, Real Madrid, Bayern Munich. These teams are famous in many countries far away from their home grounds. Taxi drivers from Bangkok to Buenos Aires, on discovering they have an English passenger, respond with, "Ah, English, Manchester United. You know Manchester United?"

South America has produced some of the most exciting soccer on earth. Many of the world's leading players have come from simple lifestyles to play on the world stage. They have been snapped up by important European teams after making their mark at home. Brazil has won the World Cup five times, Uruguay three times, and Argentina twice.

North America is the only continent where soccer has become more popular with females than males. In 1991, the U.S. won the first Women's World Cup. Interest among American men has been growing since the World Cup in Los Angeles in 1994, and more recently since the arrival of international stars such as David Beckham.

Asia: Over the past two decades, heated rivalry among Japan, China, and South Korea has increased the passion for soccer across the continent, especially after Japan and Korea co-hosted the World Cup in 2002. However, not all Asian countries share the passion: India and Pakistan prefer cricket.

The Middle East: Countries such as Saudi Arabia, Kuwait, and Qatar have lately been investing huge sums of money in soccer. They've hired the best players and coaches that money can buy.

Australia: Sports in Australia have long been dominated by cricket, rugby, and surfing. However, since they qualified for the 2006 World Cup, Australians have become much more interested in the game.

Africa has produced a number of soccer superstars, but many of them have been lost to the rich European teams. Africa is rich in talent, with thousands of gifted young players dreaming of big-time soccer. South Africa's hosting of the 2010 World Cup is very important for African soccer.

A global passion

The game of soccer is played in every nation on earth, not only by the 120 million regular team players, but also by countless others on beaches, in playgrounds, and on streets. The world's love of soccer is simple—it's because soccer is simple. All that is needed is a ball, a piece of ground, and two posts. The world's greatest players, George Best, Diego Maradona, and Pelé, all learned their skills on vacant lots. These are the places where the sport is born and why soccer has become a global passion.

VOCABULARY AND LISTENING
Things I'm passionate about

1 Work with a partner. Look at the words and expressions in the box. Which are positive, which are negative? Which are neutral?

+ ing (n)

kind of like *neutral*	crazy about *P*
adore *positive*	can't stand *negative*
loathe *negative*	don't mind *neutral*
into *p*	detest *negative*
not that into *negative*	fond of *positive*

2 Rewrite the sentences using the words in parentheses.

1. She likes ice cream very much. (*absolutely adore*)
   She absolutely adores ice cream.
2. He likes all water sports. (*very into*)
3. I hate opera. (*detest*)
4. My brother loves playing video games. (*crazy about*)
5. My sister doesn't really like any sports. (*not that into*)
6. I don't like people who always talk about themselves. (*can't stand*)
7. My mom likes going to musicals. (*very fond*)
8. I like tea but I prefer coffee. (*don't mind*)
9. The thing I hate most is cleaning up my room. (*loathe*)
10. I don't hate my job, but it's time I applied for another one. (*kind of like*)

3 Look at the photos of the people. Read what they say about their passion. Can you figure out what their passion is?

4 **CD2** **31** Listen to the people. Were you right? What are their passions?

5 Listen again. Answer the questions about each person.

1. How long have they had their passion?
2. What first created their interest?
3. Why do they like it so much?

6 Use some of the expressions from the box in Exercise 1 to talk about the people.

What do you think?

- Which of the people's passions most interest you? Why? Which interest you least?
- Is there anything in your life that you feel passionate about? Tell the class about it.

1 **Julia**
"I enjoy it, I think, because it's a very psychological game. I mean, if you're playing badly, you have to push yourself to continue."
"... there's only about 3 months that you can't play."

Paul **2**
"They're so big and powerful, but so beautiful when you see them racing around a field or on a track."
"Of course, I have fallen off a few times, but it seems that the more you fall, the less it hurts."

3 **Andrew**
"I felt the power of the words—the thing I like so much about it is that you can say so much with just a few words."
"It's all about saying what often goes unsaid, and with passion."

James **4**
"... they complain about it all the time, but I love it."
"Here, you really appreciate the sunshine, and you notice the seasons."

5 **Kim**
"... the thing I love best about it is that you are away from everything and everyone, out in the water, just waiting, with nothing around you."
"Once we capture it, we carefully release it, and it's not harmed."

EVERYDAY ENGLISH
Making the right noises

1 Look at the words in the boxes. They are all possible responses in conversation. What do they express? Write in the correct heading.

- Agreement • Sympathy • Pleasure • Surprise

Pleasure	*Agreement*	*Surprise*	*Sympathy*
How fantastic!	Absolutely.	Did you?	What a pity!
That's great!	Definitely.	You didn't! *No!*	That's a shame.
Awesome! *good*	Of course.	That's amazing!	Oh, no!
Congratulations!	Fair enough.	You're kidding!	That's too bad.
Wonderful!	Fine.	You did what?	How awful!
Good for you!	OK.	Really?	Bad luck.

No way!   Too bad
so sad.

Music of English ♪

1 **CD2 32** Listen and repeat these expressions with a wide voice range.

How fantastic! *Absolutely.* *Did you?* *What a pity!*

2 **CD2 33** Listen and practice.

---

2 **CD2 34** Listen and complete B's responses. Practice the conversation with a partner.

A My grandfather hasn't been too well lately. *recently*

B *Oh, no! That's too bad.*

A He's 79. Don't you think at his age he should slow down a little?

B *Definitely / Absolutely*

A But he won't listen to me. He says he wants to enjoy his life to the fullest.

B *Good for him!   Fair enough*

A Last summer he went on a two-week cycling trip in South America.

B *That's amazing!   You're kidding!*

A We're going to give him a big party for his 80th birthday.

B *That's great! / Wonderful!*

A But before that I'm going to have a word with him and tell him to take things easier.

B *Good for you.*

What other responses from Exercise 1 are suitable in Exercise 2?

---

3 Read the lines of conversation. Write in a suitable response. There are sometimes several possibilities.

1. **A** My boyfriend's just asked me to marry him. *did he*   ✗
   B *Really?* (surprise) *Good for you* (pleasure) *did you say yes*

2. **A** Will spaghetti Bolognese be OK for dinner?
   B *OK.* (agreement) *That's great* (pleasure)

3. **A** There's a strike at the airport so my trip's been canceled.
   B *Oh, no!* (sympathy) *That's too bad* (sympathy)

4. **A** I failed my driving test again.
   B *Did you?* (surprise) *Bad luck* (sympathy)

5. **A** We're expecting a baby.
   B *That's amazing* (surprise) *Congradulations!* (pleasure) *are you*

6. **A** So you think I should save to buy a car, not borrow the money? *You're have a lot of debt*
   B *Definitely!* (agreement)

7. **A** I told him I never wanted to see him again.
   B *You're kidding* (surprise) *How awful!* (sympathy) *touch*

CD2 35 Listen and compare. What is B's further comment?

4 Practice the conversations with a partner. Continue them if you can.

5 Work with a partner. Have a conversation about a good or bad day you have had recently. React as you listen and talk.

Last Sunday was the worst day of my life!

Well, …

Oh, no! What happened?

8 No fear!

Grammar: Verb patterns
Vocabulary: Body language
Everyday English: Travel and numbers

STARTER Match a sentence with a cartoon.

1. They stopped to talk to each other.
2. They stopped talking to each other.

What's the difference in meaning between Sentences 1 and 2?

DON'T WORRY, MOM!
Verb patterns

1 **CD2 36** Read and listen to the e-mails sent home to parents by young travelers. Where are the travelers? What has happened that gives their parents reasons to worry?

1

From: kate@oneworldmail.net
Subject: I'm fine

Hey there! Just a quick e-mail to say, Mom, please don't freak out about the photos. It looks much worse than it was!! I don't remember anyone taking the pics, and I've no idea who posted them on my Facebook website! It was pitch-black dark that night and I was trying to climb up to the top bunk bed. Unfortunately my head hit the corner of the bed—a METAL bunk bed! Anyway, a scream of pain and, oh! I forgot to mention the ambulance ride to the hospital—but, no, I'm fine. I know you'll hate to hear this, but I had to get some stitches. Don't worry! It's impossible to see the scar on my head!! I didn't want to say anything at the time for obvious reasons. Sorry if it shocked you!!!

Talk soon—lots of love from hot and rainy California.

miss you and love you SO MUCH
Kate x x x x x x x x

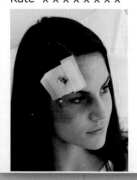

2

New Message

From: Dan [dantheman@fastwebmail.net]
Subject: Hey Ma

Hey Ma,

Must be quick 'cause late.

Just feel I need to warn you, I met some awesome Aussies last night. They're planning to go to New York next month. I said I was sure you'd like to meet them, so I gave them your number. Hope you don't mind putting them up for a few nights. They're all good guys. Can't remember their names, but I know you'll make them feel at home. They're looking forward to meeting you. Hope to speak to you soon.

XXX Dan

💬 **Bill**   ↩ <u>Reply</u> | ▽

Hello, Mom, Dad, and Izzy,

Had a great time yesterday. We went <u>piranha</u>
fishing on the Amazon in a canoe. Victor told
us to throw pieces of meat into the water to
attract the fish, but we didn't manage to catch
anything. We stopped to camp on the banks in
the evening and really enjoyed watching the
sunset and swimming in the dark. Unfortunately,
we'd forgotten to bring a flashlight, so we were
lucky to escape from the crocodiles.

Love to all,

Bill

⚫⚫⚪ ✉   4

From: jill88@adps.mail.net
Subject: **Hi from Peru!**

Dear Parents,

Last night we arrived at the most <u>fantastic</u> hotel
in Arequipa, Peru. It's great to be in a room with
a private bathroom. We <u>expected</u> to have a good
night's sleep but woke up when an earthquake
struck about 2 A.M. Don't panic, Mother! You'll
be happy to hear that no one was hurt. We fell
asleep again shortly after, and everyone felt fine
in the morning despite the holes in the walls and
ceilings. We're thinking of staying here two more
days. I'll let you know our plans.

Lots of love, Jill

Glossary

(to) freak (out) (*informal*) to have a
  completely shocked reaction to something

awesome (*informal*) very good; excellent

Aussies (*informal*) people from Australia

2 Read these sentences. Which verbs or phrases can fill the gaps?

1. **Kate** didn't _____ anyone taking the photos.
   ⓐ see   b. ask   ⓒ remember
2. She _____ to climb up to the top bunk bed.
   ⓐ wanted   ⓑ tried   c. remembered
3. She forgot _____ the hospital.
   a. mentioning   ⓑ to mention   c. mention
4. **Dan** asked his mom _____ his Australian friends.
   a. put up   b. putting up   ⓒ to put up
5. His Australian friends _____ to go to New York.
   ⓐ want   ⓑ are hoping   ⓒ are looking forward
6. He thinks his mom will make them _____ at home.
   ⓐ feel   b. to feel   c. feeling
7. **Bill** _____ to catch piranha fish.
   a. didn't succeed in   ⓑ didn't manage   ⓒ tried
8. They stopped _____ on the river bank.
   a. camping   ⓑ to camp   ⓒ to spend the night
9. **Jill** _____ having a private bathroom.
   ⓐ loved   b. wanted   c. hoped
10. She is _____ staying two more days.
    a. planning   ⓑ looking forward to   ⓒ thinking of

3 [CD2] [37] Listen and complete the lines. Who is speaking?
1. When we saw the photos we _couldn't help_ feeling worried.
2. The photos _made it_ look worse than it really was.
3. Your friends must _promise to_ keep their room clean.
4. It's really kind of you _to let_ them stay.
5. Did Victor _help you_ escape from the crocodiles?
6. He warned us not _to go_ swimming.
7. We couldn't _help feeling_ a little scared.
8. Have you _decide to_ come home yet?
   help +ing

GRAMMAR SPOT

1 Match a pattern in **A** with a sentence from the e-mails in **B**.

A	**B**
verb + *-ing*	I **need to warn** you.
verb + *to*	Victor **told us to throw** meat.
verb + sb + *to*	You'll **make them feel** at home.
verb + sb + infinitive	He **enjoyed swimming**.
(without *to*)	
adjective + *to*	We're **thinking of staying** two more days.
preposition + *-ing*	It's **impossible to see** the scar.

2 What is the difference in meaning between these sentences?

She remembered to e-mail   **She remembered e-mailing**
her mom.   **her mom.**

▶▶ **Grammar Reference 8 p. 138 Verb patterns p. 154**

she didn't forget.   _she has a memory of doing it._

PRACTICE
Calling home

1 Work with a partner. Complete Kate's phone conversation with her mother.

M   Kate! It's so good __to hear__ (*hear*) from you. Are you OK?

K   Oh, Mom, I'm really sorry for _worrying_ (*worry*) you so much. I really didn't mean to.

M   We opened our e-mails and we were so delighted _to see_ (*see*) all your photos and then we saw that one.

K   I didn't want my friends _to post_ (*post*) it on Facebook. I asked them not to.

M   But Kate, all those stitches, and you went to the hospital. We couldn't help _feeling_ (*feel*) worried.

K   I know, but honestly, Mom, my friends made me _go_ (*go*) to the hospital. I really didn't need to.

M   How is your head now?

K   Absolutely fine. Honestly. I'll e-mail you some more photos and you can see for yourself.

M   OK. Don't forget to.

K   I'll call again soon, and I promise _to text_ (*text*) regularly. Bye.

M   Bye. Take care!

2 **CD2 38** Listen and check. Practice the conversation.

SPOKEN ENGLISH *Don't forget to!* – the reduced infinitive

1 In conversation it isn't necessary to use the full infinitive if it is understood from the context.

   A *I'll e-mail some more photos.*
   B *OK. Don't* **forget to** *e-mail.*
   A *Can you and Mary come to lunch next Sunday?*
   B *Oh yes, we'd* **love to** *come.*

   Find three more examples in Kate's conversation with her mother.

2 Reply to **A**, using the verb in parentheses and a reduced infinitive.

   1. **A** Did you mail my letter?
      B Oh, sorry, I _forgot to_ . (*forget*)
   2. **A** I can't go out with you this evening. Sorry.
      B Oh, but you _promise to_ . (*promise*)
   3. **A** Why did you e-mail your mother again?
      B Because she _asked me to_ (*ask me*)
   4. **A** Do you think you'll apply for that job?
      B Yes, I've definitely _decided to_ . (*decide*)
   5. **A** Are you taking your brother to the airport?
      B Well, I _offered to_ (*offer*), but he said he _didn't want_ me _to_ . (*not want*)

   CD2 39 Listen and check your answers. Practice with a partner.

Talking about you

3 Complete the sentences so that they are true for you BUT make two of them false.

   1. I really enjoy …
   ✓ 2. I'm no good at … (*adj*)
   3. I shouldn't forget …
   4. I will always remember …
   5. I just finished …
   6. I sometimes find it difficult …
   7. My parents made me … when I was young.
   8. I'm looking forward to …
   9. I'd love …

4 Work in small groups. Read some true and some false sentences aloud to each other. Make comments and ask questions to find the false ones.

I really enjoy riding bikes.

Do you? Do you bike to work?

I don't believe you. You don't even have a bike!

LISTENING AND SPEAKING
Fears and phobias

1 What are typical phobias that people have? Make a list. Are you afraid of anything?

2 Work with a partner. Match the phobias in the chart with their definitions. Compare answers as a class.

We think autophobia is fear of …

It might be …

We've no idea what … is.

Autophobia		washing. **the color blue.**
Ablutophobia	is a	flying. **birds.** feeling cold.
Aviophobia	fear of	
Frigophobia		fridges. being alone. **cars.**

3 **CD2 40** Some people have strange phobias. Listen to Jodie, Dave, and Melissa talking about theirs. After each one discuss these questions as a class.

1. Which part of the cartoon would make them panic?
2. How did their phobia start?
3. How does it affect their lives?
4. What caused their panic attack?
5. Have they tried to cure their phobia?

4 Work in small groups to retell the stories. Use the prompts to help.

Jodie
When she was a little girl … grandmother asked her … opened the cabinet … dark green cardigan … started screaming … her grandmother managed to … now it's difficult to … tries to find … a year ago … a colleague's jacket … has decided to … embarrassed …

Dave
His dad used to … he didn't like watching him … when seven started feeling … his dad had to stop … problem got worse … supermarkets … asked his wife never to … wouldn't go to restaurants … oyster … only hamburger restaurants … started to see … hasn't succeeded in …

Melissa
Since she was five … trying to blow up … popped in her face … can remember … her friends enjoy … think it's fun to … last time … a panic attack … they refused to … difficulty in … worst thing … parties … can't imagine ever … even on TV … starts to shake …

What do you think?

5 Discuss these questions in your groups.

1. Which of the three people do you think has the most difficult phobia to live with? Why?
2. Why do people get phobias?
3. Why do some people and not others get them?
4. How do you think they can be cured? Suggest ideas.

The psychologist's view

6 **CD2 41** Listen to psychologist Dr. Lucy Atcheson talking about phobias. How does she answer questions 2–4 in Exercise 5?

Language work

Look at CD2 40 on page 123. Choose a story and <u>underline</u> examples of different kinds of verb patterns.

READING AND SPEAKING
Dangerous trips in history

1 Close your eyes. Imagine you are one of 90,000 people. You are traveling together, on foot, over mountains, rivers, and plains. It's winter. What problems would you face?

2 You are going to read about two famous leaders, Hannibal Barca and Mao Zedong. They both undertook remarkable trips with thousands of people. Look at the maps. What difficulties can you anticipate?

3 Divide into two groups.

Group A Read about HANNIBAL.
Group B Read about Mao Zedong.

First read about your leader's *Early Years*. Answer the questions with your group.
1. How did his father influence his life?
2. Who was the enemy?
3. Where did he move to?
4. Why did they set off on such a long trip?

4 Read about the trip and answer the questions.
1. When did the trip start?
2. How many began it? Who were they?
3. What kind of leader was he?
4. What problems did they face on the way?
5. How long did the trip last?
6. How did it end? How many survived?

5 Read the final part. What happened to the leader after the trip?

6 Find someone from the other group. Go through the questions again and compare the leaders and their trips. Use the maps to help. What similarities can you find? How many years separate the two trips?

What do you think?

• Which trip was more dangerous? Why?
• Can you imagine such a trip on foot taking place today? Where and why might it happen?

▶▶ **WRITING** TELLING A STORY (2) *p. 106*

HANNIBAL
CROSSES THE ALPS
247-182 BCE

EARLY YEARS

Hannibal Barca was born in Carthage, North Africa (now a suburb of Tunis, Tunisia) in 247 BCE. At that time this once prosperous seaport was losing a long and exhausting war with the Romans over who should rule the western Mediterranean. His father, Hamilcar, was a general in the army, and it is said that he made his son promise to hate the Romans forever.

The 23-year-long war was finally lost in 241 BCE. Hannibal and his family moved to Spain, where the Carthaginians were trying to build a new empire. Hannibal grew up to be a bold and fearless fighter like his father, and eventually became commander of the army. In 218 BCE the Romans again threatened to attack. In a daring and dangerous plan Hannibal decided to march from Spain to Italy before the Romans had even declared war. This march was to be a trip of 1,500 miles across both the Pyrenees and the Alps.

Mao Zedong
and the Long March
1893–1976

Early years

Mao Zedong (Mao Tse Tung) was born in Hunan province in Southern China in 1893. His father was an ambitious but illiterate farmer, who wanted his son to have the education he didn't have.

At his university Mao became active in revolutionary student groups and, in 1921, he helped found the Chinese Communist Party. He established a base in the remote Jiangxi province, where they formed the Red Army to fight against the Nationalist Government under Chiang Kai-shek. However, in 1934, after many bloody battles, they were forced to escape from the area. They set off on a remarkable trip, which became known as the Long March.

THE JOURNEY

In May 218 BCE, Hannibal left Spain with an army of about 90,000 men and 37 elephants, which he believed were needed to get them over the mountains. In the next few months under his inspiring leadership, they marched through Spain to the Pyrenees and then to the South of France. They moved about 10 miles a day, and were frequently attacked by local tribesmen. They reached the River Rhone and accomplished the unbelievable task of building huge rafts to ferry the elephants across. Some fell off but managed to swim using their trunks as snorkels. It was now fall, and snow started to fall as they approached the Alps. The army, helped by the elephants, struggled on, slipping and sliding over ice and snow, over the main pass. Finally, they were in sight of Italy. Their five-month trip at an end, Hannibal's army of 90,000 was reduced to 36,000—over half his men had perished or deserted on the way. Winter storms had killed all but one of his elephants.

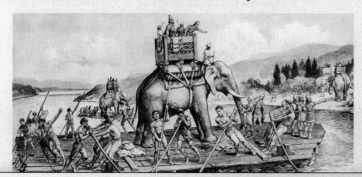

FINAL YEARS

In some ways Hannibal's march was hugely successful because he took the Romans by surprise and initially defeated them in numerous battles. However, after many years and many more battles, his army failed to overcome Rome's superior resources and manpower. Hannibal, who had been 29 at the start of his trip, sailed back to North Africa at the age of 45. He finally committed suicide in 182 BCE, at the age of 65. Despite his final defeat, he is still recognized as one of the greatest military leaders in history.

He was one of the

The Long March

The march began on October 16th. No one was sure where they were going, but 86,000 men and 30 women, including Mao's wife, set out to walk from the south to the north of China. The trip took one year, ending in the northwestern Shaanxi province.

They started the march fairly well, armed with 33,243 guns, but five weeks later suffered their first disastrous defeat at the Xiang River crossing. They lost 56,000 men and much of their equipment was thrown into the river.

It was at this time that Mao Zedong became leader of both the Red Army and the Communist Party. He was a tough but popular leader.

One of the worst experiences was crossing the Great Snowy Mountains, over 16,000 feet high. Many men died from lack of oxygen. Exhausted, they knew that to stop to rest meant certain death. If they managed to reach the top, it was best to sit down and slide to the bottom on the ice. Many men were catapulted over cliffs.

It was now September 1935 and the army had to cross the Marshland, between the Yangtze and Yellow Rivers. It looked innocent, covered with flowers, but beneath the flowers were bogs that could swallow a man in a minute. Mao lost more men during this seven-day trek than in the Snowy Mountains.

Eventually, on October 19th, after marching for 370 days and about 7,800 miles, they reached Shaanxi province. Of the 86,000 who began, only 4,000 remained.

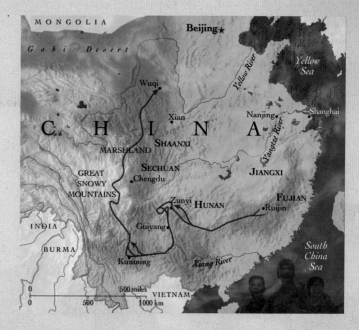

Later years

The Long March began the ascent to power of Mao Zedong. On October 1, 1949 he proclaimed the People's Republic of China, and the Great Cultural Revolution followed. This radically changed every aspect of Chinese society. In October 1966, Mao's *Little Red Book* was published, and his ideas were taught throughout the country. Mao's image was displayed everywhere: in homes, offices, stores, and streets. He finally died on September 9th, 1976, at 82.

VOCABULARY AND IDIOM
Body language

1 As a class, brainstorm all the parts of the body. Fill the board with all that you can think of.

2 Work in small groups. Which parts of the body do you use to do the following things?

bite	blow	clap	climb	hit	hug	kick	kneel
lick	march	point	scratch	stare	whistle		

3 Which verbs in Exercise 2 go with these nouns and phrases?

climb a ladder	*bite* your nails
stare out of the window	*blow* up a balloon
whistle a tune	*scratch* an insect bite
hug someone close *to you*	*clap* your hands to the music
kick a soccer ball	*point* at a place on the map
lick an ice cream	*hit* a nail with a hammer
kneel down to pick something up	*march* like a soldier

CD2 42 Listen and check. What is the situation for each expression?

4 The sentences all contain idioms that use parts of the body. Work out the meanings from context.

1. I don't get along with my brother. We don't **see eye to eye** on anything. *agree*
2. I saw a show on TV about quantum physics, but I'm afraid **it went straight over my head**. *I didn't understand a word*
3. **Don't waste your breath** trying to explain it to me. I'll never understand. *It's not worth*
4. Did you hear about Millie's party? Too many people came and the whole thing **got out of hand**.
5. The house was such a mess! When her parents came back, they **kicked up** such **a fuss**. I don't blame them. *were furious*
6. Can you help me? I've **hit a snag** installing this program on my computer. *I'm having trouble with*
7. My dad keeps chocolate in his desk. He **has** such **a sweet tooth**. *loves sweet things*
8. I feel silly. I got so excited when he said I'd won the lottery, but he was only **pulling my leg**. *joking / really*

5 Replace each idiom in Exercise 4 with a literal meaning from the box. Read the sentences aloud with both expressions.

loves sweet things	I didn't understand a word	
agree	were furious	I'm having trouble with
got out of control	it's not worth	joking

6 What other idiomatic expression do you know for each of these parts of the body? Share them with the class.

heart	head	hand	foot	hair

EVERYDAY ENGLISH
Travel and numbers

1 Read aloud these numbers.

15   50   **406**   72   178   **90**   19   850   **1,520**

17.5   36   247   5,000   **180,575**   2,000,000

CD2 43 Listen and check.

Notice the way we use points and commas in English.
$6.50 (six fifty)
2,500 (two thousand five hundred)
3.14 (three point one four)

---

2 Match a question with a number. Ask and answer them with a partner. Practice saying the numbers aloud.

Questions	Numbers
1. What time does the train leave?	212-555-2111
2. How far is it to Montreal?	27 pounds
3. How long's the flight?	1,915 miles
4. How much does it cost?	1:45
5. What's your credit card number?	17.5%
6. What's the expiration date?	About 1½ hours
7. How much does it weigh?	6356 5055 5137 9904
8. What's your cell number?	$34.99
9. What's the tax rate?	02/14

CD2 44 Listen and check. Practice again.

3 Work in pairs. Find the numbers in the pictures and practice saying them.

4 **CD2 45** Listen to the conversation.
  1. Where is it taking place? *airport, check-in counter*
  2. Who are the people? *passenger airline*
  3. Where does the woman want to travel to?
  4. What is the problem?

Listen again. Write down all the different numbers you hear. What do they refer to?

  one (bag), 60 pounds

Practice the conversation with a partner.

5 **CD2 46** Listen to another conversation and do the same again.

6 Work in groups. Write down some numbers that are important to you. Can the others guess what they refer to? Explain what they are.

> Nineteen.

> Is it your age?

> No. It's the day I go on vacation. July 19th!

9 It depends how you look at it

Grammar: Conditionals
Vocabulary: Words with similar meaning
Everyday English: Dealing with money

STARTER

Ideas can be looked at in different ways.

Work in groups. Think of some pros and cons of being a teenager.

+ You aren't a kid anymore.
  You are becoming more independent.

− You aren't a child, but you aren't an adult.
  You don't have any money.

Compare ideas as a class.

BILLY'S STORY
Conditionals

1 Why are some kids bullied? Why do some kids become bullies?

2 Read about Billy. What are his problems?

Billy enjoyed school. He tried hard, but studying wasn't easy for him.

He didn't have many friends. He felt lonely and insecure.

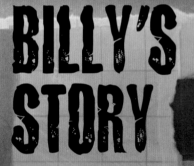

The other kids started bullying Billy. They called him "Billy no friends" and stole his money.

They sent him texts. They threatened to hurt him.

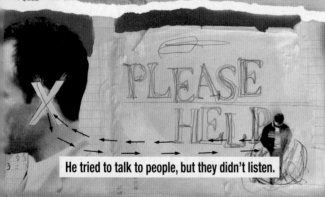

He tried to talk to people, but they didn't listen.

Billy started missing school. He felt desperate. He didn't know who to go to for help.

3 What would *you* do if you were …?

Billy's mom	Billy's sister	Billy's dad
Billy's teacher	a counselor from Kidcare	Billy

> If I were Billy's mom, I'd go to the teacher and explain what was happening.

> I wouldn't. I'd talk to Billy and …

4 **CD3 2** Listen. Who are the six speakers imagining they are?

I'd organize a school day which tried to educate everyone about bullying, and I'd invite social workers, police, and psychologists. – The teacher.

5 Look at the Kidcare Report. Read what the counselor wrote about Billy. What *did* Billy do?
Answer the questions.

- Did people listen to Billy?
- Did his father stay?
- Did he talk to Kidcare?

Look at the sentences in **bold** in the Kidcare Report.

CD3 3 Listen and repeat.

Things got tough for Billy and his sister when their dad walked out.

WITHDRAWN

WHERE'S BILLY

Then the attacks started. Every day after school the bullies waited for him.

So what would you do…?
If you're being bullied, contact *KIDCARE*.
We're on your side. Call 212 364 8888.

MISSING

KIDCARE REPORT

Client: Billy Simmons
Age: 14
Counselor: Carmen Delanie

Billy ran away from home because he was being bullied at school. He has now been missing for six months. He had tried to talk to his mother and his teachers. **If they'd listened to him, they'd have understood** how he was feeling.

Billy's father walked out on the family. **If his father had stayed, Billy might have felt happier** and less insecure.

If he'd talked to us, we could have helped. He should have come to us a long time ago.

We are doing all we can to locate Billy. We suspect that he is somewhere in New York.

6 Make a sentence using *If* and the prompts.

1. People didn't understand what Billy was going through.
   understood … wouldn't … run away
   If they'd understood, he wouldn't have run away.

2. He didn't go to Kidcare.
   gone … could … talked … problems

3. His father left.
   left … Billy might … felt more secure

4. The bullies threatened him.
   threatened … he wouldn't … run away

CD3 4 Listen and check.

> **GRAMMAR SPOT**
>
> **1** Second conditional sentences express an unreal situation about the present.
>
> If I **was** in trouble, **I'd** (= would) **come** to you for help. (*But I'm not in trouble.*)
>
> Third conditional sentences express an unreal situation about the past.
>
> If you'**d** (=had) **told** me about your problems, **I'd** (= would) **have helped**. (*But you didn't tell me, so I didn't help.*)
>
> How do we form second and third conditional sentences?
>
> **2** Which two of these modal verbs express a possibility?
>
> I **would** / **might** / **could** have helped you.
>
> **3** Look at this sentence.
>
> Pete **shouldn't have stolen** the money.
>
> Is this good advice? Did Pete steal the money?
>
> ▶▶ **Grammar Reference 9.1–9.6 pp. 138–9**

PRACTICE
It all went wrong

1 Work in pairs. Read about three robberies that went wrong. What were the robbers' mistakes?

Easy arrest

A bank robber in Montreal, Canada, held up a sign that said "Give me all the money." The cashier handed over the money, and the bank robber fled, leaving the note behind. Unfortunately, he had written the note on the back of an envelope. On the other side was his address. He was arrested later the same day.

Smile!

Car thief Lee Hoskins took pictures of himself stealing a Honda Civic with a camera he found in the glove compartment. Lee and his girlfriend took turns posing before crashing the car and fleeing the scene, leaving the camera on the back seat of the car. "It's amazing just how stupid some criminals can be," said a spokesman for the Atlanta police.

Have a loan instead

A bank manager in Arlington, Virginia, stopped a robbery by persuading the three criminals to take out a loan instead. The robbers burst into the bank near Washington, D.C., and demanded $50,000. The manager put the money on the table, but suggested that a loan would be more sensible. He offered them a $20 cash advance and told them to return in ten minutes to sign the loan papers. Police were waiting for them.

2 Rewrite the sentences about the robberies using the words in parentheses.

1. It was a mistake to write his note on an envelope. *(shouldn't)*
   <u>He shouldn't have written his note on an envelope.</u>

2. It would have been better to take the note with him. *(should)*
   _____

3. He left his address. The police found him. *(if)*
   _____

4. It was stupid to take his picture. *(shouldn't)*
   _____

5. They crashed the car. They didn't escape. *(if, could)*
   _____

6. He left pictures of himself. He could have gotten away with it. *(if, might)*
   _____

7. They were so stupid. They didn't escape with the money. *(if)*
   _____

8. They listened to the manager. They didn't steal the money. *(if, could)*
   _____

9. It was silly to go back to the bank. *(shouldn't)*
   _____

10. It would have been better to just run away. *(should)*
    _____

You're an idiot!

3 Your friend did some really stupid things.

> I drove home even though I was falling asleep at the wheel.

> You're an idiot! You might have had an accident! You could have killed someone!

How do you react when he tells you these things? Use *might have* or *could have*.

1. I went walking in the mountains for three days with no food or equipment.
2. I didn't feel like going to work, so I called in sick. I went shopping instead.
3. I had a temperature of 102, but I went out dancing all night.
4. I told Sandra I couldn't see her, then went out with Danielle.
5. I used to be really good at tennis—I was an under-14 champion—but then I gave it all up.

CD3 5 Listen and compare.

Speaking

4 Think of a time in your life when things went wrong.

> I went to a party with my boyfriend.
> I danced with another boy.
> I had a fight with my boyfriend.
> We broke up.

Make sentences like these.

> I shouldn't have danced with the other boy.

> If I hadn't danced with him, I wouldn't have had a fight with my boyfriend.

> I should have just said sorry to my boyfriend. Then we wouldn't have broken up.

SPEAKING AND LISTENING
A social conscience

1 Work in small groups. Do you have a social conscience? Discuss situations 1–5 and decide what you would do.

I'd...   I wouldn't...   I might...

Tell the class.

2 **CD3 6** Listen to five people describing a situation they were in. Answer the questions.

1. Where was he/she? *bank*
2. Who were the other people involved?
3. What was the problem?
4. Did he/she do anything? Say anything?
5. What was the other person's reaction?
6. What was the result?

Talking about you

3 What would *you* have done in the same situations? Discuss in your groups, then tell the rest of the class.

I wouldn't have done what she did.
I'd have told him . . .

SPOKEN ENGLISH *just*

1 Look at the use of *just* in these sentences.

*I'd **just** reached the front of the line . . .*
*I **just** need to ask a quick question.*
*. . . I was **just** furious!*

In which sentences does *just* mean . . . ?

really   a short time before   only/simply

2 Find other examples of *just* in CD3 6 on page 124.

3 Write the word *just* where you think it goes best in these sentences.

1. Miwako isn't here. She left. *just*
2. I'm sorry I'm in a bad mood. I'm tired, that's all.
3. I love your new coat!
4. I finished the most wonderful book. You have to read it!
5. I don't want any coffee. A glass of water, please.
6. John's so generous. I think he's amazing!
7. "Who's coming tonight?" "Me."
8. Hold on a minute. I'm going to the restroom.

CD3 7 Listen, check, and repeat.

Do you have a social conscience?

What would YOU do?

1 You are on the sidewalk. A man who says he's penniless and homeless is asking for money, so you give him some. As you're walking away, his phone starts ringing. He pulls out a really nice cell phone and starts talking to a friend.

2 You're in a store. You see a woman shoplifting some food. She has three small children who look hungry.

3 You're in a clothing store where eating is forbidden. A woman opens a bag of chips and starts eating in front of you.

4 Your best friend is cheating on her boyfriend, Bill. She's been going out with him forever, but she's also seeing a guy named Mark.

5 You see some kids on the street dropping litter. There is a trash can ten feet away.

READING AND SPEAKING
The victim meets the burglar

1 Have you or has anyone you know ever been the victim of a crime? Discuss the questions.
   - What happened?
   - Were the police involved?
   - Was the criminal arrested?

2 There is an organization called the Restorative Justice Consortium. It brings together criminals and their victims.
   - What do you think it hopes to achieve by this?
   - What might the victim of a crime have to say?
   - What might the criminal learn?

3 Read the headlines and the introduction to the newspaper article. How do you think the burglar and the victim became friends?

4 Work in two groups.

   Group A   Read about the victim.
   Group B   Read about the robber.

   Answer the questions.
   1. What personal details do you learn? (*name, age, background …*)
   2. What was he doing in the moments before their first encounter?
   3. What was his first reaction? How did he feel? What did he think?
   4. How does he describe the act of violence?
   5. How did he feel after the crime took place?
   6. What was his reaction when asked to meet the other person?
   7. What made Will so angry?
   8. What did this outburst of anger make him realize?
   9. What does he think of the experience of restorative justice?

5 Find a partner from the other group. Compare your answers to the questions in Exercise 4.

What do you think?

1. Is bringing together the criminal and the victim a good idea? Could it help with all crimes? Could it help with bullying?

2. 60% of people released after serving one year in prison are convicted of another crime. What does this statistic suggest?

3. The purposes of imprisonment are …
   - to punish the criminal.
   - to protect society from the criminal.
   - to rehabilitate the criminal.

   Do you think these goals are achieved?
   What other forms of punishment might be more effective?

▶▶ **WRITING** PROS AND CONS *p. 108*

I'M SORRY
How a burglar and his victim became the best of friends

THE VICTIM

BUSINESSMAN Will Riley, 50, lives in the city with his wife and daughter …

I WAS getting ready to go to the gym when I walked into my hallway and stopped dead in my tracks. There, standing on the stairs, was a man about the same age as me, dressed in a scruffy leather jacket.

"What are you doing here?" I asked in shock. He said he was a neighbor who'd gotten lost. But it was obvious who he was.

I was suddenly scared. I thought, "If he has a knife, he could kill me." We kind of fought with each other. A passerby saw us and called the police. Somehow I managed to hold him until the police arrived. It was only after they arrested him and took him away that a policeman asked if I was OK. I put my hand to my head and felt blood. I hadn't realized what he'd done to me. It's incredible, but I just didn't register that he'd hit me really hard. He'd smashed a flower pot on my head, and all the pieces were on the ground. I went to the hospital and needed stitches.

After the burglary, my whole life changed. I've always lived in big cities, and I've never been afraid of urban crime, but suddenly I became too frightened to open my front door. All I could think was, "What if my daughter had been at home? Would he have attacked her?"

PETER WOOLF, a life-long criminal, broke into Will Riley's home one March evening. Will found Peter standing in his hallway, his pockets stuffed with money and jewelry.

Peter was jailed for three years for the burglary. So it's hard to think of them becoming friends.

Here, Will and Peter describe their first encounter, and why meeting each other again was the best thing for both of them ...

By VICTORIA KENNEDY

CLOSE FRIENDS: Peter Woolf and Will Riley

I was asked to meet the burglar in prison. I wasn't sure what the purpose was, but I went anyway. I was curious.

We sat in the prison library, and he explained how he'd come from a dysfunctional family and spent his life in and out of jail. He spoke without any emotion. But it was when he suddenly said, "Last time we met ..." that I exploded.

I screamed at him, "Why me? Why did you ruin my life?"

"We didn't meet in a bar! You broke into my house!" I was so angry. I screamed at him, "Why me? Why did you do this to me? Why did you ruin my life?"

I could see from his face that I had gotten through to him. He looked stunned. It was then I realized he was just an ordinary guy. And I wanted to help him ...

When I got home, I felt relieved. All my fears disappeared. Because I could see Peter was just a normal human being, he became less frightening.

When he was finally released, we stayed in touch. I've met him dozens of times since, and the change in him is amazing. It's hard to believe he's the same person who broke into my home. He's totally different.

I'm delighted that I've done something to help Peter get his life back.

THE ROBBER

PETER WOOLF, 50, is married to Louise, and works as a counselor to rehabilitate criminals ...

IT WAS easy to break into Will's house. Just one push and the lock broke. I quickly took some gold jewelry and some money from upstairs. I was feeling lucky.

But when I was coming downstairs and I bumped into Will in the hallway, I suddenly felt frightened. I thought, "He's a big guy. If he wanted to, he could hurt me."

I tried to escape. I didn't want to hit him, but I did. I'm not a violent guy, but I just did what I had to do. There was a flower pot, and I smashed it on his head.

After I was arrested, all I felt was a big sense of relief. I was going back to a place I knew well. I'd been in and out of prison for 18 years, for theft, burglary, and fraud.

I'd hit rock bottom. I stole because it was the only thing I knew how to do. I knew it would only lead me back to prison.

I was given a three-year sentence. It was while I was in jail that someone mentioned Restorative Justice. I couldn't see the point, but I agreed to do it because I was bored.

It wasn't until I started walking down the hall toward the library that I got scared.

When I got there I sat down and just looked at the floor. I said the same things I always used to say to the police. But Will was furious, and I was shocked. I thought, "My God, I did all this."

I felt angry with myself, and ashamed. I was determined to make things better.

I suddenly realized that I was responsible for this man's pain. He wasn't just a faceless nobody that I'd stolen from. I felt angry with myself, and ashamed. I was determined to make things better.

I started a course to be a counselor. It was at the counseling class that I met Louise. I was over the moon. And my life changed completely ...

I was released early after 18 months, and Louise and I got married. Life hasn't been easy, but I've worked hard to get things together.

I'm now helping others. I haven't committed another crime. I feel proud of myself. These days, I consider myself lucky that I broke into Will's house that day. If I hadn't—and if we hadn't become friends—I don't know what I would have done. I guess I'd have gone back to my old ways.

VOCABULARY
Words with similar meaning

1 Match the words in **A** with their similar meanings in **B**. They all appeared in the newspaper article on pages 70–71.

A	B
prison	frightened
burglar	bump into
scared	stunned
purpose	completely
meet	furious
angry	normal
shocked	jail
ordinary	point
delighted	over the moon
totally	robber

2 Complete the sentences with pairs of words from Exercise 1. The first word is from **A**, the second word is from **B**.

1. "Did you _____ anyone you know in town?"
   "Yes, I _____ Carlos as I was coming out of a store."

2. "Aren't you _____ with your test grade?"
   "You bet. I'm _____ . It's great!"

3. "The _____ of this meeting is to brainstorm ideas."
   "Sorry, but I don't see the _____ . Why bother?"

4. "You must be _____ with Tim for crashing your car."
   "I'm absolutely _____ with him."

5. "I was _____ when I heard that Joe had died. Weren't you?"
   "I was _____ . He was only 48."

6. "I'm _____ of dogs. I was bitten once."
   "I'm not _____ of them. They're usually really friendly."

3 These words are similar but not the same. Choose the correct word.

1. **alone / lonely**
   live _____ happily
   feel _____ and unhappy

2. **big / great**
   _____ house/mistake/feet
   _____ artist/Wall of China/party

3. **tall / high**
   _____ person/building/trees
   _____ mountain/wall/ceiling

4. **small / little**
   _____ old lady/boy/finger
   _____ room/glass of water/dress size

5. **quick / fast**
   _____ car/train/food
   _____ look/worker/thinking

4 Which verb goes with which phrase?

win	the other team
beat	the championship

clean	my hair
wash	the apartment

make	a mess
do	your best

listen	a noise
hear	to music

talk	to my friends for hours
speak	to my bank manager

rob	a bank
steal	some jewelry

pay	someone a present
buy	at the cash register

borrow	money from someone
lend	money to someone

burglar

robber

EVERYDAY ENGLISH

Dealing with money

1 **CD3 8** Listen to the beginnings of five conversations. Match each conversation with a photo.

- Who are the people?
- What are they talking about?
- What questions are asked?

2 **CD3 9** Listen to the whole conversations. Check your answers to the questions in Exercise 1.

3 Work with a partner. Look at 1–5. Try to remember the full conversations. The words in **blue** will help.

1
A Here's … check.
B Thank … Is the tip …?
A No … hope … enjoyed …
B … nice, …
A Can you … here? … card … receipt.
B Thanks. … for you.
A … kind. … hope … again soon.
B Bye!

included sign

2
A How … standard …?
B $120 …
A … everything?
B That … two people, but it … breakfast.
A Is that…?
B Yes, … afraid … But … $120 does … tax.

per night extra

3
A … tickets … MasterCard.
B Can you … number?
A 5484 6922 3171 2435.
B … date?
A 09/12.
B And the three … security number …?
A 721.

expiration digit

4
A … give me … my account?
B Sure. … number.
A 4033 2614 7900.
B Bear … one moment. The … cleared balance … is $542.53 …

balance credit

5
A … cappucino … bottles … water, please?
B … $14.50.
A Thank you.
B And here's your change. 50 cents.
A Thanks. Um …? How much …? I think … mistake!
B Sorry?
A I think you must … I … $20, but … given me … $15.
B No, I …
A Well, I … pretty … I gave you …
B Oh, …? Um … Here …
A Thanks.

change made a mistake

4 **CD3 9** Listen again to the conversations. Check your answers in CD3 9 on page 124.

5 Discuss the questions.

- What's the exchange rate between your currency and the U.S. dollar?
- Are you overdrawn at the end of the month? Can you economize if you have to?
- What credit cards do you have? Do you have any store cards? Do you stay within your credit limit?

10 All things high tech

STARTER

1 Underline the nouns in these sentences.

My brother has the best computer in the world.
Mine is just an old laptop.

Find ... a definite article an indefinite article
a possessive adjective a possessive pronoun

2 Underline the reflexive pronouns in these sentences.

Mike programs his computer himself.
I live by myself, which suits me fine.

CHIPS IN EVERYTHING
Noun phrases

1 Work with a partner. Read the text about microprocessors. Answer the questions.

1. Do you agree with these statements? Why/Why not?

   Microchips are huge.   Microchips are tiny.

2. What things in our daily lives have microchips in them?
3. In what way are computers very simple?
4. How long does it take to make microprocessors?
5. Why do designers put pictures on the chips?
6. In what ways is the future exciting?

Microprocessors
The biggest thing since the invention of the wheel

How do they work?

Transistors are microscopic electronic switches that turn on and off billions of times a second. It's hard to believe that basically that is all a computer does — it either says *Yes* or *No*.

To process the words, images, and sounds we use every day, computers and other devices (such as CD players) transform these communications into a simple code that uses the numerals 0 and 1 to represent the on and off states of a transistor. This language of 0s and 1s is known as digital information.

What are they?

A microprocessor—(also known as a microchip, or just a chip)—is a small, thin piece of silicon that has been printed with transistors. One chip can contain hundreds of millions of transistors, performing billions (yes, billions) of calculations each second. The smallest are just a few mm^2. The microchip is the most complex product that has ever been made.

What do they do?

Microprocessors are the brains of your personal computer. They control everything in our lives. They are used in all digital devices — calculators, cameras, radios, ovens, fridges, washing machines, DVDs, and watches. Without microprocessors, modern cars wouldn't start or stop (there are about 60 per car), TV remotes wouldn't switch channels, and we couldn't text each other on our cells. Doctors and surgeons wouldn't be able to diagnose, treat, or operate. Nearly all of their equipment contains microchips.

How are they made?

It takes months to make a microprocessor and involves over 250 manufacturing steps, but it can take years to design one. Sometimes the engineers put pictures on the surface of the chip because they want to show it's theirs. The pictures are incredibly tiny, and can only be seen with a microscope. They are like the designers' signature.

What about the future?

The digital world is only a few decades old. There are still countless more things we could do with microprocessors. Soon they'll be able to fix themselves and even make themselves. No one knows what will happen. Only time will tell.

2 Look back at the text on page 74. Find and complete these sentences.

Microprocessors are the biggest thing since …
A microchip is a …
The smallest … mm².
… most complex product …
Microprocessors control …
They are used in all …
We couldn't text …
Doctors and surgeons … Nearly all …
It takes months …
Microprocessors will be able to … and even …

GRAMMAR SPOT

Noun phrases can consist of:

Articles

A chip is **a** small piece of silicon.
It is **the** biggest thing since **the** invention of **the** wheel.

Possessives

All of **their** equipment contains microchips.
They want to show it's **theirs**.
The pictures are like the designers' signature.

all/everything

Microchips control **everything** in our lives.
They are used in **all** digital devices.

Pronouns

Microchips will be able to fix **themselves**.
We couldn't text **each other**.

▶▶ **Grammar Reference 10.1–10.5 pp. 139–41**

---

3 Read these facts. Which surprise you most?

Did you know ...?

There are **20 billion** microchips in use in the world today. Every year another **5 billion** are produced.

Every **18** months, the technology develops to allow **twice** as many transistors to fit on a chip, **doubling** its speed and capacity.

The smallest wire on a chip is less than **0.1 microns** wide. A human hair is **100 microns** thick.

PRACTICE

Articles – *a/an/the*/no article/*one*

1 Discuss the use of articles in these sentences.

I bought **a** laptop and **a** printer on Saturday.
The laptop has **an** *Intel* microprocessor.
Intel is **the** largest manufacturer of computer chips in **the** world.
One chip contains millions of transistors.
I don't understand **(-)** computers.

2 Complete the text with *a/an/the*, or no article.

THE FIRST COMPUTER

Charles Babbage (1791–1871) was (1) _____ scientist and (2) _____ engineer. He had the idea for (3) _____ first programmable computer. He wanted to build (4) _____ machine that could do (5) _____ calculations without making the mistakes that human "computers" made.

He designed a machine called the Difference Engine, and (6) _____ British government provided funds. (7) _____ machine was never completed because Babbage ran out of (8) _____ money.

In 1991, (9) _____ team of engineers from (10) _____ Science Museum in London built one of Babbage's machines using his original designs, and it worked perfectly.

CD3 10 Listen and check.

3 Complete the sentences with *a/an/the*/no article, or *one*.

1. "Where's Han?" "In _____ kitchen cooking _____ lunch."
2. Washington, D.C., is _____ capital of _____ United States.
3. We had _____ dinner in _____ best restaurant in _____ world.
4. _____ day I'm going to be _____ rich man.
5. Victor's in _____ hospital. He's had _____ operation.
6. Certainly _____ computers have changed _____ modern life.
7. "How do you like your coffee?" "Black with _____ sugar, please."
8. I have two daughters. _____ daughter is _____ teacher, _____ other works in _____ advertising.
9. Today is _____ first day of _____ rest of your life. Enjoy it.

Speaking

CD3 11 Work in small groups. Listen and then answer the questions. Be careful with articles.

Where did you have lunch today?   **I had lunch in a cafe/in the school cafeteria.**

Possessives

4 In these sentences, which word is a possessive adjective? Which are possessive pronouns?

> I'm very proud of **my** children.
> Don't touch that! It's **mine**!
> James is an old friend of **ours**.

Don't touch that! It's mine!

Underline the correct word.

1. "Is that *her / hers* book?" "Well, it isn't *my / mine*."
2. "*Who's / Whose* car is that?" "It's *our / ours*. Nice, huh?"
3. Microsoft owes *it's / its* success to Windows. That's why *it's / its* the biggest software company in the world.
4. Those aren't *your / yours* socks. These blue ones are *your / yours*.
5. Mary, this is Pete. Pete's an old friend of *me / mine*.
6. My sisters borrow *my / mine* clothes, and I borrow *their / theirs*.

5 In these sentences when does the apostrophe come before *s*? When does it come after?

> My wife**'s** family lives in the northeast.
> I went to a boy**s'** school.

Put the apostrophe in the correct place in these sentences.

1. I borrowed my dads car.
2. My parents new house is great.
3. I like Julianas boyfriend.
4. The childrens room is upstairs.
5. I really like my brothers girlfriend.

its or *it's*

6 **CD3 12** Listen to the sentences. Underline the words you hear.

1. its   it's
2. theirs   there's
3. there   their
4. it's   its
5. they're   their
6. there's   theirs

all and *every* . . .

7 Correct the mistakes in these sentences.
1. I buy ~~my all~~ ^{all my} clothes in secondhand stores.
2. All was stolen in the burglary.
3. "Did they take any of your CDs?" "All."
4. In my family we like all baseball.
5. All enjoyed the party.
6. All of employees in my company work hard.

8 Complete the sentences with *all/everything/everybody/everyone*.

1. Two plus two is four. **Everybody** knows that.
2. _____ I want is you.
3. I'm having a terrible day. _____ is going wrong.
4. My girlfriend calls me _____ the time.
5. My sister is really popular. She knows _____ , and _____ knows her.

Reflexive pronouns and *each other*

9 Look at the sentences.

> I cut **myself** shaving.
> They send **each other** e-mails.

Which sentence expresses the idea: ⇄ ?
Which sentence expresses the idea: ↻ ?

Complete the sentences with *myself/yourself* . . . or *each other*.

1. We love _____ and we're going to get married.
2. He's crazy! He could have killed _____ !
3. Do you like the cake? I made it _____ .
4. "Can you make me a cup of coffee?" "No. Do it _____."
5. My kids get along well with _____ .
6. Please make _____ at home.
7. We're very different, but we understand _____ .
8. Her kids are good. They know how to behave _____ .
9. The food's all ready, so help _____ to whatever you want.

mime

With a partner or on your own, mime these to the class. The others must say what you're doing.

- **look at yourself in the mirror**
  You're looking at yourself in the mirror.
- talk to yourself
- hate each other
- help yourself to some food
- enjoy yourself
- help each other with homework
- shout at each other
- not speak to each other

LISTENING AND SPEAKING
What do you do on the Internet?

1 Work in small groups. Do you think these statements are true or false?

> 1 billion searches are made on *Google* search engine every day.

> Over 140 million people in the U.S. have their own web page on social networking sites such as Facebook and MySpace.

> In 2005, the original Hollywood sign was sold on eBay for $450,400.

> 86 percent of the web pages on the Internet are in English.

> 1 out of 8 couples who marry in the U.S. met on an online dating site.

> 88% of websites are never visited.

> There is a web that no one knows about. It is called the deep web, and it is 500 times bigger than the surface web we all know about.

2 Put the words into the correct order to make sentences about using the Internet.

1. websites / onto / go / sports / I / about
2. Internet / mainly / Facebook / use / I / the / for
3. log / bank / onto / my / I / and / "Pay Now" / click / on
4. shopping / do / my / nearly / online / I / all
5. player / onto / download / MP3 / I / music / my

3 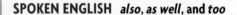 Listen to five people talking about what they do on the Internet. <u>Underline</u> what they say they do.

1 Tom
1. <u>watch videos</u>
2. talk to friends
3. learn languages
4. buy and sell things

2 Monica
1. watch movies
2. do social networking
3. look for work
4. see what's on

3 Pedro
1. pay bills
2. watch sports
3. book and buy things
4. make friends

4 Daisy
1. watch DVDs
2. send e-mails
3. do shopping
4. get news and weather

5 David
1. make friends
2. research family history
3. practice languages
4. download music

4 Work in pairs. Choose one of the people and listen in more detail.
Tell the rest of the class about the person you chose.

SPOKEN ENGLISH **also, as well,** and **too**

1 Look at the position of the expressions *also, as well,* and *too* in these lines from CD3 13
> I'm **also** selling some of my old stuff.
> ...I update my GPS system **as well**.
> I watch the news in Spanish and French, **too**.

2 Put the three expressions in these sentences.
> I go onto social networking sites.
> I download music and videos.
> I go onto websites to get the weather.

3 Only two of the expressions sound right in these sentences.
> "Dave's nice." "His sister is _____."
> "I'm going home now." "I am _____."
> Don't forget your coat. And take your umbrella _____.
> Buy some bread. And some coffee _____.

4 Only *one* of the expressions sounds right in these sentences.
> "I like Harry." "Me, _____."
> "I'm thirsty." "Me, _____."

Talking about you

- What do *you* do on the Internet?
  What are your favorite websites?

- Do you use websites like Facebook and eBay?

- The Internet represents the democracy of ideas. Is it right that it has no censorship? What are the dangers of this?

READING AND SPEAKING
21st century city

1 What do you want from a city? Put these features in order for you.
(1 = the most important)

____ earning a living
____ beautiful architecture
____ things of cultural interest
____ a variety of entertainment
____ a good transportation system
____ career opportunities
____ good shops and restaurants

Compare your answers with a partner, then with the class.

2 Look at the photos of Dubai, and read the introduction to the article.

Discuss what you can see in the photos.

3 Read parts 1–6 quickly. What superlative adjectives can you find?

What do they refer to?

Complete the chart.

superlative adjective	Things referred to
the most exciting	new city
the most popular	
	prize money
	hotspot
	centers of learning
the world's first	
	airport
the fastest	
the most expensive	

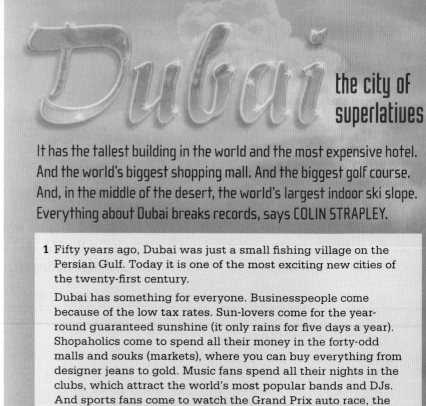

Dubai the city of superlatives

It has the tallest building in the world and the most expensive hotel. And the world's biggest shopping mall. And the biggest golf course. And, in the middle of the desert, the world's largest indoor ski slope. Everything about Dubai breaks records, says COLIN STRAPLEY.

1 Fifty years ago, Dubai was just a small fishing village on the Persian Gulf. Today it is one of the most exciting new cities of the twenty-first century.

Dubai has something for everyone. Businesspeople come because of the low tax rates. Sun-lovers come for the year-round guaranteed sunshine (it only rains for five days a year). Shopaholics come to spend all their money in the forty-odd malls and souks (markets), where you can buy everything from designer jeans to gold. Music fans spend all their nights in the clubs, which attract the world's most popular bands and DJs. And sports fans come to watch the Grand Prix auto race, the Open Tennis Tournament, the Desert Classic Golf Tournament, or the Dubai World Cup horse race (which has the biggest prize money —$6 million—in the world).

Reasons for success

2 There are several reasons why Dubai has become the world's latest hotspot. One is its location. It is situated midway between Europe and Asia, and on the doorstep of Africa, thus providing easy access from Europe, India, Southeast Asia, Japan, and Australia. Another is tradition. Arabic nations have been traders for over five thousand years. Doing business, buying and selling, is in their blood. And another very important reason is opportunity. The wealth from oil has been invested to create an ultra-modern city, a financial center, a world-famous place of learning, and a year-round tourist destination.

A global city

3 Dubai is one of the seven United Arab Emirates (UAE). It is ruled by crown prince Sheikh Mohammed bin Rashid al-Maktoum. He has declared that he wants to make Dubai "a pioneering global city," whose revenue comes not from oil but from tourism and business. To this end, the country has invested more than $100 billion in new projects.

Dubai has established a growing number of free trade zones, where international companies are encouraged to locate with the promise of zero percent taxes and few regulations. A zone

called Media City has attracted CNN and Reuters, and Microsoft and IBM opened regional headquarters in nearby Internet City. Dubai Knowledge Village has partners from universities across the globe and is one of the world's largest centers of learning.

Ten million tourists

4 Dubai's 10 million tourists a year come for the beaches but especially for the stores. There is an annual Shopping Festival in January and February that attracts 3.5 million people who spend $2.5 billion.

If the beach and the desert lose their appeal, visitors can always go skiing at Ski Dubai, an indoor ski resort. While temperatures outside can soar above 104°F, the ski center is covered with real snow all year round. It has five runs, including the world's first indoor black run.

The new airport will eventually be able to handle more than 150 million passengers a year, making it the world's busiest airport.

The world's biggest building site

5 New buildings are going up all the time. Dubaians joke that they go to sleep at night alone and wake up next to a skyscraper in the morning. Dubai has nearly 20% of the world's construction cranes—that's more than 22,000.

The building that has become the symbol of Dubai is the Burj Al Arab hotel. It is shaped like a sail and is the world's first seven-star hotel. It has a helicopter pad on the 28th floor.

Another building, the Burj Dubai tower, is designed to be the tallest in the world, at over 2,300 feet, with more than 200 floors, and the world's fastest elevators, traveling at 40 miles per hour.

There are even manmade islands. On Palm Jumeirah there are hotels, villas, restaurants, and shops. Another artificial archipelago, called The World, is, at $14 billion, one of the most expensive pieces of real estate ever built.

What's next?

6 Marinas, gyms, theme parks, sports stadiums, underwater hotels, rotating skyscrapers, subways— all these are under construction. Dubai's getting better, but the best is yet to come.

4 Answer the questions.

Part 1
1. What five of groups of people are mentioned?
2. Why do these people find Dubai attractive?

Part 2
3. What are the three reasons that explain Dubai's success?
4. Explain each reason.

Part 3
5. What is special about free trade zones?
6. What are three of them called?
7. Who has been attracted to them?

Part 4
8. What three things are mentioned that visitors can do in Dubai?

Part 5
9. What is the joke about building?
10. Give five facts about construction and buildings in Dubai.

5 Here are some numbers from the article. What do they refer to?

50 - *Fifty years ago Dubai was just a small fishing village.*

a. 5	f. 0%
b. 40	g. 10 million
c. 6 million	h. 104°
d. 5,000	i. 20%
e. 100 billion	j. 200

CD3 14 Listen and check.

What do you think?

- How does Dubai rate according to the features of a city mentioned in Exercise 1?
- What would you like most if you lived in Dubai? What would you miss from your own country?
- What are your favorite old buildings in your country? What is your favorite new building? Which building would you like to knock down?

VOCABULARY AND SPEAKING
Compound nouns

1 Nouns can be combined to make a new word.
Here are some examples from the text on pages 78–9.

| shopping mall | tax rates | skyscraper | real estate |

Where is the stress on these compound nouns?

2 Look at the dictionary entries. Practice saying the words.

3 Answer the questions.
1. Why do people take aspirin?
2. Where do you find the words *Here lies James Barlow – RIP*?
3. What can you do if you want to listen to music without disturbing other people?
4. What are the front lights on a car?
5. What's the first thing you read in a newspaper?
6. Where are the headquarters of the United Nations?
7. Are *you* making headway in English?

4 In these lists, one compound noun doesn't exist. Which one is it?

sun	sunglasses	**sunpool**	sunscreen	**sunset**
card	**running card**	**parking card**	birthday card	**business card**
tea	**tea bag**	teacup	**teatime**	tea cars
case	money case	**briefcase**	suitcase	**bookcase**

CD3 **15** Listen and repeat.

5 Put one word in each box to form three compound nouns.

dining
1 waiting [   ]
dressing

lights
2 [   ] sign
jam

antique
3 secondhand [   ]
shoe

Spider
4 mail [   ]
chair

brush
5 [   ] dresser
cut

secret
6 travel [   ]
real estate

brows
7 [   ] glasses
witness

wrapping
8 toilet [   ]
wall

---

headache /'hedeɪk/ *noun* [C] **1** a pain in your head: *I've got a splitting* (= very bad) *headache.* ⊃ note at **ache 2** a person or thing that causes worry or difficulty: *Paying the bills is a constant headache.*

headlight /'hedlaɪt/ (also **headlamp**) *noun* [C] one of the two large bright lights at the front of a vehicle ⊃ picture on **page P9**

headline /'hedlaɪn/ *noun* **1** [C] the title of a newspaper article printed in large letters above the story **2 the headlines** [pl] the main items of news read on TV or radio

headphones /'hedfəʊnz/ *noun* [pl] a piece of equipment worn over or in the ears that makes it possible to listen to music, the radio, etc. without other people hearing it ⊃ note at **listen**

headquarters /'hedkwɔːtərz/ *noun* [pl, with sing or pl verb] (*abbr* **HQ**) the place from where an organization is controlled; the people who work there: *Where is/are the firm's headquarters?*

headstone /'hedstəʊn/ *noun* [C] a large stone with writing on, used to mark where a dead person is buried ⊃ look at **gravestone, tombstone**

headway /'hedweɪ/ *noun*
IDM **make headway** to go forward or make progress in a difficult situation

Oxford Wordpower Dictionary (third edition) © Oxford University Press 2006

6 Work with a partner. Use your dictionary to find some compound nouns made with one of these words.

| hand | foot | finger | fire | air | water |

Describe them for the other students to guess.

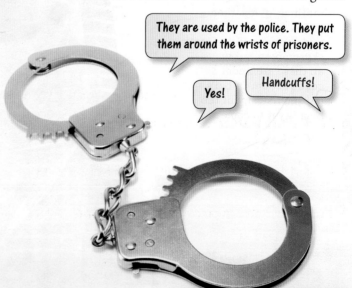

> They are used by the police. They put them around the wrists of prisoners.

> Yes!

> Handcuffs!

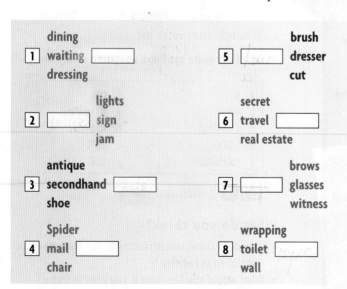

EVERYDAY ENGLISH
I need one of those things . . .

1 **CD3 16** Listen to five students each describing one of the things in the pictures, but they don't know the word. Which object are they describing?

2 Listen again and complete the lines.
1. *"I need _____ when you want to open a bottle."*
2. *"I'm looking for _____ when you want to clean between your teeth. It's _____ . It's white."*
3. *"They're _____ , and the Chinese _____ to pick up food."*
4. *"It's _____ , and it's used _____ flies."*
5. *"They're _____ you're cooking and you want to pick up something that's hot."*

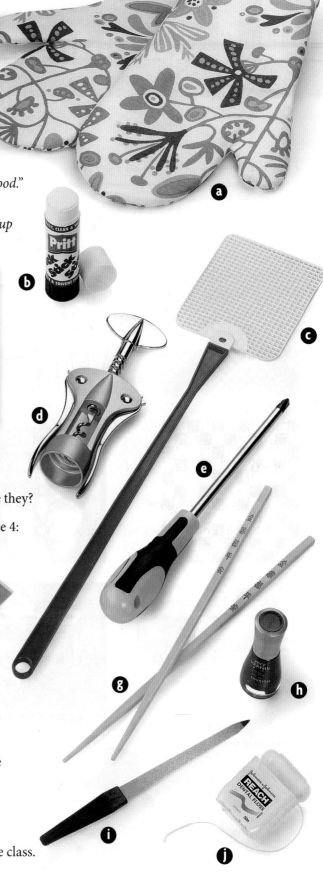

> ### Music of English ♪♩
>
> **1** **CD3 17** Listen to the stress patterns in these sentences. Practice them.
> *I need one of those things you use to open a bottle.*
> *I'm looking for some of that stuff you use when you want to clean your teeth.*
> *They're long and thin, and the Chinese use them to pick up food.*
>
> **2** Practice the other sentences in Exercise 2.

3 Work in groups. Describe the other things in the pictures.

4 **CD3 18** Listen to the descriptions. What objects do you think are being described? Turn to page 147. Listen again. Which objects are they?

5 Look at the language the people used in the descriptions in Exercise 4:

- It's one of those things you . . .
- It's long and thin and . . .
- It looks like . . .
- It's the stuff you . . .
- It's used for . . .
- They're made of . . .
- It's a kind of . . .
- It's something you use when . . .
- You know! It has a . . .

CD3 19 Listen and complete these lines. Practice saying them.

6 Work with a partner. Turn to page 147. Take turns describing some of the other objects.

7 **CD3 20** Listen to two conversations in a store. What does each person want to buy?

8 In pairs, write a similar conversation in a store. Act it in front of the class.

11 Seeing is believing

Grammar: Modals of probability
Vocabulary: Phrasal verbs (2)
Everyday English: Expressing attitude

STARTER Work with a partner. Look at the optical illusions. Can you find . . . ?

eight people   three animals   an old lady   five young ladies
a word   the color red   parallel lines   a musical instrument

1.
2.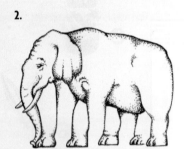
3.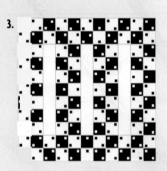
4.
5.
6.
7.
8.
9.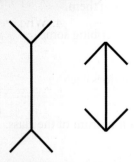

OPTICAL ILLUSIONS
must be / can't be / looks like

1 Two people are discussing the optical illusions on this page. Here are some lines from their conversation. Which optical illusion does each line refer to?

a. It **looks like** a man playing the saxophone.
b. That **must be** a candlestick in front of her face.
c. They **can't be** the same color.
d. She **might be wearing** a feather in her hat.
e. It **can't have** five legs.
f. It **could be** a duck or a rabbit.
g. The one on the left **must be** longer.
h. It **looks like** someone wearing glasses.
i. It **looks wobbly, like jelly**.
j. The dots **must be creating** the illusion.

2 **CD3 21** Listen to the full conversation. As you listen, point to the picture they are talking about.

• What is the truth about each one?
• Which *two* optical illusions can the woman *not* see?

GRAMMAR SPOT

1 Which of these sentences is the most sure? Which two sentences are less sure?

It **must be** a duck.
It **could be** a duck.
It **might be** a duck.

2 The above sentences all mean *I think it's possible that it is a duck.*
What does *It can't be a duck* mean?

3 Compare the sentences. When do we use *like*?

It **looks like a man** playing the saxophone.
It **looks red** to me.
You **look like your mother**.
You **look hot and tired**.

4 Look at the example of the continuous infinitive (*be + -ing*).

She **might be wearing** a feather.

Find another example in Exercise 1.

▶▶ **Grammar Reference 11.1–11.2 p. 141**

82 Unit 11 • Seeing is believing

PRACTICE
Fact or fiction?

1 Work with a partner. Do you believe these statements are true or false? Use modal verbs in your comments. Discuss ideas as a class.

1. Lightning never strikes in the same place twice.

> That must be true. I've often heard this.

> It could be true but I'm not so sure.

2. Hurricanes always have female names.
3. Women have a higher pain threshold than men.
4. The sea is blue because it reflects the sky.
5. A penny dropped from a skyscraper can kill a person.
6. Hair and nails continue to grow after death.
7. Birds are bird-brained and stupid.
8. No two snowflakes are the same.
9. Bats are blind.

2 **CD3 22** Listen and check your ideas. Did you learn anything that surprises you?

Grammar and speaking

3 Work with a partner. Take turns reading aloud the statements, and respond using the words in parentheses.

1. I think I lost my passport. (*must, worried*)
   You must be very worried.
2. Your phone's ringing! (*might, Jane*)
3. Paul's taking his umbrella. (*must, rain*)
4. Marcelo and Valeria never go on vacation. (*can't, much money*)
5. Hannah's not in class. (*could, coffee shop*)
6. Look! Three fire engines! (*must, somewhere*)
7. Tom hasn't seen Zoë in a long time. (*can't, go out together anymore*)
8. Whose jacket is this? (*might, John's*)
9. You got the highest score in the class! (*must, joke!*)

CD3 23 Listen and check your answers. Practice again.

What are they talking about?

4 **CD3 24** Listen to five short conversations. With a partner, guess the answer to the questions. Give reasons for your conclusions.

1. A A cup of coffee and a glass of water, please.
   B Tap or bottled?
   A Bottled, please.
   B Did you want ice and lemon with that?
   A Just ice, thanks. How much is that?

   Where do you think the people are? *At home? In a restaurant? In a coffee shop?*

   They can't be at home because they're paying for the drinks. They could be in a restaurant, but... They must be in ...

2. What are they talking about? *A TV? A cell phone? A computer?*

3. What do you think she's talking about? *An exam? A job interview? Her driving test?*

4. Who are the people? *Two friends? A husband and wife? A brother and sister?*
   What are they talking about? *A birthday present? A wedding present? An anniversary present?*

5. What do you think they are doing? *Watching a movie? Having dinner? Dancing?*

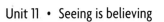

WHAT ON EARTH HAS HAPPENED?

must have been/can't have been

1 **CD3 25** Christina is calling Rachel. Read and listen to Rachel's side of the conversation. What do you think has happened?

R Hello.

C …

R Hi, Christina, what on earth's wrong? Tell me.

C …

R Oh, no! That's terrible. When?

C …

R They must have known no one was at home. What did they take?

C …

R Did you save everything?

C …

R Thank goodness. What else is missing?

C …

R Not your camera! Well, at least you still have your photos. Oh, but Lisa's expensive leather jacket! Does she know?

C …

R She's going to be so shocked when she gets back— and she has her final exams soon.

C …

R Yeah, that's good. I know she always takes it with her to lectures. Have you called the police?

C …

R Good. Do they have any idea who might have done it?

C …

R So it wasn't just *your* apartment then. Is it messy? Did they turn the place upside down?

C …

R Oh, how awful! Your nice clothes. Did they take any of them?

C …

R Yes, of course, and anyway, it must be really difficult to see exactly what's missing.

C …

R Look, Christina, you're obviously really upset. I'm coming over. I'll help you clean up. I'll be there in 15 minutes.

C …

2 What can you work out from Rachel's side of the conversation? Read the questions. Discuss and check (✓) the most likely answer.

1. What is the relationship between Rachel and Christina?
   - [ ] They must be friends.
   - [ ] They could be sisters.

2. What do you think has happened?
   - [ ] Christina's apartment must have been broken into.
   - [ ] Christina's apartment might have been broken into.

3. When did it happen?
   - [ ] It could have happened during the night.
   - [ ] It may have happened while she was at work.

4. Who is Lisa?
   - [ ] She must be Christina's roommate.
   - [ ] She can't be a student.

5. What was taken from the apartment?
   - [ ] Christina's laptop computer could have been taken.
   - [ ] Lisa's laptop may have been taken.

6. Has Christina told Lisa about her jacket?
   - [ ] She might have told her.
   - [ ] She can't have told her.

7. Has she called the police?
   - [ ] She can't have.
   - [ ] She must have.

8. What happened to Christina's clothes?
   - [ ] They can't have been stolen.
   - [ ] They must have been thrown onto the floor.

What do you think?

3 Go through the questions in Exercise 2 and tell the class what you think.

> We think Rachel and Christina must be friends and that Christina's apartment ...

4 **CD3 26** Listen to the full conversation and check your answers.

SPOKEN ENGLISH *What on earth ...?*

1 Questions with *... on earth ...?* are often used in spoken English to express disbelief.

> ***What on earth*** *has happened?*
> ***Where on earth*** *have you been?*
> ***Who on earth*** *left the window open?*

CD3 27 Listen and repeat. Pay attention to the stress and intonation.

2 Work with a partner. Read the statements aloud and respond with disbelief.

1. I can't carry all these shopping bags. *What ...?*
2. Tom's broken his arm in three places. *How...?*
3. There's someone at the door! *Who ...?*
4. My aunt left all her money to her cat. *Why ... that?*
5. I can't find my car keys. *Where ...?*

CD3 28 Listen and compare your answers. Practice them.

GRAMMAR SPOT

1 These sentences all express **past** probability. What is the present?

> They **must have been** friends.
> They **might have caught** the burglar.
> It **can't have been** my jacket.

2 What is the past of these sentences?

> He **must love** her very much.
> She **can't be** at home.

3 Remember that *must* also expresses obligation. What is the past of this sentence?

> I **must call** the police.

▶▶ **Grammar Reference 11.3 p. 141**

PRACTICE
Grammar and pronunciation

1 Match the phonemic script with the words.

1. /məstəv/	**could have**
2. /kæntəv/	can't have
3. /kədəv/	**may have**
4. /maɪtəv/	might have
5. /meɪəv/	**must have**

CD3 29 Listen and repeat.

2 **CD3 30** Listen and read these lines aloud as a class.

1. It must have been stolen.
2. I can't have lost it.
3. He could have taken it.
4. I might have dropped it.
5. She may have found it.

3 Work with a partner. Read aloud the following situations. Take turns responding using the words in parentheses.

1. I can't find my ticket. (*must, drop*)

> You must have dropped it.

2. John didn't come to school yesterday. (*must, sick*)
3. Why is Isabel late for class? (*might, oversleep*)
4. I can't find my notebook. (*must, leave at home*)
5. The teacher's checking Maria's exercise. (*can't, finish already*)
6. Why is Carl looking so happy? (*may, do well on the test*)

CD3 31 Listen and check. Practice again with your partner.

Discussing grammar

4 How many of these modal verbs can you fit naturally into each sentence? Discuss as a class. What are the different meanings?

can	can't	could	must	might	should

1. He _____ have been born in the 1960s.
2. _____ you help me wash the dishes, please?
3. You _____ see the doctor immediately.
4. _____ we go out to eat tonight?
5. I _____ stop eating candy.
6. I _____ learn to speak English.

1 Sherlock Holmes is probably the most famous detective in the world of English literature. What do you know about him?

1. Sherlock Holmes lived in *Chicago / London / Edinburgh*.
2. Stories about him first appeared in the *19th / 20th / 21st* century.
3. He was helped in all his adventures by *Dr. Krippen / Dr. Jones / Dr. Watson*.

2 You are going to read a Sherlock Holmes story called "The Three Students." Look at the picture and headings. What can you guess about the story?

3 Read **Part 1** and answer the questions.

1. Where was Sherlock Holmes staying? Why?
2. Who is Hilton Soames?
3. What did Mr. Soames receive that afternoon?
4. What was lying on the floor when he returned to his room after tea?
5. Why did Mr. Soames refuse to call the police?
6. Who is Bannister?
7. What clues did Mr. Soames find?
8. What does he think has happened?

4 Read **Part 2**. Who and what can you see in the picture? Are these sentences true (✔) or false (✗)? Correct the false ones.

1. The tutor's room was on the same floor as the three students'.
2. Holmes couldn't see into the room through the window.
3. He found a clue on the carpet.
4. The papers were next to the window because it was easier to read them in the light.
5. Holmes found another clue in the bedroom.
6. The intruder saw Mr. Soames returning.
7. He escaped through the study window.

5 Read **Part 3**. What motives did each of the students have? Who do you think copied the papers? Why? Discuss with a partner and then the class.

I think it could have been . . .   No, it can't have been . . .

THE THREE

PART 1 ❖ *Who copied the exam questions?*

Sherlock Holmes and Dr. Watson were in one of England's most famous university towns doing some research. One evening, Holmes received a visit from an old acquaintance, Mr. Hilton Soames, a tutor at one of the colleges. Mr. Soames looked very nervous and agitated.

"I hope you can spare me some of your valuable time, Mr. Holmes. Something very serious has happened at my college."

Holmes was very busy. "Why don't you call the police?" he said irritably.

"No, no that's impossible. We can't have a scandal at the college. I should explain. You see, tomorrow is the first day of the university exams, and this afternoon I received the Greek translation papers. I put them on the desk in my room while I went to have tea with a friend. When I returned, I saw immediately that the papers had been disturbed. Indeed some were lying on the floor by the window."

"I see," said Holmes. "Please continue."

"Well, at first I thought that perhaps my servant, Bannister, was responsible because he'd been in the room after I left, but he denied touching the papers and I believe him. He is a good and honest man. I examined the room very carefully."

"And what did you find?" asked Holmes impatiently.

"On the table by the window I found a broken pencil. Also, there was a cut, about three inches long, in the red leather top of my desk and next to it, a small lump of black mud. There were no signs of entry at the window. Please help me, Mr. Holmes. Someone must have copied the exam questions. If I don't find who did it, I will have to cancel the exam and there will be a scandal."

"We need to visit your room," said Holmes. "Come on, Watson."

STUDENTS

PART 2 ❖ *Looking for clues*

They walked towards the tutor's room, which was on the ground floor. Holmes tried to look in through the window, but he wasn't tall enough. He had to stop and stand on tiptoe. Above lived three students, one on each floor. Holmes entered the room and examined the carpet.

"Nothing," he said. "Let me look at the table by the window. Ah, yes, I see what might have happened. Someone took the papers from your desk over to the window table to copy them, because from there he could see when you were returning."

"Actually, Holmes, nobody could see me. I came back through the side door."

"Ah, so you may have surprised him, and he had to leave in a hurry. Did you hear someone running away as you entered?"

"No, I didn't."

"Interesting. So, our only clues are the cut in the leather and one small lump of black mud. Now tell me, where does that door go to?"

"My bedroom."

"Can I examine it?"

"Yes, of course."

Holmes followed Soames into his bedroom.

"Hello," said Holmes, "What's this? Another small lump of black mud, exactly like the one on the desk. Clearly your visitor came into the bedroom."

"I don't understand. Why did he do that?"

"Well, when you came back so suddenly, he must have run into your bedroom to hide. Look at the bedroom window, it's open. That must be how he escaped."

PART 3 ❖ *The three suspects*

"Now," said Holmes, "The three students who live above you. Are they all taking this examination?"

"Yes."

"Tell me about them."

"Well, on the second floor is Gilchrist, an excellent student and an athlete. He plays rugby and cricket and is particularly good at the long jump. He's hardworking but poor. His father gambled away all the family money."

"And the third floor?"

"Daulat Ras lives there. He is from India, very quiet and hardworking, but Greek translation is his weakest subject. And finally there's Miles McLaren on the top floor. A very intelligent student, one of the best when he chooses to work — but he's been very lazy this term. He's been playing cards until late at night and I think he must be worried about this exam."

"Now tell me," said Holmes, "how tall are these young men?"

"How tall? What a strange question. Um … I think Miles is taller than Daulat, but Gilchrist is the tallest, over six feet."

"Ah, that's important. Now, Mr. Soames. I wish you goodnight. I'll return tomorrow."

Next morning Sherlock Holmes left his house at 6 A.M. He returned at 8 A.M. to pick up Watson, and they made their way to the tutor's rooms. Mr. Soames was waiting nervously for them.

Listening

6 **CD3 32** Listen to **Part 4**. Whose ideas in Exercise 5 were correct? Did you guess who copied the papers? Now answer these questions.

1. What was it about the culprit that made Holmes suspicious?
2. Where did Holmes go to solve the mystery? What did he discover there?
3. What was Holmes's explanation? Describe what happened.
4. What does Watson say to congratulate his friend? How does Holmes reply?
5. Why does Bannister apologize?
6. Why can the examinations take place?

What do you think?

- What were the cleverest parts of Holmes's investigation?
- How might the mystery be solved by detectives today?
- What methods of detection are used now which were not available 100 years ago?

Language work

1 Work out the meanings of the highlighted words from their contexts.

2 Here are some things that Sherlock Holmes could have said while he was working out who did it. Rewrite the sentences using the words in parentheses.

1. One of the students is undoubtedly the culprit. (*must*)
2. I don't think Bannister did it. (*can't have*)
3. The lump of mud is possibly a clue. (*could*)
4. Perhaps the leather was cut by a knife. (*might have*)
5. I don't think he escaped through the study window. (*can't have*)
6. Perhaps the culprit is still hiding in the bedroom. (*may*)
7. Maybe he jumped out of the bedroom window. (*could have*)
8. I'm pretty sure that Gilchrist did it. (*must have*)

Telling the story

Tell the story to the class in your own words. Begin:

Student 1 Sherlock Holmes was working in a university town, probably Oxford.

Student 2 His friend Mr. Soames, who was a tutor, asked Holmes to help him because …

Student 3 …

VOCABULARY
Phrasal verbs (2) with *out* and *up*

1 Read the dictionary entries for two phrasal verbs. Answer the questions.

1. What are the verbs?
2. What do *sth* and *sb* stand for?
3. Which groups of phrasal verbs are separable? Which are inseparable?

> **PHR V** **work sth out 1** to find the answer; to solve sth: *I can't work out how to do this.* **2** to calculate sth: *I worked out the total cost.*
>
> **work out 1** to progress in a good way: *I hope things work out for you.* **2** to do physical exercise to keep your body fit: *We work out to music at my exercise class.*

> **PHR V** **make sth up 1** to invent sth, often sth that is not true: *to make up an excuse.* **2** to form sth: *the different groups that make up society.*
>
> **make up (with sb)** to become friends again after an argument: *Has she made up with him yet?*

2 Complete the sentences with the correct form of one of the phrasal verbs in Exercise 1.

1. Sherlock Holmes _____ who committed the crime.
2. That's a lie. You _____ that _____, didn't you?
3. I know we argue a lot, but we always kiss and _____ afterwards.
4. Don't worry, things will _____ in the end. They always do.
5. He's determined to lose weight. He _____ at the gym every day.
6. Women _____ 56 percent of the students in this university.
7. Can you _____ this bill for me? I don't understand all those figures.
8. You must have _____ the answers by now.

3 Many more phrasal verbs are formed with *out* and *up*. Match a verb in **A** with a line in **B**.

A	B
1. find out	a problem
2. break up	in a Chinese restaurant
3. break out of	golf
4. eat up	with a boyfriend/girlfriend
5. eat out	all your vegetables and you'll be healthy
6. save up	what time the train leaves
7. sort out	a good idea
8. take up	to buy a new car
9. come up with	jail

4 Replace the words in *italics* with one of the phrasal verbs from Exercise 3 in the correct form.

1. You need to learn to relax. Why don't you *start doing* yoga?
2. He's just *thought of* a brilliant plan to save the business.
3. There's no dessert until you've *finished* all your meat and vegetables.
4. Anne and Tony aren't talking to each other. They may even have *ended their relationship*.
5. Did you hear the news? Three dangerous prisoners have *escaped from* the local prison.
6. You must learn to *solve* your problems without your parents' help.
7. We *aren't spending much money* so we can buy a house.
8. Have you *discovered* why you didn't get the job?

CD3 33 Listen and check.

5 Work with a partner. Complete these sentences in any suitable way. Read them aloud to the class and compare ideas.

1. I've just found out …
2. I never eat out …
3. I can't figure out …
4. I'm saving up …
5. I need to sort out …
6. I've just come up with …
7. It's important to make up …

CD3 34 Listen and compare. What are the responses?

eureka!

Archimedes works it out.

EVERYDAY ENGLISH
Expressing attitude

1 **CD3 35** Read and listen to the conversation. Who are they talking about? What has happened?

A Have you heard about Sam?

B No, I haven't.

A Well, I haven't spoken to him myself, but **apparently** he was caught cheating on his math exam.

B **No kidding!** I can't believe that. Does he have a problem with math?

A No. **Actually,** math is his best subject.

B **Really?** So why would he cheat? He doesn't need to.

A **Exactly.** And **anyway,** Sam's not the type to cheat.

B He must be very upset. **Presumably,** he's going to complain.

A Yeah, he's seeing the principal this afternoon. **Obviously,** he's going to deny it completely.

B Well, **hopefully,** the principal will believe him. Let me know what happens.

A I will. **Personally,** I think he'll be OK.

B I hope you're right. See you later.

A Yeah. Fingers crossed for Sam. Bye.

2 **CD3 35** Read and listen to the conversation again. The words in **bold** express the attitude of the speaker.

3 Choose the correct word or phrase to complete the lines.

> Did you hear about Marcos? You know, the guy who works in my office. Well, **apparently / obviously** he is going to be promoted. **Of course / To be honest,** I don't understand why. **Exactly / Personally,** I think he's hopeless at his job. He never does any work. **In fact / Naturally,** all he does all day is talk to his friend on the phone and drink coffee. **Unfortunately / Really,** his desk is next to mine. **Generally / Presumably,** he'll move to another office now, so **hopefully / really** I won't have to work with him anymore. **Anyway / Apparently,** enough about me. How's your work going? Are you still enjoying it?

CD3 36 Listen and check. Read the lines aloud with a partner.

4 Complete the sentences with your own ideas.

1. A Hi! You're Emily, aren't you?
   B **Actually,** _____ .

2. A What did you think of the movie? Great, wasn't it?
   B **Personally,** _____ .

3. A What's the latest gossip about Kate and her boyfriend?
   B **Apparently,** _____ .

4. A What's the weather like in spring?
   B **Generally,** _____ .

5. A What time will we arrive?
   B **Hopefully** _____ .

6. A I've called and left messages for them but no reply.
   B **Presumably,** _____ .

7. A What did you do when you saw the accident?
   B **Obviously,** _____ .

8. A How did you feel when they offered you the job?
   B **To be honest,** _____ .

CD3 37 Listen and compare your answers. Practice with your partner and continue the conversations.

▶▶ **WRITING** EXPRESSING ATTITUDE *p. 112*

12 Telling it like it is

Grammar: Reported speech
Vocabulary: Ways of speaking
Everyday English: You know what they say

STARTER

1 Look at the reported speech. What were the girl's words?

She said she was a student.
She asked me what I was doing in Miami.
She told me she'd arrived on Monday.

2 Here are some reported thoughts. What were my thoughts?

I thought she worked in an office.
I knew I'd seen her somewhere before.
I wondered if she'd called me.

I READ IT IN THE PAPERS ...
Reported speech

1 Read the newspaper article. Who is Jack Neal? What did he do? What happened in the end?

2 Work with a partner. Complete the article by reporting the words and thoughts in 1–10. **CD3 38** Listen and check.

Look, Mom! I bought a car on eBay for $15,000

A three-year-old boy used his mother's computer to buy a $15,000 car on the Internet auction site eBay.

Jack Neal's parents only discovered their son's successful bid when they received a message from the website.

> **1.** You have bought a pink Nissan Figaro.

The message said they (1) **had bought** a pink Nissan Figaro.

> **2.** We can't understand it.

Mrs. Neal, 36, said that they (2) _____ it. She (3) _____ on the Internet the day before, but (4) _____ anything.

> **3.** I was on the Internet yesterday.

> **4.** I didn't buy anything.

> **5.** I'm so happy!

"Jack kept telling us that he (5) _____ so happy, and that we (6) _____ soon get a big surprise."

> **6.** You'll soon get a big surprise!

Mrs. Neal, from Houston, Texas, thought Jack (7) _____. He often used the computer, and she was pretty sure that he (8) _____ her password.

> **7.** He's joking.

> **8.** I'm pretty sure he knows my password.

Her husband, John, 37, called the seller of the car, and explained that there (9) _____ a mistake.

> **9.** There has been a mistake.

"Fortunately, he saw the funny side and said he (10) _____ the car again."

> **10.** I'll advertise the car again.

Mr. Neal has told Jack to be more careful, and he has asked his wife to change her password.

3 Here are Mr. Neal's words to Jack and his wife.

You have to be more careful, son.
Do you think you could change your password, dear?

How are these words reported in the article?

4 Report these sentences.

1. "My Jack is very clever," his mother said.
   Mrs. Neal said her son was very clever.
2. "He usually plays computer games," she told me.
3. "I bought the computer for my work," his father explained.
4. "I won't use eBay anymore," Mrs. Neal decided.
5. "I don't know how it happened," said Jack.
6. "I've always liked computers," he told reporters.
7. "Please clean up your room," his mother asked Jack.
8. "Go and play soccer," his father told him.

CD3 39 Listen and check.

Reported questions

5 Read the newspaper article below. Match the direct questions and thoughts to numbers 1–7 in the article, then report them.

Has there been a road accident?
Why did you do it?
Are you going to arrest me?
What's happening?
Where did the money come from?
Why are you giving away all your money?
Do you know the man?

CD3 40 Listen and check. Repeat the reported questions.

Grammar Reference 12.1–12.3 p. 142

GRAMMAR SPOT

1 When we report words or thoughts, we usually move the tense back.

"**I'm** tired." She said she **was** tired.

Complete the reported speech.

"I've seen the movie before." She told me _____.
"You'll like it." She was sure I _____.

2 What does *tell* mean in these two sentences?

She **told me that** she loved me.
She **told me to** go away.

3 When we report questions, there is no inversion, and no *do/does/did*.

"Where do you live?" **He asked me where I lived.**
Report these questions.
"How long are you staying?" **She asked me . . .**
"Do you know Mike?" **She wanted to know if . . .**

---

6 Imagine you were stopped by the police and asked these questions. Report them.

"Where are you going?" (*ask*)
They asked me where I was going.
"Where have you been?" (*ask*)
"Do you live in the area? (*want to know*)
"How old are you?" (*wonder*)
"Have you been with friends?" (*demand to know*)
"What time did you leave home?" (*ask if I could remember*)

CD3 41 Listen and compare. Look at CD3 41 on page 127 and practice the conversation with a partner.

Man throws away $30,000 in town center

Daily Mail Reporter

A mystery man started a riot in a busy town center yesterday by hurling $30,000 into the air.

Traffic was stopped at 11.00 A.M. as money rained down from the sky.

Local store clerk Anthony Jones, 55, said "I couldn't understand it, so I asked my neighbor (1) **what was happening** ." They saw people on their hands and knees grabbing banknotesmiw. "No one knew (2)_____," he said. "They were just stuffing it in their pockets."

Passerby Eleanor Morris said, "I wondered (3) _____, because the traffic was at a complete standstill."

Florist Jane Thomas saw the man, who was wearing a red shirt. "I asked him (4)_____ all his money, but he didn't answer. He just laughed."

Police asked Jane if she (5) _____. "I told them I'd never seen him before. He certainly wasn't from around here."

The police confirmed that a local forty-year-old man had been questioned. "He refused to tell us (6) _____," a spokesman said, "so it's a complete mystery. He wanted to know if we (7) _____ arrest him, but giving away money isn't against the law."

PRACTICE

But you said ...!

1 Complete the conversations with an idea of your own.

1. **A** Bill's coming to the party tonight.
   B Really? I thought you said <u>he wasn't feeling well</u>.

2. **A** I'm making dinner for Joe tonight.
   B I didn't know you _____!

3. **A** Oh, no! I spilled ketchup on my white shirt!
   B I told you to be careful. I knew _____.

4. **A** Did you get me something to eat?
   B Sorry. I didn't realize _____. What would you like?

5. **A** I'm 25 today!
   B Are you? I didn't know _____. Hope you have a great day!

6. **A** Oh, no! It's raining!
   B Really? But the weather forecast said _____.

7. **A** You left the doors and windows of the apartment open this morning.
   B I'm sorry. I was pretty sure I _____ all the doors and windows.

8. **A** Where did Tom go last night?
   B I have no idea _____.

CD3 42 Listen and compare. Practice the conversations.

The interview

2 Work with a partner. Think of questions you are asked when you have a job interview.

Where have you worked before?
Do you like working in a team?

> **Full-time RECEPTIONIST**
> required in ★★★★ Boston hotel
> Experience and
> foreign language preferred
> Annual salary $30k
> Please send CVs to:
> info@hotelcharles.com

3 Julia has just been for a job interview as a receptionist. She's telling her friend about it.

They asked me why I wanted the job.
They asked me if I had any experience.
They wanted to know if I could do word processing.

What other questions do you think they asked?
Use ideas from Exercise 2.

CD3 43 Listen and compare.

Reporting verbs

4 Match the reporting verbs in the box with the direct speech.

> a. invite   b. persuade   c. explain   d. promise
> e. ask   f. remind   g. offer   h. encourage

1. _e_ "Can you help me?" she said to me.
2. __ "Don't forget to mail the letter," he said to her.
3. __ "I will really study hard for my exams," she said.
4. __ "Come to my party," he said to me.
5. __ "You really must travel. You'd love it," she said to me.
6. __ "I'll give you a lift to the airport," he said to me.
7. __ "I'm not sure about this job." "Go on! Apply for it! You'd be good at it," he said. "OK, I will," I replied.
8. __ "I've been very busy," she said.

5 Report the sentences using the reporting verbs.

She asked me to help her.

CD3 44 Listen and check.

She didn't say that!

6 **CD3 45** Listen to the conversations. What mistakes do the people make when they report the conversations?

1. Merinda called from work. She said she'd call you again later.

   She didn't say she'd call later. She asked Jenny to call her.

2. I got a job as manager! I'm going to earn $50,000 a year!

3. My mom said you couldn't have a turn.

4. James — Sue called. Meet her outside the theater at 7:45.

5. Tom offered to fix my computer. He said he was sure he could do it. He wanted $130!

▶▶ **WRITING** A THANK-YOU E-MAIL *p. 113*

VOCABULARY AND SPEAKING
Ways of speaking

1 There are many verbs that describe ways of speaking.

> to discuss   to promise   to agree

Add two more verbs from the box to each category in **red** on the diagram.

advise	chat	scream	fight	accuse
recommend	whisper	criticize	gossip	
order	quarrel	demand	protest	deny

2 Write in a verb from the diagram. Sometimes there is more than one possibility.

1. _____ to a colleague in the office about football
2. _____ with your parents about staying out late
3. _____ at the kids because they're annoying you
4. _____ that you made a mistake
5. _____ to the waiter about the cold soup
6. _____ if you see blood/your favorite movie star/a rat
7. _____ against the war/about pay and conditions
8. _____ that your friend should see a doctor

3 Complete the sentences with the correct preposition (or no preposition).

1. I talk _____ my kids _____ everything.
2. My boss criticizes _____ me _____ my work.
3. I agree _____ you _____ most things, but not politics.
4. I discuss _____ everything _____ my wife.
5. People love gossiping _____ celebrities.
6. The teacher accused me _____ cheating on the test.

4 Work with a partner. Think of a sentence to complete these ways of speaking.

My mother told me to clean up my room.

1. My mother The teacher My doctor	advised told persuaded	me the students …	to …

2. My friends I My brother	suggested admitted complained	that	we … the teacher … …

5 With your partner, write a conversation that illustrates some of the verbs on this page. Act it in front of the class.

A Have you been out spending money again?
   We just can't afford it!

B Don't be so mean! It's only a few dollars!

The others must say who the people are and what they're talking about.

It's a husband and wife. They're arguing. He's complaining that she spends too much money. She accuses him of being mean.

---

suggest

argue

good idea

disagreeing

talk

social

shout

volume

ways of speaking

admit

in a court of law

expressing dislike

giving commands

complain

tell

READING AND SPEAKING
People who changed the world

1 Do you have a hero or heroine?
Is he/she in the world of ...?

art	politics	entertainment
style	science	sports

Tell the class.

2 Read the introduction to "Movers and shakers." Look at the pictures of the four people. Write down anything you know about each person.

Compare your lists as a class.

3 Work with a partner. Discuss these questions. How many can you answer?
1. Who is known simply as "The King"?
2. Who is seen as "the principal fighter for women's equality in the UK"?
3. Who is referred to as the "father of modern science"?
4. Who is known as the "Great Master"?

Read the four texts *quickly* to check.

4 With your partner choose one of the texts and answer the questions.
1. What century did he/she live in?
2. What was his/her area of activity (politics, science ...)?
3. What was an important year for him/her? Why?
4. Why were his/her ideas opposed?
5. What did he/she say? What did others say about him/her?

Compare and exchange information with other students.

5 Discuss the questions.
1. How did each of the people change the world?
2. What prevailing ideas did they challenge?
3. What happened as a result?

What do you think?

• What *mover and shaker* would you add from your country?
• What did he/she do?
• How did other people react?

Movers

It's hard to imagine that what we now believe to be true wasn't always so. There was a time when people believed the earth was flat . . .

Every now and then, someone comes along with new ideas. ANN WILSON profiles five people who left the world a different place.

Confucius 551 BCE–479 BCE

Confucius was a Chinese thinker and social philosopher known as the "Great Master." He spoke and dreamed of a world where happiness, good, and peace would replace misery, corruption, and war. He established principles for life that have lasted over 2,500 years. Perhaps his most famous is the Golden Rule, or ethic of reciprocity, that teaches the importance of treating others with respect.

Confucius traveled throughout China encouraging people to trust their own moral judgment. He taught that rulers should lead by example to create a truly great empire. He was persecuted by his critics, who feared that these thoughts might lead to chaos and rejection of the ruling system. Once, he was imprisoned and nearly starved. In 484 BCE, at the age of 67, he returned home and spent his last years writing. These writings formed the basis for the dominant Chinese ideology known as *Confucianism*.

His teachings and philosophy have deeply affected Chinese, Korean, Japanese, and Vietnamese thought and life and have influenced thinkers worldwide.

HE SAID

"What you do not wish for yourself, do not do to others."

THEY SAID

"In a society where relationships are considered more important than laws, there will be corruption and nepotism."

AND shakers

Galileo Galilei 1564–1642

Galileo was born in Pisa, Italy. He spent years observing the movements of the planets through a telescope. At the time it was generally thought that the earth was the center of the universe. Galileo believed, as Copernicus had done seventy years before, that the earth rotated on its axis once daily and traveled around the sun once every year. At the time, this was a fantastic concept that was considered dangerous by the Church.

In 1633 he was found guilty of heresy and spent the final years of his life imprisoned in his own home.

Galileo is referred to as the "father of modern science." He paved the way for the separation of science and religion.

HE SAID

"All truths are easy to understand once they are discovered; the point is to discover them."

THEY SAID

"The proposition that the sun is in the center of the world is absurd, philosophically false, and heretical; it is contrary to Holy Scriptures."

Emmeline Pankhurst 1858–1928

Emmeline Pankhurst is seen as "the principal fighter for women's equality in the UK." Women were not given the vote because they were considered to be incapable of rational thought. Their place was in the home.

In her twenties Emmeline Pankhurst belonged to the suffragists, who wanted to achieve equal voting rights for women by peaceful means. She later led the suffragettes, who had a more militant approach. Their tactics for attracting attention included smashing store windows, burning down buildings, slashing paintings in art galleries, organizing marches, and chaining themselves to railings.

In 1908–09 Pankhurst was sent to prison three times. She experienced force-feeding after going on a hunger strike.

The British government changed the law on voting rights for women in 1918. In 1928, women finally achieved equal voting rights to men.

SHE SAID

"We are here, not because we are law-breakers; we are here in our efforts to become law-makers."

THEY SAID

"These women are hysterical and unreasonable. Heaven help us if they had the vote. They have abandoned their duties as wives and mothers."

Elvis Presley 1935–77

Elvis Presley is known simply as "The King." When he arrived on the pop scene in 1956, he changed teenagers' attitudes towards music, sex, language, and fashion. Before his arrival, adolescent kids dressed like their parents. Then Elvis shook his hips and changed everything. This new sex symbol mesmerized one generation and at the same time alienated another. Boys wanted to be him, girls fell instantly in love with him, and—most importantly—their parents all hated him. The teenager was born.

He did more than anyone else to invent youth culture, and as such he was considered a dangerous threat to society.

John Lennon said, "Nothing really affected me until I heard Elvis. If there hadn't been an Elvis, there wouldn't have been a Beatles."

HE SAID

"If you like rock 'n' roll, if you feel it, you can't help but move to it. That's what happens to me. I can't help it."

THEY SAID

"He was an indifferent singer, a mediocre musician, and a totally uninteresting person. In five years' time, he will be totally forgotten."

LISTENING AND SPEAKING
What the papers say

BOY SUES BURGER CHAIN
"Eating burgers made me fat"

1 Which newspaper in your country …?
- has the best reputation
- is the most popular
- is the best for sports
- is the best for entertainment

DOG WITH TWO HEADS BITES MAILMAN – TWICE!

2 Do you believe everything you read in the newspapers? Do you think some stories are made more sensational?

3 **CD3 46** Listen to an interview with the singer Jamie Seabrook. Answer the questions after each part.

COACH LEAVES WIFE FOR CHEERLEADER

Part 1
1. What are some of the highs and lows of Jamie's career?
2. What was he doing in Texas?
3. What does he like about all the media attention? What doesn't he like about it?
4. What does he think of reporters?

JAMIE CHECKS INTO PRIVATE CLINIC
Last chance to save my marriage, says pop star Jamie Seabrook

Part 2
5. Complete the chart.

	What did they say about him?	What did *he* say?
reporters		
ex-friends		
police officers		
Barbara James		

6. Why did he go into the clinic?

Part 3
7. How has Jamie's life changed?
8. Why has he changed his attitude to life?
9. What did the news anchor refuse to do? Why?
10. How does he reply? What does he say about himself?

SPOKEN ENGLISH *don't mind / don't care*

1 Look at these sentences from the interview.

   I don't mind the media attention.
   I don't care what people think.

   I don't mind = I'm easy. I have no strong opinions.
   I don't care = Other people's opinions aren't important
                    to me. (Careful! This can sound rude.)

2 Reply to these sentences with *I don't mind* or *I don't care*.

   1. "Tea or coffee?" "_____. Whatever you're making."
   2. "I hate your haircut!" "_____. *I* like it."
   3. "What should we do today?"
      "_____. I'm happy doing whatever."
   4. "She's so upset!" "_____. That's *her* problem."

What do you think?
- Who do you believe — Jamie, or all the other people in his life?
- When you read a story in the news, how do you know whether to believe it?
- What are the big stories (political, environmental, sports, scandal) in the news right now?
  What are the different angles on the story?
  Do people agree on the basic facts, or are there different opinions?

EVERYDAY ENGLISH
You know what they say . . .

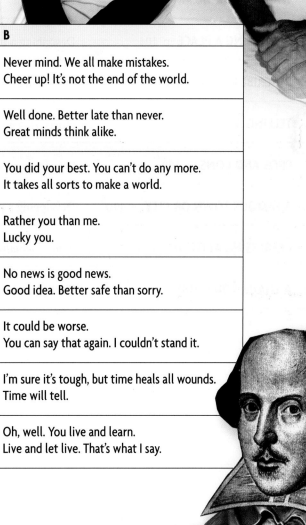

1 Some people like to bring a conversation to an end with a cliché. Nothing else needs to be said, the cliché says it all! Underline the clichés in these conversations.

> "I didn't get that job I applied for. They said I need more experience."
> "Oh, well! You win some, you lose some."

> "Did you know 25% of the world speaks English?"
> "Well, I never! You learn something new every day!"

2 Match the lines in **A** with the clichés in **B**.

	A	B
1	I'm so fed up! I lost my cell phone yesterday! I got the time wrong, and I missed my plane.	Never mind. We all make mistakes. Cheer up! It's not the end of the world.
2	I forgot her birthday, so I sent her a text. Hey! You're reading the same book as me!	Well done. Better late than never. Great minds think alike.
3	Tim's strange. He's not like me at all. I studied so hard for that exam, and I still failed.	You did your best. You can't do any more. It takes all sorts to make a world.
4	I have ten exams in the next two weeks. I have three months' vacation!	Rather you than me. Lucky you.
5	I'm going to pack some anti-malaria tablets. I haven't heard from my kids for weeks!	No news is good news. Good idea. Better safe than sorry.
6	That party was awful. I hated it. I couldn't stand it. I backed into a wall and broke a headlight.	It could be worse. You can say that again. I couldn't stand it.
7	She's been so sad since her husband died. I wonder if their relationship will last.	I'm sure it's tough, but time heals all wounds. Time will tell.
8	Our neighbors are extreme right-wing. I trusted Peter, and he stole all my money!	Oh, well. You live and learn. Live and let live. That's what I say.

3 **CD3 47** Listen and check.

And finally . . .

In the words of William Shakespeare …

Writing

REFERENCE

1 It is important to try to correct your own mistakes when you write. Look at the symbols in the box. What kind of mistakes do they signify?

2 Read the letter that Valeria, a student from Argentina, has written to her Canadian friend, Stephanie. Use the symbols to help you correct her mistakes.

T Tense	WW Wrong word
Prep Preposition	P Punctuation
Gr Grammar	Sp Spelling
WO Word order	λ Word missing

> 23 St. Mary's Road,
> Philadelphia, PA
> Tuesday, May 10
>
> Dear Stephanie,
>
> How are you? I'm very well. I came in (Prep) Philadelphia two weeks ago for to (Gr) study at a language school. I want λ learn english (Gr) because λ is a very important language. I'm stay (Gr) with a (Gr) American family. They have two son (Gr) and a dauhgter (Sp). Mr. Kendall is λ teacher and Mrs. Kendall work (Gr) in a hospital. The Americans is (Gr) very kind, but they speak very quickly!
>
> I study in the morning. My teachers (P) name is Ann. She said (WW) me that my English is OK, but I do (WW) a lot of mistakes. Ann don't (Gr) give us too much homework, so in the afternoons I go always (WO) sightseeing. Philadelphia is much more big (Gr) than my town. I like very much art (WO) and I'm very interesting (Gr) for (Prep) history, so I visit monuments and museums. I met a girl named Carla. She came (T) from Mexico and go (Gr) to the University of Pennsylvania. Last night we go (T) to the movies, but the movie wasn't very exiting (Sp).
>
> Do (WW) you like to visit me? Why don't you come for a weekend?
>
> I'd love to see you.
>
> Write to me soon.
>
> Love, **Valeria**
>
> P.S. Here's my new e-mail address:
> Valet@intermail.net

3 Answer the questions.
  1. Where is Valeria? Where is she staying?
  2. Why is she there?
  3. What does she do each day?
  4. What does she do in her free time?
  5. Who has she met?

4 Imagine that you are a student in another town. Answer the questions in Exercise 3 about *you*.

5 Write a similar letter to a friend. Swap letters with a partner. Try to correct your partner's letter using the symbols.

1 Read lines 1–10 from some letters and e-mails. Which are formal and which are informal? Which are beginnings? Which are endings?

1. *Great to hear from you again.*

2. *I am writing in response to your advertisement in today's newspaper for an IT consultant.*

3. *Give my regards to Robert and all the family.*

4. *I'm sorry I haven't been in touch for so long, but you know how it is.*

5. *Thank you for your invoice of April 16th. Please find enclosed a check for the full amount.*

6. *Write, or better still, e-mail me soon.*

7. *We trust this arrangement meets with your satisfaction.*

8. *Just a note to say thank you so much for having me to stay last weekend.*

9. *Take care. I can't wait to see you next week.*

10. *I look forward to hearing from you at your earliest convenience.*

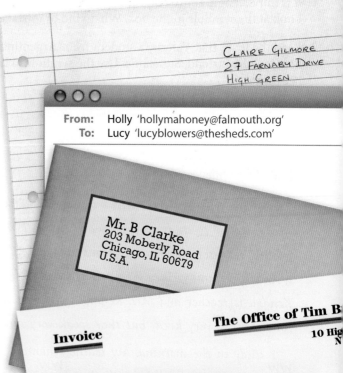

2 Read the **beginnings** of these letters and e-mails. Match them with their **next lines** and **endings**.

Beginnings	Next lines	Endings
1. Dear Jane, thanks for your e-mail. It's great to hear from you after so long.	**a.** We had no idea John was such a good cook!	**e.** Let me know a.s.a.p. All the best, Danny
2. Dear Mr. Smith, We have received your order and payment for the Children's Encyclopedia CD-ROM.	**b.** It's good to catch up on all your news. I've been pretty busy lately, too. I've just started a new job.	**f.** We apologize for the inconvenience. Your order will be processed as soon as we receive the additional amount. Yours sincerely, Pigeon Publishing
3. Hi Pete, Any chance you're free next Saturday evening?	**c.** Unfortunately, your check for $90 did not include postage of $7.50.	**g.** Let's meet soon. Give my love to Alan and the boys. Yours, Julie
4. Dear John and Liz, Thank you so much for a great evening and meal.	**d.** Chris and Nick are coming over and we wondered if you'd like to join us.	**h.** Thanks again. We hope to see you both soon. Love, Vicky and Jamie

3 Which letter or e-mail in Exercise 2 is …?

- an invitation
- a formal request
- exchanging news
- saying thank you

<u>Underline</u> the words or phrases which helped you decide.

4 You have just found the e-mail address of an old friend. Write to him/her. Give news about your personal life and work. Ask about his/her news.

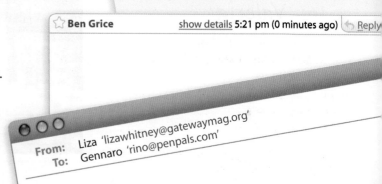

1 Read the story. Look at the picture. Who are the people?

The Farmer and his Sons

There was once an old, dying farmer **(1)** _____ . Before he died, he wanted to teach his three sons how to be good farmers. So, he called them to his bedside and said, "My boys, I have an important secret to tell you: there is a great treasure buried in the vineyard. Promise me that you will look for it when I am dead."

The sons gave their promise and **(2)** _____ , they began looking for the treasure. They worked very hard in the hot sun **(3)** _____ . They pictured boxes of gold coins, diamond necklaces, and other such things. **(4)** _____ , but they found not a single penny. They were very upset **(5)** _____ . However, a few months later the grapes started to appear on the vines. Their grapes were the biggest and best in the neighborhood and they sold them for a lot of money. Now the sons understood **(6)** _____ and they lived happily ever after.

2 Where do clauses a–f go in the story?

a. ☐ as soon as their father died
b. ☐ who had worked hard in his vineyard all his life
c. ☐ what their father had meant by the great treasure
d. ☐ and while they were working, they thought about what their father had said
e. ☐ because they felt that all their hard work had been for nothing
f. ☐ Soon they had dug up every inch of the vineyard

3 Read the lines from another story. Who are the people in the picture?

The Emperor and his Daughters

There was once an emperor **(1)** _____ lived in a palace.

He had three daughters **(2)** _____ no sons.

He wanted his daughters to marry **(3)** _____ he died.

He found three princes. **(4)** _____ his daughters didn't like them.

They refused to marry the princes, **(5)** _____ the emperor became very angry.

He said they must get married **(6)** _____ they were 18 years old.

The three daughters ran away **(7)** _____ the night and found work on a farm.

They fell in love with the farmer's sons **(8)** _____ they were working there.

They married the sons **(9)** _____ they were 18.

4 Complete the lines using a linking word from the box.

before	as soon as	while	during
when	but	However,	so	who

5 In what ways are the lines below different from the ones in Exercise 3?

There was once an old emperor who lived in an enormous, golden palace in the middle of the city Ping Chong. He had three beautiful daughters, but unfortunately no sons ...

Continue rewriting the story, adding more detail to make it more interesting.

6 Write a folk tale or fairy story that you know. Write about 200 words.

Begin: *There was/were once ...*

End: *... and they lived happily ever after.*

Mother Teresa of Calcutta (1910–1997)

1 What do you know about Mother Teresa? Share ideas as a class.

2 Work with a partner. Look at the information about Mother Teresa's *Early years*. Compare the sentences in **A** with the paragraph in **B**. Note the different ways the sentences combine.

A Early years	B
Mother Teresa was a missionary. She worked among the poor people of Calcutta, India. She was born Agnes Gonxha Bojaxhiu. She was born in Skopje, Macedonia. She was born on August 26, 1910. Her father was Albanian. He died when she was eight years old. Her mother was left to raise the family.	Mother Teresa was a missionary who worked among the poor people of Calcutta, India. She was born Agnes Gonxha Bojaxhiu, in Skopje, Macedonia on August 26, 1910. Her father, who was Albanian, died when she was just eight years old, leaving her mother to raise the family.

3 Read the sentences in *Working as a teacher*. Work with your partner and use the information in **A** to complete the paragraph in **B**.

A Working as a teacher	B
Agnes was very young. She wanted to become a missionary. She left home in September 1928. She joined a convent in Ireland. She was given the name Teresa. She was sent to India in January 1929. She taught in St. Mary's High School Convent. St. Mary's was in Calcutta. She worked in St. Mary's for over 20 years. At first she was called Sister Teresa. She was called Mother Teresa in 1937.	From a very young age Agnes had wanted …, so in September 1928 she … to join … in Ireland, where she was given … . A few months later, in …, she was sent to … to teach in … in Calcutta. Here she worked for …, first as Sister … and finally, in 1937, as Mother Teresa.

4 Do the same with the information in *Working with the poor*. Read your completed paragraph aloud to the class.

A Working with the poor	B
In 1946 Mother Teresa felt called by God. She was called to help the poorest of the poor. She left St. Mary's convent on August 17, 1948. She started visiting families in the slums of Calcutta. She looked after sick and dying children. She started a religious community in 1950. It was called the Missionaries of Charity. The communities spread all over the world in the 1960s and 70s. Mother Teresa was awarded the Nobel Peace Prize in 1979. She developed severe health problems. She continued to work amongst the poor. She died on September 5, 1997. Thousands of people from all over the world came to her funeral.	Mother Teresa finally left … on August 17, 1948. Two years earlier, in …, she had felt called by … to help…, so she started visiting …, looking … sick …. In 1950, she started … called the Missionaries of Charity, which by the 1960s and 70s had spread …. In 1979 Mother Teresa …. She continued to work … despite developing …. When she finally … on September 5, 1997, thousands of people ….

5 Research some facts about a famous man or woman, dead or alive, that you admire. Write a short biography.

1 What topics are in the news at the moment? Are they national or international? Are they about the environment, politics, crime, sports …? Discuss any that concern you with the class.

2 **CD2** **10** Read and listen to a girl talking about a topic that concerns her.

1. What is her cause for concern?
2. Why does she have a personal interest?
3. How did Craig use to be?
4. What does research tell us about the addiction?
5. Do most children become addicts?
6. What concerns Dr. Griffiths?
7. What other concerns does the girl have?

3 Now read the speech carefully and answer the questions.

1. <u>Underline</u> the phrases that introduce each paragraph. Why are these words used?
2. Find examples of the speaker talking from her own experience.
3. Find examples where she quotes research.
4. How does the girl conclude her talk?
5. Read the paragraph beginning "Research shows …" aloud to a partner.

Preparing your talk

4 Choose a cause for concern from the topics you discussed. Make notes. Say why it concerns you.

5 Write a speech to give to your class, of 200–300 words. Use your notes and these guidelines to help.

1. Introduce your topic
   My cause for concern is …
   I want to talk about X because …
2. Give the reason why
   Let me explain why.
   Two years ago …
   I've always been interested in …
3. List your research
   Research shows that…
   A recent study found that …
   I read in the newspaper/heard on the news that …
4. Introduce new points
   I have two more concerns .
   Firstly, … secondly, …
   Another thing is …
5. Conclude
   Finally, I'd like to say …
   Thank you all very much for listening to me.
   Are there any questions?

My cause for concern

The thing I'm concerned about at the moment is the influence that video games may have on children.

Let me explain why. I've been reading lots of newspaper articles on the subject, and I also have a personal interest. You see, I have a younger brother, Craig; he's 13 years old, and I'm afraid he's becoming a video game addict. Just a few years ago, Craig had many interests. He played basketball, he was learning judo, he went out on his bike with his friends. He was a happy, fun-loving boy. Now he spends hours every day in front of a screen, in a virtual world, playing virtual games, usually violent ones, and he becomes really angry if our parents tell him to stop.

Research shows that today 40% of family homes have computers, so there is plenty of opportunity for very young children to start using them, and by the age of seven, many have developed an interest in video games. This is not a problem for most of them. However, by their early teens, a small minority have become addicts, playing for at least 30 hours a week. Dr. Mark Griffiths, an expert in video addiction, finds this figure very worrying. He says that children may become so addicted that they stop doing homework, start missing school, and even steal money in order to buy the games.

I have two more concerns. First, I worry that the violence in the games could cause children to become more violent. My brother isn't violent, but he is certainly bad-tempered if he is stopped from playing. Second, I worry that sitting without exercise for so long is unhealthy. Craig often plays five hours a day, and some days his thumbs are really sore and he can't sleep because he is overexcited. His schoolwork is going from bad to worse.

Finally, Dr. Griffiths says that more research is needed, but I don't need to read more research to conclude that video games cause problems. He should come and meet my brother. That's all the evidence he needs.

6 Practice reading your speech aloud first to yourself, then to a partner. Give your speech to the class. Answer any questions.

My favorite room

1 Think of your favorite room. Draw a plan of it on a piece of paper. Write down why you like it and some adjectives to describe it.

My favorite room is . . .   I like it because . . .

Show a partner your plan and talk about your room.

2 Read the description "My favorite room." Why is this kitchen more than just a room where you cook and eat?

3 Complete the description using the relative clauses below:

> . . . which tells the story
> . . . that we're going to next Saturday
> . . . where we cook and eat
> . . . whose family has emigrated
> . . . which is the focal point of the room
> . . . which means
> . . . we haven't seen
> . . . I like best
> . . . who are irritable and sleepy
> . . . where family and friends
>   come together

GRAMMAR SPOT

1 Underline the relative pronouns in Exercise 3. What do they refer to? When do we use *which, who, that, where,* and *whose*?

2 Look at the these sentences. We can omit the relative pronoun from one in each pair. Which one? Why?

This is the room **that** I like best.
This is the room **that** has the best view.

He's a friend **who** we haven't seen for years.
He's a friend **who** lives in London.

3 Look at these examples of participles. Rewrite them with relative pronouns.

I have so many happy memories of times spent there.

There is a large window looking out on two apple trees in the garden.

▶▶ **Grammar Reference 6.3 and 6.4 p. 136**

The room in our house (1) _____ is our kitchen. Perhaps the kitchen is the most important room in many houses, but it's particularly so in our house because it's not only (2) _____ but also the place (3) _____ .

I have so many happy memories of times spent there: ordinary daily events such as making breakfast on dark, cold winter mornings for children (4) _____ before sending them off to school; or special occasions such as family reunions or cooking holiday dinners. Whenever we have a party, people gravitate to the kitchen. It always ends up the fullest and noisiest room in the house.

So what does this special room look like? It's pretty big but not huge. It's big enough to have a good-sized rectangular table in the center, (5) _____ . There is a large window above the sink looking out on two apple trees in the garden. There's a big, old stove at one end and at the other end a wall with a huge bulletin board (6) _____ of our lives, past, present, and future: a school photo of the kids; a postcard from Aunt Nancy, (7) _____ to Canada; the menu from a takeout Chinese restaurant; an invitation to a wedding (8) _____ ; a letter from a friend (9) _____ for years. All our world is there for everyone to read!

The front door is seldom used in our house, only by strangers. All our friends use the back door, (10) _____ they come straight into the kitchen and join in whatever is happening there. Without doubt, some of the happiest times of my life have been spent in our kitchen.

4 Link these sentences with *who, which, that, where,* and *whose*.

1. The blonde lady is Pat. She's wearing a black dress.
2. There's the hospital. My sister works there.
3. The postcard arrived this morning. It's from Aunt Nancy.
4. I passed all my exams. This made my father very proud.
5. Did you meet the girl? Her mother teaches Portuguese.

5 Complete the sentences with a word from the box in the present or past participle.

play	give	stick
listen	arrange	

1. I spend hours in my room _____ to music.
2. I have lots of posters _____ on the walls.
3. My brother is in his bedroom _____ on his computer.
4. There are photos of my family _____ on my shelves.
5. I also have a color TV _____ to me on my last birthday.

6 Write about your favorite room. Use relative pronouns and participles.

1 Think of someone in your family and write three sentences about them. Read your sentences aloud to the rest of the class.

2 Which relative did you choose? Why? Did you write about their character, their appearance, or both?

3 Read the description of crazy Uncle Joe. Which sentence below accurately describes the writer's opinion of him?

– *The writer likes Uncle Joe but is critical of his way of life.*

– *The writer admires everything about Uncle Joe.*

4 The text consists of *factual description* and *personal opinions*. Work with a partner and read through the text again. Underline like this _____ what is factual, and like this _ _ _ _ what is personal opinion.

5 Find words and lines which describe:
- his physical appearance
- his character
- his past life
- his current lifestyle

6 Find the following words:

much (line 2)	really (line 13)
so (line 4)	pretty (line 13)
completely (line 10)	particularly (line 15)
absolutely (line 11)	extremely (line 18)

How do they change the meaning of the adjectives which follow them?

7 Write a similar description of a member of your family in about 200 words. Include your sentences from Exercise 1 and the following:
- your relation to him/her
- your opinion of him/her
- a little about his/her past life
- his/her physical appearance
- his/her character
- his/her current lifestyle

MY CRAZY UNCLE JOE

1   Of all my relatives, I like my Uncle Joe the best. He's my mother's much younger brother. He was only nine when I was born, so he's been more like a big brother to me than an uncle. He is in his mid-20s now and he is always so fun to be with.

5   He studied at a drama school in California, and then he moved to New York a year ago to try his luck in the theater. He shares an apartment with three other aspiring actors, and he works as a waiter and a part-time DJ. He's passionate about his music. It's called House Music, and it's a kind of electronic dance music. When
10 he "deejays," he goes completely wild, waving his arms and yelling at the crowds. His enthusiasm is infectious. He's absolutely great! I'm proud that he's my uncle.

Also, I think he is really good-looking. He's pretty tall with dark hair, and twinkly, dark brown eyes. He's had a lot of
15 girlfriends, but I don't think there is anyone particularly special at the moment. He has a great relationship with his roommates, they are always laughing and joking together. He knows how to have fun, but he's also an extremely caring person. I can talk to him about all kinds of problems that I could not discuss with my
20 parents. He's very understanding of someone my age.

He works hard, and he plays hard. He's had a lot of auditions for various theatrical roles. He hasn't had much luck yet, but I'm sure that one day he'll be a highly successful actor. I think he's really talented, but he says he doesn't want to be rich or famous, he just
25 wants to prove to himself that he's a good actor.

1 What do you know about the sinking of the Titanic?

It happened at the beginning of the twentieth century.
There was a movie about it starring Leonardo DiCaprio.

2 Work with a partner. Look at the pictures and tell the story in your own words. Then read **Text A**, and match the lines with the pictures.

On April 10, 1912, the Titanic left Southampton on her way to New York. There were many rich passengers on board. Everyone believed the ship was unsinkable, so she didn't have many lifeboats.

On the night of April 14, the passengers were having dinner and listening to the band. The Titanic was traveling fast because the owner wanted his ship to beat the record for crossing the Atlantic. Some ships nearby warned of icebergs, but the messages were not delivered. A look-out sounded the alarm, but it was too late. The Titanic hit an iceberg, and the ship sank quickly. The band played until it sank. The lifeboats only saved some of the people. Most of them died in the sea.

People today are still interested in the Titanic. The movie *Titanic* was very popular.

3 Now read **Text B**. Compare it with **Text A**. Which is the more interesting text? Why? Give some examples.

| Text B | **The Unsinkable Titanic, 1912** |

On April 10, 1912, the liner Titanic, the luxurious ship they called unsinkable, left Southampton on her maiden voyage to New York. Her passengers were a mixture of the world's wealthiest in their magnificent first-class accommodations and immigrants packed into steerage. The ship was believed to be so safe that she carried only 20 lifeboats, enough for only half her 2,235 passengers and crew.

On the evening of April 14, there was no wind and the sea was calm. The band was playing as the rich enjoyed their evening meal in the sumptuous dining room. At 9:40 p.m. nearby ships warned of icebergs. However, the messages were not delivered. The Titanic was traveling at 22 knots. The owner of the ship was on board, encouraging the captain to go faster to beat the record for crossing the Atlantic. Finally, a look-out on the bridge sounded the alarm, but it was too late. At 11:40 p.m. the Titanic struck an iceberg. Passengers felt only a slight bump and carried on dancing and dining. After all, this ship was unsinkable. In fact, the ship was sinking fast, but it was not until nearly 12:45 that an SOS signal was sent and the first lifeboat was lowered. The last one was lowered at 2:05 A.M., and at 2:20 A.M. the ship sank, just two hours and forty minutes after hitting the iceberg. 713 people were saved. The remaining 1,522 all met their death in the dark waters of the Atlantic Ocean. These included most of the men and third-class passengers, the crew, and all of the band members. Amazingly, they had kept playing until the ship disappeared beneath the waves.

The ship sank almost 100 years ago, but interest in the Titanic continues. Books and movies have kept its memory alive. *Titanic* is the most watched film in movie history. Incredibly, in 1985, the wreck itself was discovered and photographed on the sea bed.

4 Go through the Titanic texts again with your partner. Discuss the differences. Consider the following questions.

The general organization
How is the scene set?
What forms the main part?
How is the story concluded?

Telling the story
What information is given?
How is interest created?
What is the order of events?

The language
Which adjectives and adverbs are used?
How are the sentences constructed?

5 With your partner, discuss what you know about the story of the Trojan Horse. Look at the pictures and prompts to help.

THE TROJAN HORSE

1 Greek army / camped / the city of Troy / Greek king Odysseus / good idea / decided / build a huge, hollow, wooden / big enough / soldiers / hide.

2 horse / built / soldiers / inside / others set fire / camp / pretended / sail back / Greece / hid nearby.

3 Trojans, delighted / came out / gates / found / horse / very curious / Greeks / left one soldier / Trojans asked about / said / offering to / goddess Athena.

4 Trojans / pull / horse into the city / so big / tear down / city wall / took to / temple of Athena / big party / celebrate / end of the war.

5 finally / asleep / Greek soldiers crept out / killed guards / signaled / Greeks / to attack Troy.

6 bloody battle / Greeks won / Trojan men / killed women / children / back to Greece / slaves.

6 Work together to write the story. Remember to set the scene, create interest, and use adverbs and adjectives.
Begin like this: **The Greeks and the Trojans had been at war for ten years.**

7 Read some of the stories aloud to the class. Compare with the story on pages 146–47.

1 Do you think childhood is the best time of your life? Discuss as a class.

2 Read the text about the pros and cons of childhood. Replace the underlined words and phrases in the text with those in the box.

> For instance
> One advantage is that
> pros and cons
> One disadvantage is that
> Finally,
> All things considered
> in my opinion,
> In conclusion
> In fact,
> Another point is that
> Moreover,

3 There are four paragraphs. What is the purpose of each one?

Pros and

Childhood — the best time of your life?

1 **Some people say that childhood is the best time of your life. However, being a child has both <u>advantages and disadvantages.</u>**

2 <u>On the plus side</u> you have very few responsibilities. <u>For example</u>, you don't have to go to work, pay bills, or do the shopping, cooking, or cleaning. This means you have plenty of free time to do whatever you want — watch TV, play on the computer, go out with friends, play sports, or pursue other hobbies. <u>On top of that</u>, public transportation, movie theaters, and sports centers cost much less for children. <u>All in all</u>, being a child is an exciting, action-packed time in life.

3 However, for every plus there is a minus. <u>For one thing</u>, you have to spend all day, Monday to Friday, at school. Studying usually means you have to do homework, and you have to take exams. <u>What is more</u>, you may have a lot of free time, but you are rarely allowed to do whatever you want. You usually have to ask your parents if you can do things, from going shopping in town to staying out late or going to a party. <u>Last of all</u>, although there are often cheaper prices for children, things are still expensive — and parents are not always generous with allowance. There's never enough to do everything you want. <u>The reality is that</u> sometimes there's not enough to do anything at all!

4 <u>To sum up</u>, although some people see childhood as the best time in life, <u>I think that</u> children have no real choice, independence, or money. Nevertheless, it is true that choice, money, and independence all bring responsibilities and restrictions — which increase with age.

4 Match the pros with the cons.

pros	cons
1. don't have to go to work	are never given enough allowance
2. can go out to parties with friends	have to do homework and take exams
3. don't have to cook and clean	have to go to school Monday to Friday
4. pay less for things	need to ask your parents' permission

5 Work with a partner. Choose one of these subjects and briefly discuss the pros and cons.

1. Restorative justice (where criminals meet their victims to talk about the effect of their crimes)
2. Getting older
3. Having children while young

6 Work together to complete these phrases with your ideas from Exercise 5.

On the plus side …
For example, …
Another point is that …
However, there are also disadvantages …
For instance, …
What is more, …
Last of all, …
In my opinion, …
In conclusion, …

7 Use the ideas from Exercises 5 and 6 to write four paragraphs on your chosen subject. Read your essay aloud to the class. Do they agree with your conclusion?

1 Write down everything you know about New York City. Collect all your ideas as a class.

2 Work with a partner and study the diagram about New York. Compare the information with your ideas.

Geography
- Hudson River
- same latitude as Naples and Madrid

History
- Dutch 1614 / New Amsterdam
- British 1664 / New York
- 19th c./ immigration
- 20th c./ economic boom
- Sept. 11, 2001

Its people
- densely populated / 8,214,246
- 36% foreign born
- 170 languages

"The Big Apple"

NEW YORK CITY

"The city that never sleeps"

Transportation
- 12,000 taxis
- 3 airports
- Grand Central Station
- subway / 1.4 billion passengers

Sports
- baseball
- marathon / 37,000 runners

Tourism
- shopping / 5th Ave.
- Empire State Building, etc.
- 40 million visitors

Food
- variety
- haute cuisine / hot dogs

NEW YORK CITY

Although New York City is not the capital of the United States, its influence is seen throughout the world. Its nickname, (1) "_____," was given to it by early immigrants because the city seemed so huge and full of promise.

Geography

It is located at the mouth of the (2) _____ and lies on the same latitude as the European cities of (3) _____.

History

The Dutch founded the city in 1614, calling it (4) _____. However, in (5) _____ it was captured by the British and renamed New York. The city grew in importance and was the U.S. capital until 1790. During the 19th century it was transformed by (6) _____, and from the early 20th century, it became a world center for industry, commerce, and communication. With the economic (7) _____ came the construction of its distinctive skyline of skyscrapers, two of which, the Twin Towers of the World Trade Center, were destroyed in the attacks of (8) _____, when nearly 3,000 people died.

Its people

New York is the most (9) _____ and cosmopolitan city in the United States with 8,214,246 inhabitants speaking (10) _____ languages. 36% of the city's population is (11) _____ . Five of the largest ethnic groups are: Puerto Ricans, Italians, West Indians, Chinese, and Irish.

Transportation

One in three New Yorkers uses public transportation to get to work, whereas in the rest of the U.S. 90% of commuters go by car. The New York City Subway, which is open 24/7, is used by (12) _____ a year. New York is also home to the famous Grand Central Station, three major airports, and (13) _____ distinctive, yellow taxi cabs.

Sports

The New York Marathon, held annually on the first Sunday of November, is the largest marathon in the world. It attracts (14) _____ . However, many New Yorkers prefer a less energetic jog around Central Park. New Yorkers are also passionate (15) _____ fans. The two most popular teams are the New York Yankees and the New York Mets.

Tourism

About (16) _____ tourists visit New York City each year. Major attractions include the Empire State Building, the Metropolitan Museum of Art, Times Square, Central Park, and, of course, the (17) _____ along Fifth Avenue. Tourists are also attracted by the incredible (18) _____ of places to eat, from diners, with their burgers, bagels, and pizza, to many of the finest haute cuisine restaurants in the U.S., not forgetting the Grand Central Oyster Bar and the steaming (19) _____ sold on every street corner.

Finally

With so much to do and see, it is no surprise that New York is often called (20) "_____."

---

3 Read and complete the text using the information from the diagram in Exercise 2.

4 Read the text again. What extra information not in the diagram can you find? Give some examples.

5 Find these words and expressions in the text and discuss why they are used.

Although	its	However	distinctive
two of which	whereas	is home to	with (so much to do)

6 Complete these sentences with the words or expressions from Exercise 5.

1. Tokyo is the biggest city in the world. _____ population is over 28 million.
2. The U.S. has many big cities, _____ are Chicago and Los Angeles.
3. Mexico City _____ one of the biggest stadiums in the world, Estadio Azteca.
4. The temperature in Canada can be as low as -13°F in the winter. _____, in summer it is often over 86°F.
5. _____ most people in Canada speak English, French is also an official language.
6. It is easy to recognize pictures of San Francisco because of its _____ bridge.
7. Brasilia is located in the center of Brazil, _____ Rio de Janeiro is on the coast.
8. _____ so much to see, it is impossible to do a tour of the city in two days.

7 Choose a famous town or city. Research it, make notes (you could draw a diagram), and then write about it. Use the headings about New York, or choose headings of your own.

1 Join the sentences in different ways using the words in parentheses.

  1. George was rich. He wasn't a happy man. (*but / although / however*)

  2. Jo called me from a phone booth. She lost her cell. (*because / so*)

2 Look at these words and expressions. They prepare people for what you are going to write or say next. Read and complete the sentences with your own ideas.

in fact
actually
of course
naturally
fortunately
unfortunately
nevertheless
anyway

  1. **In fact/Actually** *(I'm going to add more information to support this statement.)*

    Peter doesn't like working in Houston. **In fact**, he's thinking of changing jobs.

    Alice and I are in love. **Actually**, we _____.

  2. **Of course/Naturally** *(What I am going to say is obvious.)*

    Of course, having a baby has totally changed our lives.

    Naturally, when I was a child I didn't _____.

  3. **Fortunately/Unfortunately** *(What I am going to say is/is not good news.)*

    She tried really hard, and **fortunately**, she passed the exam.

    She stood and waited for over an hour, but **unfortunately**, _____.

  4. **Nevertheless** *(I am going to tell you about a result or effect which is unexpected.)*

    The accident wasn't her fault. **Nevertheless**, she felt terrible.

    My father didn't do very well at school. **Nevertheless**, _____.

  5. **Anyway** *(I am going to finish talking about the subject and move on to something new.)*

    What traffic! I thought I'd never get here. **Anyway**, now let's get on with the meeting.

    Anyway, you've heard enough about me. What _____?

3 Read the letter and write the word or words that fit best.

Dear Melody,   *August 15th*

  I hope you're all well. Things are busy here. Maya moved out last week. She found a small apartment not far from here, (1) _____ (so / anyway) we still see her all the time. She also got a new job at a radio station. (2) _____ , (Unfortunately / Because) it doesn't pay very well, (3) _____ (of course / but) at least she likes it. Now that Maya has moved out, it's only Joe and me at home. After 24 years of having kids around the house, it's a little strange to have the place all to ourselves. (4) _____ , (However / In fact) it's nice to come home to a clean house at the end of the day.

  Samantha is going to graduate from Columbia University this year. We're all very proud, and (5) _____ (however / of course) we're going to have a party for her. (6) _____ , (So / Actually) it's going to be a surprise party! So, shhh! Samantha says she wants to travel somewhere interesting in the fall, (7) _____ (but / because) she hasn't decided where to go yet. Joe's fine, (8) _____ (although / so) he's been in a bad mood lately. He hasn't been able to do much in the garden (9) _____ (because / actually) it's rained every day for the last two weeks! (10) _____ , (In fact / Nevertheless) it's been the rainiest summer in 20 years. (11) _____ , (Anyway / Of course) that's enough of our news. How are you all? What are you up to?

Write back and tell me everything!

Love, Jackie

1 Valeria was a student of English in Philadelphia, where she stayed with the Kendall family. She has now returned home. Read the e-mail she has written to Mr. and Mrs. Kendall. Her English has improved, but there are still over 25 mistakes. How many can you find?

To: GillandBobKendall@lightspeed.net   Attachment: GoodbyePhilly.jpg
Subject: **Hello from Valeria**

Dear Mr. and Mrs. Kendall,

I am home now since two weeks, but I have to start work immediately, so this is the first time is possible for me to write. How are you all? Are you busy as usual? Does Tim still work hard for his exam next month? I am miss you a lot and also all my friends from Philadelphia. :-)

Yesterday I've received an e-mail from my Mexico friend, Carla, and she told me about some of the other people I met. She say that Atsuko and Yuki will write me from Japan. I am lucky because I made so many good friend during I was in the U.S. It was really interesting for me to meet people from so many different countries. I think that we not only improved our English (I hope this!) but we also knew people from all over the world, and this is important.

My family are fine. They had a good summer vacation at the beach. We are all very exciting because my brother will get married in December, and we like very much his girlfriend. They have looked for an apartment in the city, but it is no easy to find one. If they won't find one soon, they will have to stay here with us.

Please can you check something for me? I can't find my red scarf. I think maybe I have forgotten it in the closet in my bedroom.

Please write soon. My family send best wishes to you all. I hope I can come back next year. Stay with you was a very wonderful experience for me. Thank you for all things, and excuse my mistakes. I already forget much words.

Love and best wishes to you all,

Valeria x x

P.S. I hope you like the attached photo. It's nice, isn't it?
It's the one you took when I was leaving!

2 Compare the mistakes you have found with a partner.
Correct the e-mail.

3 Write a thank-you e-mail to someone you have stayed with.

Audio Scripts

UNIT 1

CD1 2 **One World Quiz**

1. In which country do men and women live the longest?
   Women and men live longest in Japan. Women live on average 86 years and men 79. The average life expectancy in Japan is 81.25 years. In the U.S. it is 77.8 and in Germany 78.8.
2. In which year did the world population reach 6 billion?
   The world population reached 6 billion in 1999. There are now over 6.5 billion people in the world.
3. If you are standing on the equator, how many hours of daylight do you have?
   If you are standing at the equator you have 12 hours of daylight every day of the year. You also experience the fastest sunrise and sunset in the world, between 128 and 142 seconds depending on the time of year.
4. Where does most of the world's oil come from?
   Most of the world's oil comes from Saudi Arabia. It produces 10.9 million barrels per day. Russia produces 9.4 million, and Venezuela 3.2 million.
5. Which of the seven wonders of the world is still standing?
   Of the seven wonders of the ancient world only the pyramids of Egypt are still standing. The Colossus of Rhodes and the Lighthouse of Alexandria were destroyed by earthquakes hundreds of years ago.
6. Why didn't dinosaurs attack humans?
   Dinosaurs didn't attack humans because they became extinct 65 million years ago. Human beings didn't appear on earth until 130,000 years ago.
7. Where was the Titanic sailing to when it sank?
   The Titanic was sailing to New York from Southampton when it hit an iceberg on April 14th, 1912.
8. How long has Hawaii been a U.S. state?
   Hawaii has been a U.S. state since 1959. It was the 50th state to be admitted to the union.
9. How many people have won the Nobel Peace prize since it started in 1901?
   94 people have won the Nobel Peace prize since it started in 1901. These include Nelson Mandela in 1993 and Mother Teresa in 1979.
10. How long have people been using the Internet?
    People have been using the Internet since 1969. It was invented by the U.S. Department of Defense as a means of communication. It first went live in October 1969, with communications between the University of California and the Stanford Research Institute.
11. Which language is spoken by the most people in the world?
    Chinese is spoken by the most people in the world. Over one billion people speak it. English is the second most spoken language in the world, with about half a billion speakers.
12. In which country were women first given the vote?
    New Zealand was the first country in the world to give women the vote in 1893. Canadian women were given the vote in 1917, but women in Paraguay weren't allowed to vote until 1961.

CD1 3 **You're so wrong!**

1. A The Pope lives in Montreal.
   B He doesn't live in Montreal! He lives in Rome. In the Vatican.
2. A Shakespeare didn't write poems.
   B You're wrong. He wrote hundreds of poems, not just plays.
3. A Vegetarians eat meat.
   B Of course they don't eat meat. They only eat vegetables and sometimes fish.
4. A The Internet doesn't provide much information.
   B That's not true! It provides a lot. Sometimes I think that it provides too much!
5. A The world is getting colder.
   B It isn't getting colder, it's getting hotter. Haven't you heard of global warming?
6. A John F. Kennedy was traveling by plane when he was killed.
   B No, you're wrong. He wasn't traveling by plane. He was traveling by car, in Dallas, Texas.
7. A Brazil has never won the World Cup.
   B Brazil *has* won it, five times. My dad goes on about it all the time.
8. A The 2008 Olympics were held in Tokyo.
   B No, they weren't held in Tokyo. They were held in China, in Beijing.

CD1 4 ***is* or *has*?**

1. My brother's just started a new job.
2. He's working in South America.
3. He's been there three months.
4. He's having a great time.
5. He's never worked overseas before.
6. His company's called Intext Worldwide.

CD1 5 **Making conversation**

R = Ruth (mother)   N = Nick (son)
L = Lily (daughter)
R So kids, did you have a good day at school?
N No.
L Yes, I did. We were practicing for the school concert.
R Oh, wonderful! Do you have a lot of homework?
L Ugh! Yes, I do. I have Geography, Spanish, and Math! Do you have a lot, Nick?
N Yeah.
R Nick, did you remember your soccer uniform?
N Um …
L No, he didn't. He forgot it again.
R Oh, Nick, you know we need to wash it. Are you playing soccer tomorrow?
N No.
R Lily, do you need your uniform tomorrow?
L Yes, I do. I have a softball game after school. We're playing our rival team.
R Didn't they beat you last time?
L Yes, they did. But we'll beat them tomorrow.
N No, you won't! Your team's terrible.
R OK. That's enough, children. Put on your seatbelts! Let's go!

CD1 6

R So kids, did you have a good day at school?
N No, I didn't. Not really. We didn't have any of my favorite subjects.
L Yes, I did. We were practicing for the school concert.
R Oh, wonderful! Do you have a lot of homework?
L Ugh! Yes, I do. I have Geography, Spanish, and Math! Do you have a lot, Nick?

N Yes, I do. I have to work on my science project. I have to finish by Friday!
R Nick, did you remember your soccer uniform?
N Oh no, I didn't—sorry, Mom.
R Oh, Nick, you know we need to wash it. Are you playing soccer tomorrow?
N No, I'm not, thank goodness. The game was cancelled.
R Lily, do you need your uniform tomorrow?
L Yes, I do. I have a softball game after school. We're playing our rival team.
R Didn't they beat you last time?
L Yes, they did. But we'll beat them tomorrow.
N Ummm—I'm not so sure about that.
R OK. That's enough, children. Put on your seatbelts! Let's go!

CD1 7 see page 5

CD1 8 **A world in one family**

An interview with Xavier
I So, Xavier—how old are you?
X I'm 21.
I And I know you have an interesting background. What nationality are you?
X Well, I have an American passport …
I … so you're American, but your parents—what nationality are your parents?
X Well, my dad's Peruvian. He was born in Peru, in South America, but he's had an American passport for the last 20 years. My mom was born in Spain, in the Basque country, and she still has her Spanish passport.
I So, how did they meet and end up having children in the U.S.?
X Ummm … they met when they were both studying English in the U.S. Ummm … and um … and about three years after that that they got married and here I am, and then my brother.
I And what was it like growing up in the U.S. with a Spanish mother and a Peruvian father?
X I don't think I actually noticed nationality for years—um … probably the first time I really noticed a difference was in high school. The U.S. was playing Spain in the 2004 Olympic Games, and my classmates made me choose which country to support.
I So which country did you support?
X I stayed neutral. Actually, I didn't care which team won.
I And which nationality do you feel now?
X I'd say I was American—um, but I'm also very proud of my parents' heritage, half Basque and half Peruvian. I like that.
I What contact have you had with your family abroad?
X Well, I've only actually been to Spain once—um, when I was a baby. I've had more contact on my dad's side. My Peruvian grandparents visit us in the U.S., and when I was growing up, we always went to Peru in the summer, and …
I Very nice.
X … and if I'm home I speak to them—um, to my grandparents, on the phone—um … maybe once a week.
I And do you think that your Spanish heritage has influenced you at all?
X Well, yes, I think so. I think it influenced my degree choice. I'm studying modern languages at Syracuse University—Spanish and French. I'm in my third year. I have one more year to do.

I And what are you hoping to do in the future?

X Umm—That's a very good question. Um … hopefully a job that offers some kind of opportunity to travel, but ultimately, I want to settle down for good in the U.S. I've always been interested in my background, but I think that I realize the U.S. is my home and it is where I see myself living.

I Thank you very much, Xavier.

X You're welcome.

CD1 9 I = Interviewer A = Ana

I Ana, you're Spanish, aren't you?

A Yes, I am. I'm from Bilbao, in the Basque country.

I And how long have you lived here in New York?

A Um … 23 years.

I And how did that happen?

A Well, I wanted to improve my English so I came to the U.S. to study. Originally, I came for six months but—um … I met my husband—um … we met at college—actually we met on the way to the college, in the street.

I You met in the street?

A Yes, it was the first day and I was walking up the hill to the college, and Teo, that's my husband, was driving up the hill, and he stopped and offered me a ride, which I refused.

I You refused?

A Yes, but we ended up in the same class. I went into the class, and there he was.

I And your husband's from Peru, isn't he?

A Yes, he is.

I So that means you speak the same language.

A Yes, Spanish.

I So, why did you decide to live in the U.S.?

A Well, mainly because my husband had a job here and, um—we kind of decided we wanted a place in the middle, between Spain and Peru.

I A nice idea. And you have two sons.

A Yes, I do. Xavier is 21, nearly 22, and James is 19.

I So, what's it been like for them growing up in the U.S. with parents of different nationality?

A Well, I think because we live in New York, a cosmopolitan city, they didn't notice it too much.

I They are both bilingual presumably?

A No, not really.

I Oh.

A … because, when they were children, even though we spoke to them in Spanish, they always replied in English.

I Um, interesting. Tell me, how much contact has your family here had with the families in Spain and Peru?

A I think more with my husband's family in Peru because it's closer. We always spent summer there—um—two or three weeks usually.

I And the Spanish side?

A Well, I keep in touch all the time, but my family has never been here.

I Never?

A Never. We went to Spain once when Xavier was 18 months old. James has never been.

I So what are the children doing now?

A Xavier's in college and James just finished high school. He's been working in a restaurant, saving money to travel.

I And what do they want to do in the future?

A Well, James, he's going to travel to Spain at last! Then he's going to college to study Biology.

I And Xavier?

A I think he wants to work in foreign affairs.

I Ana, is it possible to sum up the pros and cons of bringing up a family in another country?

A Well, I think in a way it's good because you can take the best things from both cultures, but I don't think my sons will ever feel 100% American because their parents aren't American. It's very tricky.

CD1 10 **Pronunciation**

1. rose   goes   does   toes
2. meat   beat   great   street
3. paid   made   played   said
4. done   phone   son   won

CD1 11

mother   enjoy   apartment   holiday   population

CD1 12 **Everyday situations**

1. **A** I need to make an appointment. It's pretty urgent. I've lost a filling.
   B We have a cancellation this afternoon. 2:45, if that's OK?
   A That's great. I'll be there.
2. **A** A medium latte and a muffin, please.
   B For here or to go?
   A Here, please.
   B That'll be $3.90 please.
3. **A** I can't make the meeting. I'm stuck in traffic.
   B Don't worry. We'll start without you and brief you later.
   A Oh, hold on! We're moving again. I should be there in about an hour.
4. **A** Can you put in your PIN number and press "Enter"?
   B Oh, no! I can't remember my number for this card. Oh, what is it?
   A Do you have another card you could use?
5. **A** Bottled or tap? And do you want ice and lemon in it?
   B Bottled, please. Ice but no lemon.
   A No problem. Is that all?
6. **A** I don't think you've met Greg. He's joining us from our New York office.
   B Hello. Good to meet you. I've heard a lot about you.
   C Yeah, at last we meet. I'm looking forward to working together.
7. **A** How many bags are you checking in?
   B Just the one.
   A And did you pack it yourself?
   B Yes, I did.
8. **A** The elevator's on your right. Would you like someone to help you with your bags?
   B No, thank you. I'll manage.
   A OK. If you insist. Here's your key. Enjoy your stay.
9. **A** Please hold. Your call is important to us. All our operators are busy at the moment, but one of them will be with you shortly.
   B If I have to listen to that again, I'll go crazy!
   C Can I help you?
   B At last a real person! Do you know how long I've been waiting?
10. **A** There are still tickets for the 5:45 performance, but the 8:45 is sold out, I'm afraid.
    B That's fine. We'll have two, please, one adult, one child.
    A OK. Two for 5:45. The doors open at 5.

CD1 13 **Role play**

1. **A** Maria, this is my friend Peter. We came to the U.S. together. We come from the same town in Canada.
   B Hello, Peter. Nice to meet you. I hope you're having a good time.
2. **A** Excuse me. I don't think this is mine. I ordered a medium latte and a muffin.
   B Oh, sorry. My mistake. This is for the next table.
3. **A** Good evening. Reception? I'm in room 216, and my TV isn't working. Can you send someone to fix it?
   B Of course, sir. I'll send someone immediately.
4. **A** Excuse me. Can you tell me which is the check-in desk for Bangkok? I can't see my flight on the screen.

B Oh no. You're at the wrong terminal. Flights to Bangkok leave from Terminal 2. You can take a bus to the terminal over there.

5. **A** OK, everyone. Dinner's ready! Can you all come to the table? Bring your drinks and just help yourselves to the food.
   BCD Mmmm. It smells good. Can we sit where we like?

UNIT 2

CD1 14 **"Blue Monday" by Fats Domino**

Blue Monday, how I hate Blue Monday
Got to work like a slave all day
Here come Tuesday, oh hard Tuesday
I'm so tired got no time to play

On Wednesday, work twelve hours, then
Go home, fall into bed at ten
'Cause Thursday is a hard working day
And Friday I get my pay

Saturday morning, oh, Saturday morning
All my tiredness has gone away
Got my money and my honey
And I'm out on the town to play

Sunday morning my head is bad,
But it's worth it for the fun that I had
Sunday evening it's goodnight and amen
'Cause on Monday I start again

CD1 15 **My favorite day of the week**

Vicky

I go to a boarding school, so I don't live with my parents during the semester. Um … what I like is being with my friends all the time. Whether we're working or just chatting, it's great to know there's always someone there. There's also a lot of freedom. I don't have to tell my parents where I'm going, who I'm going with, you know … Normally Monday is my favorite day because I only have two classes on Mondays, but I'm having a very bad day today because I have homework from every one of my teachers, and I have to do it now!

Terry

I work in a restaurant in Miami. I have two days off a week, usually Monday and Wednesday, but my favorite day of the week is in fact Friday, even though I work that day. It's the best night because all my friends come into the restaurant, and we have a great time. There's a real buzz to the place, and it doesn't feel like work at all. Time just flies by. The restaurant's being redecorated right now, so everything's a little crazy.   *passive*

Dave

I'm a police officer. I like my job because it's challenging, but I live for surfing. I go as often as I can. I'm opening two shops that sell surfboards in the next few months. The boards are made here in the U.S. Sunday is my favorite day of the week. I hardly ever work on Sundays. I get up as early as I can, and spend the day at the beach.

Jenny

Mike and I live on a beautiful farm in Missouri. I know we're very lucky, but it's hard work. We never have a day off on weekends or holidays, or any day of the year. We have to feed the animals and take care of the fields. Now we're harvesting, so we aren't getting any rest at all. But I suppose our favorite day is Wednesday because that's the day we generally get together with friends and prepare a wonderful meal.

What's your background?

D I'm 35, and I'm single. I live in Los Angeles, California. I'm a police officer. I've been in the police force for over ten years. I love my job, but my passion is surfing.

What hours do you work?

D I work different shifts. The morning shift starts at 5:00, and I can't stand that because I have to get up at 4:30. My favorite shift is 2:00 in the afternoon until midnight because I get home about 12:30. What's good is that I work ten hours a day for four days then have three days off.

What do you think of your job?

D My job is extremely busy and very hard. But I like it because it's challenging, and I never know what's going to happen. I like working in a team. We look after each other and work together.

Why do you like surfing?

D My work is very stressful, so I surf to get away from it all. It's just me and the sea, and my mind switches off. I concentrate so hard on what I'm doing that I don't think about anything else.

How often do you go surfing?

D I go surfing whenever I'm not working. Sometimes I'm on the beach before 7:00 in the morning. I go all over the world surfing. Next month I'm going to Costa Rica, and in the fall I'm going to Thailand.

Do you have a business?

D I have a surfing school. I teach all ages, from kids to seniors. The business is doing well. I'm also opening two shops that sell surfboards. The boards are made here in the U.S.

What is your favorite day of the week?

D I like Sundays best of all. I work as a lifeguard, then around 6:00 me and my friends barbecue some burgers and relax. Awesome! I've been all around the world, but when I look around me, I think there's nowhere else I'd rather be.

CD1 17   Questions and answers

1. Where does he live?
   In Los Angeles, California.
2. Is he married?
   No, he is single.
3. Why doesn't he like the morning shift?
   Because he has to get up at 4:30.
4. How many hours a day does he work?
   Ten.
5. What does he like about his job?
   He likes it because it's challenging, and he likes working in a team.
6. What does he think about while he's surfing?
   He only thinks about surfing, nothing else.
7 Where's he going next month?
   Costa Rica.
8 Is his business doing well?
   Yes, it is. He's opening two shops.
9 What do he and his friends do on Sunday evenings?
   They eat burgers and relax.

CD1 18   The office

A = new employee B = established employee

A Gosh! I don't know anybody! Can you help me? Who are all these people?
B Uh, well, that's Simon. He's sitting at the head of the table reading something.
A He's the one wearing a sweater, right?
B Yeah, that's him.
A And what does he do?
B He's the Managing Director. He's the man in charge.
A The boss, in other words.

B Uh-huh. He shouts a lot, but he listens as well. Then there's Edward. He's wearing a suit. He's standing up talking to Anna. Edward's the sales director. He's charming. He always has a nice word to say to everyone. Anna's standing next to him. She's drinking coffee. She's wearing a jacket and she has a scarf around her neck.
A And Anna is the …?
B Anna's the accountant. Money, money, money. Very bright, very quick.
A Oh, OK. And who's that talking on her phone?
B In the blue skirt? That's Jenny, the Human Resources Manager, HR manager. She deals with all the personnel. She's a sweetheart. Everyone loves her. Then there's Matthew. He's the IT manager. He's only working here for a few months. He's from our New York office. I don't really know him very well.
A He's the guy working on his laptop?
B That's him. Wearing a shirt, no tie. He knows everything about technology. And finally that's Christina talking to Simon. She's his PA. She …
A Sorry. What was that?
B She's Simon's PA, Personal Assistant. She organizes his schedule, but she helps all of us, really. We couldn't cope without her. She runs the whole place, actually. She's the one in a black suit and fabulous earrings. Very sharp.
A Right. I think I got that …

CD1 19   Who earns how much?

Part 1

A Well, I guess that doctors earn a lot.
B Yeah. I think so, too. They have a lot of responsibility and a lot of training. I'd say that doctors get about … $140,000? What do you think?
A Could be … or it could be even more, $200,000.
B One of those two, anyway. Should we look at the high earners first?
A Uh-huh. $750,000 …
B There's one higher …
A Oh, is there? Oh, yes. A million. Mmm.
B I'd say … that has to be the basketball player.
A Yes, definitely. They do earn ridiculous amounts of money, don't they? So what about $750,000? Who earns three quarters of a million?
B Um … I think that's the lawyer.
A As much as that? What about the Senior Director? Do lawyers earn more than them?
B Maybe, maybe not. I suppose the lawyer could be $140,000, and the Senior Director $750,000. Senior Directors are in charge of huge companies.
A OK. Now … the pilot. Pilots earn a lot, don't they? They need a lot of experience. They have people's lives in their hands … I think they get … oh, at least a hundred, a hundred fifty.
B Mmm. I know what you mean, but I don't think they get that much.
A Don't they? Oh! Anyway, there isn't 150 on this list, so …
B I guess pilots get about $65,000 …
A OK. I'd say that's about right …

CD1 20

Part 2

B Let's go on down to the bottom. What's the lowest salary?
A $20,000. I guess that's the nurse. They don't get paid much, nurses.
B I thought they earned more than that, actually. I know they don't get much, but even so …
A Then there's $25,000, and the next up is $30,000.
B Oh, look! Supermarket cashier. I don't suppose they get much. $25,000, I'd say?
A OK. That seems about right. What about farmers? How much do they get?
B I don't know. It depends what sort of farmer. They can earn a fortune, can't they?

A I suppose so, yes … But they're always complaining that supermarkets don't pay them enough for what they produce.
B I still think they get a decent salary. They own so much land! I bet they get 50 or 60 thousand.
A No, I think it's much lower. I'd say $30,000.
B Hmm. Not so sure. Then we have … teachers. What do they earn?
A I guess they get … um … $40,000?
B But it all depends how many years they've worked and how many qualifications they have.
A Yes, I know, but we're talking about the average.
B Don't teachers and police officers earn about the same?
A Do they? I'm not so sure. I'd say that police officers get more. What do we have? $40,000 … $48,000.
B I think 40 for the police officer and 48 for the teacher.
A Well, actually I'd say the other way around. 48 for the police officer and 40 for the teacher. My mother's a teacher, and she doesn't earn anything like that!
B What does that leave? We haven't decided about the farmer or the nurse yet.
A I think the nurse gets less than the farmer. She gets the least.
B Why she? Nurses can be men, you know.
A True. Sorry. Nurses—men *and* women—earn less than farmers.
B Men AND women.
A Absolutely.

CD1 21   Free time activities

John

My favorite hobby is cooking, and that's a thing you do at home, obviously. I cook most days, though not every day. We also like eating out. What clothes and equipment do I need? Well, I always wear an apron to protect my clothes, because you can make a mess when you're cooking, and tomatoes and spices change the color of your clothes forever! The most important piece of equipment is knives, and I'm very particular about my knives. They're German, and very sharp, and I really take care of them. Obviously in the kitchen you need all sorts of things like pots and pans and baking dishes and chopping boards and food mixers, but I don't really have a lot of gadgets. I like to keep things simple. What I like about cooking is the fact that it's creative and it's real. We have to eat, and what we eat is really important, so I like to know that what I'm eating, and what my family is eating, is good. I actually like all the preparation. Going out shopping, seeing the food, feeling it, smelling it, talking to the people who are selling it, is half the fun. People often ask me what I like cooking, and I don't really have an answer. Whatever looks good, and whatever I feel like cooking that day. The best part is of course seeing people enjoy my food, but what's also very important to me is seeing everyone happy, and enjoying being at the table. It's about the occasion as much as the food.

CD1 22

A = Ann J = Joaquim

A So what do you think of Chicago, Joaquim?
J It's really interesting. Chicago's such a great city. There are some beautiful buildings, and the people are so friendly!
A Yes, they are. When did you get here?
J Two days ago. I took a flight from Miami. We were a bit late landing, but it didn't matter.
A Oh, good. Where are you staying in Chicago?
J At the Avenue Hotel. It's very convenient for the office. My room isn't very big, but it's OK.
A That's too bad! Don't worry. Where are you from?
J From Brazil. I was born in São Paulo, but I live in a suburb of Rio de Janeiro. It's very pretty, and it's not far from the sea.

A Really? It sounds beautiful. Your English is very good. Where did you learn it?

J That's very kind of you, but I know I make a lot of mistakes. I learned it in school for years, and I've been to the U.S. many times.

A Oh, have you? How interesting! And what are you doing here in Chicago, Joaquim?

J I'm attending a conference. I'm here for five days, and I'm going home on the 17th.

A Oh, so soon! And have you managed to get around our city yet?

J I haven't seen very much. I've been for a walk along the lakefront path and I've taken a boat tour from the Navy Pier, but I haven't been to the John Hancock Observatory yet.

A Well, I hope you enjoy it. Don't work too hard!

J I'll try to enjoy myself! Bye. It was nice to talk to you.

CD1 23

1. Who do you work for?
2. Do you enjoy your job?
3. Where do you come from?
4. Have you been to New York?
5. What do you do when you're not working?
6. The weather's amazing right now, isn't it?
7. Are you going on vacation this year?
8. This city's very exciting, isn't it?
9. What's your favorite TV show?

CD1 24

1. **A** Who do you work for?
   B Siemens. I've been with them for four years. They're a good company. How about you?
2. **A** Do you enjoy your job?
   B Yes, I do. It's quite hard, but it's very challenging. I don't earn very much. What about you? Do you like your job?
3. **A** Where do you come from?
   B I was born in Michigan, and I've lived there all my life with my parents. I'd like to live abroad some time.
4. **A** Have you been to New York?
   B No, I haven't, but I'd love to. I've heard it's one of the most amazing cities in the world. Have you been there?
5. **A** What do you do when you're not working?
   B Well, I like horseback riding, and I play golf. And I love music, so I often go to concerts. Do you?
6. **A** The weather's amazing right now, isn't it?
   B Yes, it's so mild. We haven't had any real cold weather at all! Have you heard a weather forecast for the weekend? It's supposed to be good, isn't it?
7. **A** Are you going on vacation this year?
   B Yes, I'm going to Mexico with some friends. I haven't been there before, so I'm really looking forward to it. What about you?
8. **A** This city's very exciting, isn't it?
   B Really? Do you think so? There isn't very much to do. I get so bored here. What *do* you find to do?
9. **A** What's your favorite TV show?
   B I like soaps and documentaries. And game shows. And the news. I suppose I like everything. What about you?

UNIT 3

CD1 25 Vincent Van Gogh

1. Where was he born?
2. What was his job?
3. Why was he fired?
4. Why did he try to commit suicide?
5. Which artists did he meet?

6. What was he doing when he met them?
7. Who came to live with him?
8. Where did they first meet?
9. What was he carrying?
10. Why did he cut off part of his ear?
11. Which paintings were completed there?
12. What was he doing when he shot himself?
13. Why did he shoot himself?
14. Where was he buried?
15. Why didn't he have any money?

CD1 26

1. Where was he born?
   In Brabant in the Netherlands.
2. What was his job?
   He worked as an art dealer.
3. Why was he fired?
   Because he'd had an argument with customers.
4. Why did he try to commit suicide?
   Because he'd fallen in love with his cousin and she'd rejected him.
5. Which artists did he meet?
   Degas, Pissarro, Seurat, Toulouse-Lautrec, Monet, and Renoir.
6. What was he doing when he met them?
   He was studying art.
7. Who came to live with him?
   Gauguin.
8. Where did they first meet?
   In Paris.
9. What was he carrying?
   A razor blade.
10. Why did he cut off part of his ear?
    Because he'd had an argument with Gauguin.
11. Which paintings were completed there?
    Starry Night, *Irises*, and *Self-Portrait Without a Beard*.
12. What was he doing when he shot himself?
    He was painting outside.
13. Why did he shoot himself?
    Because he was depressed.
14. Where was he buried?
    In Auvers.
15. Why didn't he have any money?
    Because he'd sold only one of his paintings.

CD1 27 see page 19

CD1 28

/t/ worked published

/d/ tried moved continued died recognized

/ɪd/ rejected completed

CD1 29 I didn't do much

1. I didn't do much. I just had something to eat, watched TV for a while, and then had an early night. I was in bed by ten.
2. I went to my yoga class, then went out to eat with a couple of friends. I got home about nine and did a bit of housework, and that was it.
3. I went out with some people from work, so I didn't get home until about midnight. Well, after midnight, actually. It was a very late night for me!
4. I met some friends in town for coffee, and we talked for a while. Then I went home and did some stuff on the computer, you know, Facebook, then went to bed about eleven thirty.

CD1 30 Smash! Clumsy visitor destroys priceless vases

A clumsy visitor to a museum has destroyed a set of priceless 300-year-old Chinese vases after slipping on the stairs.

The three vases, which were produced during the Qing dynasty in the 17th century, had stood on a windowsill at the City Museum for forty years. Last

Thursday they were smashed into a million pieces. The vases, which were donated in 1948, had been the museum's best known pieces.

The museum decided not to identify the man who had caused the disaster. "It was a most unfortunate and regrettable accident," museum director Duncan Robinson said, "but we are glad that the visitor wasn't seriously injured."

The photograph was taken by another visitor, Steve Baxter. "We watched the man fall as if in slow motion. He was flying through the air. The vases exploded as though they had been hit by a bomb. The man was sitting there stunned in the middle of a pile of porcelain when the staff arrived."

The museum declined to say what the vases were worth.

CD1 31 I = Interviewer NF = Nick Flynn

I It's 7:45, and you're listening to the *Morning Show*. The man who broke Chinese vases worth $160,000 when he fell down the stairs at a museum has been identified by a daily newspaper. He's Nick Flynn, and he's with us now. Are you all right, Mr. Flynn? You didn't hurt yourself falling down the stairs, did you?

NF I'm recovering, which is more than I can say for the vases!

I Very true! How did it happen?

NF I was coming down the stairs, looking at the pictures, and I slipped. The stairs are very slick, and it had been raining, so I guess my shoes were a bit wet. And I just went head over heels.

I It must have been a strange feeling, lying in the middle of all that priceless porcelain?

NF I was surprised that these incredibly valuable vases were left just lying on a windowsill. I'd seen them lots of times before, but I hadn't really paid them any attention.

I And I hear you've been banned from the museum? Is that right?

NF Yes, I got a letter from the director of the museum asking me not to go back. It's a shame, because I used to go twice a week. Now I have to find somewhere else to go.

I Well, thank you, Mr. Flynn, and good luck.

CD1 32 see page 21

CD1 33 Words that sound the same

knew/new read/red wore/war threw/through flew/flu

CD1 34 see page 21

CD1 35 see page 21

CD1 36 see page 21

CD1 37 see page 22

CD1 38 The first time I fell in love

Sarah

The first time I fell in love was when I was 13. It was with a boy named Max. We were on a school trip, a geography trip, so a whole group of us were traveling together for a week. I'd never really noticed this boy before, because we used to hang out with different people, but I suddenly started looking at him, and I remember thinking, "Hmm! You're nice!" and I couldn't understand why I hadn't looked at him before. He was very quiet, and he had dark eyes that seemed to see everything, and he made me go all weak at the knees. We kind of started going out. When we held hands, it was electric. I'd never felt anything like it in my life! Wow! I don't think he felt the same way. He was very cool about everything. It only lasted a few months. Then he went back to his friends and I went back to mine.

Tommy

T Well, I fell in love with a girl called Clara, but it didn't last very long.
I How long did it last?
T Well … about two weeks. It all ended last Friday.
I Really? What happened last Friday?
T I decided that I'd had enough of being in love. I didn't like the feeling.
I Was Clara upset?
T Not really. She didn't know anything about it.
I What?
T No. I hadn't told her that I was in love with her, so she didn't know that it had ended.
I Was it so bad?
T Oh, yes. I couldn't sleep, I used to get this funny feeling here in my tummy when I saw her coming, and my heart went bang, bang, bang. It was horrible!
I So how did you manage to stop loving her?
T Well, I'm only 9, and I figured that I'm too young to only love one person for the rest of my life.
I Fair enough. I'm glad you didn't hurt her feelings.
T I'm glad it's all over.

James

Well, I've only been in love once in my life, and that was when I was 22. I'd had other girlfriends, of course, but it was never more than that. Just a girlfriend. And then I met this other girl, Ruth, and my whole life just turned upside down. I remember thinking at the time that I'd never felt anything like it. Nothing looked the same, felt the same, life had never been so amazing, so colorful. I wanted to do everything—climb mountains, fly like a bird, stay up all night—life was far too amazing to sleep. It's funny, I never used to care what I looked like, but suddenly I started to care. I wanted to look good for this girl in my life. I felt that I hadn't really lived until that moment, until I'd met her and fallen in love. Thank goodness she felt the same! We're still together. Fifteen years and four kids later. Amazing, huh?

CD1 39   **see page 25**

CD1 40

1. We had a great time in Thailand, didn't we?
2. The weather was great, wasn't it?
3. The French really love their food, don't they?
4. It's a lovely day today, isn't it?
5. Karen and Tom are a really nice couple, aren't they?
6. Tom earns so much money, doesn't he?
7. They want to get married, don't they?

CD1 41

1. **A** She's very nice.
   B She's absolutely wonderful!
2. **A** The movie was good.
   B The movie was just great!
3. **A** The hotel's all right.
   B The hotel's really fabulous!
4. **A** I like dark chocolate.
   B I absolutely adore dark chocolate.
5. **A** I like Peter.
   B I really love Peter.
6. **A** The book wasn't very good.
   B The book was absolutely awful!
7. **A** I don't like noisy restaurants.
   B I just can't stand noisy restaurants!

UNIT 4

CD1 42   **Discussing grammar**

1. I don't get along with my boss. Do you think I should look for another job?
2. We're throwing Tom a surprise birthday party. You can't tell him about it.
3. Please, Dad, can I go to Tom's party? It'll be great.
4. You have to drive on the left in England.
5. Do you have to wear a uniform in your job?
6. Are you allowed to take cell phones to school?
7. I had to go to bed early when I was a child.
8. You don't have to go to the U.S. to learn English, but it's a good idea.

CD1 43   **Giving advice**

Conversation 1

A Are you going to Charlotte's party?
B I don't know if I should go or not.
A What do you mean?
B Well, her parents are abroad, and they told her she wasn't allowed to have friends over while they were away.
A Oh, come on! You have to come. It's a party. Everyone has parties when their parents are away.
B Yeah, but her mom and dad are best friends with mine.
A Look. You don't have to tell your mom and dad. Just go to the party and help clean up after.
B I'm not sure.

Conversation 2

A Do you see that woman over there?
B Yeah, what about her?
A She's eating!
B So?
A You're not allowed to eat in this store.
B Well …
A Do you think I should tell her to stop?
B No, no, you shouldn't say anything. It's embarrassing. The sales assistant will tell her.
A No! I can't just sit here. I have to say something. Um—excuse me …

Conversation 3

A I'm so mad!
B Why?
A I got a parking ticket. I had to go to the store for my dad, and when I got back to the car, there was ticket on the windshield.
B Oh, that's bad luck!
A I think *he* should pay the fine.
B Who? Your dad? Why? He wasn't driving.
A Yeah, but I was doing *his* shopping.
B But he didn't tell you to park illegally.
A OK, OK, so it's my fault. Um—I still think he should pay it.

CD1 44

Rules for life

1. Millie

Well, so many teenagers seem to think life is about just one thing, you know—money and fame, they think it will bring them happiness. Honestly, I would hate to be famous. When I read the magazines and see all the photos of these rich, famous movie stars, athletes and the like, it frightens me. They can't move without being followed and photographed. Usually they have bodyguards. When I grow up I just want to enjoy my work. If I earn lots of money, fair enough, but if I don't, I'll still be happy. I never want to be famous. That's scary stuff.

2. Richard

My rule for life is that you only get out of life what you put in. I mean, you should never ask that question people always ask "Why are we here? What is the meaning of life?"—you'll never find the answer. You've got to *give* meaning to your life by

what you *do* with your life—um … and I think you can do this in all kinds of ways. It doesn't matter if you are president of your country or a janitor. You have a place in the world, you have a part to play.

3. Frank

I believe you've got to look for the good in people and things. So many people of my age do nothing but complain about today's world—oh, on and on they go about—ooh, how bad the traffic is, or how cell phones are such a menace. Oh, and most of all they complain about young people—they're loud, they're impolite, not like in the "good old days." Well, I don't agree with all that. There's always been good and bad in the world, and I think we should look for the good. The rule I try to live by is find three things every day to be happy about.

CD1 45   **Spoken English**

1. "Isn't your mom away this week?"
   "Yeah, so Dad's got to do all the cooking, and I've got to do the ironing."
2. "Where's my briefcase? I've got to go to work."
   "It's where you left it when you came home. In the hallway by the front door."
3. "Mom, why can't I go out now?"
   "You've got to clean up your room first. Your friends will just have to wait."
4. "Won't you be late for work?"
   "Oh, no. Look at the time. I've got to go now. We'll catch up later. Bye!"

CD1 46   **"I Believe"**

I believe in bottle banks
And beauty from within
I believe in saying thanks
And fresh air on the skin

I believe in healthy walks
As tonic for the feet
I believe in serious talks
And just enough to eat

Chorus
That's what I believe
Surprising as it seems
I believe that happiness
Is well within our dreams

I believe in being nice
In spite of what you think
I believe in good advice
And not too much to drink

I believe in being true
In everything you try to do
I believe in me and you
I hope you share my point of view

Chorus
I believe in being kind
Especially when it's hard
I believe an open mind
Can show a fine regard

I believe that manners make
A person good to know
I believe in birthday cake
And going with the flow

Chorus
That's what I believe
Although it seems naïve
I believe that peace and love
Are there to be achieved

That's what I believe …

CD1 47   **Phrasal verbs**

1. **A** Who do you take after in your family?
   B Mmm … I don't think I take after anyone in particular. Although the older I get, the more I think I'm like my mother. Humph!
2. **A** Do you get along with both your parents?
   B Yes, I do. Most of the time. I do a lot of stuff with my dad. Baseball and things.

3. A Have you recently taken up any new sports or hobbies?
B Me? No! My life's too busy already!
4. A Do you often look up words in your dictionary?
B Sometimes, if I'm really stuck.
5. A Are you looking forward to going on vacation soon?
B I wish! But I just went on vacation, so I have to wait until the holidays now.
6. A Do you pick up foreign languages easily?
B Well, I picked up Italian quite easily when I was living in Milan, but I already knew Spanish, so I think that helped a little.
7. A Do you have any bad habits that you want to give up?
B Yes, I bite my nails. I just can't stop and I'm a teacher, so I have to hide my hands from the kids because I don't want to set a bad example.

CD1 48 see page 33

CD1 49 see page 33

CD1 50

Conversation 1
A Hello, it's me again. I just remembered that I have a doctor's appointment in the morning. Could we possibly make it lunch instead of coffee?
B Um … no problem. I can do lunch, too. How about 12:30 in the usual restaurant?

Conversation 2
A Would you mind if we didn't go out to eat after work? I want to watch the game on TV.
B Hey, we could have dinner at Morgan's. They have a huge screen. We could both watch the game there.
A You're on. Great idea!

Conversation 3
A So, anyway, there I was just finishing my report, when suddenly the boss calls me into his office and he starts going on about my performance …
B Sorry, darling, I really do want to hear all about it, but the baby's crying. Do you think you could go and check him? He might need a new diaper.

Conversation 4
A Help! Ugh … I don't know what's wrong with my computer. The screen's frozen again.
B I'll try and fix it if you like. I'm pretty good with computers.
A Go ahead. Be my guest. I've had it with this machine!

UNIT 5

CD2 2 **Things our grandchildren may never see**

H = Hannah   D = Dan
H Do you ever worry about what the world will be like when our grandchildren grow up?
D Hold on! We haven't had our baby yet. I'm not thinking about grandchildren.
H I know, but having a baby makes me wonder—what will the world be like when he or she grows up? Look at these pictures. Don't they make you worry about what could happen in the future?
D Mmm—OK, of course things are going to change a lot in the next hundred years, even in the next fifty, but …
H I know, and I'm getting worried. Everyone says global warming is a fact nowadays. No one says it *may* get warmer or it *might* get warmer anymore. Scientists say that it definitely *will* get warmer. It's going to be a very different world for our children and grandchildren.

D Look, Hannah, it's no good worrying. Not *all* scientists think the same …
H Yes, I know, but *most* do. It says here over 2,500 climate scientists agree. They say temperatures might rise by up to 39°F before the end of the century. Dan, this is the world our son or daughter is going to grow up in.
D Hannah, you have to take it easy. You're having a baby soon and …
H I can't help being worried. If the Arctic ice melts, there'll be floods, and the polar bears will have nowhere to live. Oh, and look at this …
D Come on, Hannah. Look here, it also says humans are clever enough to find solutions. We'll do our part, and we'll bring up our baby to do the same. Every little bit helps …
H OK, but maybe it won't help. It may be too late already.

CD2 3

1. A Do you think the earth will continue to get warmer?
B Yes, I do. The more I read about it, the more I think it will. A few years ago I wasn't so sure.
2. A Do you think all the ice will melt at the Poles?
B Well, I don't think *all* the ice will melt, but a lot has melted already. Do you know a new island near Greenland has just appeared? They thought it was part of the mainland, but it was just an ice bridge and it melted. It's called Warming Island. A good name, don't you think?
3. A Do you think Polar bears will become extinct?
B I think they might. They only live in the Arctic, and I read that the ice there has decreased by 14% since the 1970s.
4. A Do you think more people will travel by train?
B Definitely. I think lots more people will choose train travel when they can, especially across Europe. Of course it won't always be possible.
5. A Do you think that air travel will be banned to reduce CO₂ emissions?
B Well, I think it could become much more expensive to travel by air, but I don't think it'll be banned.
6. A Do you think new sources of energy will be found?
B I hope so. Some people say nuclear energy is the only answer, but I think this could cause more problems. Actually, I like wind farms. They look amazing. But I know some people hate them.
7. A Do you think there'll be more droughts or floods in the world?
B I don't really know. There might be both droughts and floods. I think parts of New York City may be flooded, including most of the lower Manhattan shoreline.
8. A Do you think our lifestyles will have to change?
B Definitely. They're already changing. We're told all the time to do things like drive smaller cars, use cleaner gas, and recycle our trash. That worries me a lot—the amount of trash we make.

CD2 4 **Discussing grammar**

1. A Have you decided about your vacation yet?
B No, not yet. We've never been to Costa Rica, so we might go there.
2. A Are you going to take an umbrella?
B No, I'm not. The forecast says it'll be fine all day.
3. A Why are you making a list?
B Because I'm going shopping. Is there anything you want?
4. A Would you like to go out to dinner tonight?
B Sorry, I'm working late. How about tomorrow night? I'll call you.

5. A What are you doing Saturday night?
B I'm not sure yet. I may go to a friend's, or she may come here.
6. A Are you enjoying your job more now?
B No, I'm not. I'm going to look for another one.
7. A Your team's no good! It's 2 to nothing Brazil!
B Come on. It's only half-time. I think they could still win.
8. A You won't pass your exams next month if you go out every night.
B I know, I'll study harder. I promise.

CD2 5
1. Thailand
A prolonged period of heavy rain and thunderstorms will affect parts of the country on Friday and into Saturday. Rainfall could total 1 to 2 inches in the south, but there may be up to 2 to 4 inches in the north. The heavy rain might lead to flooding in some areas.

2. Canada
High winds following in the path of Hurricane Gloria will head north from the U.S. overnight. They could reach up to 100 miles per hour and may cause damage to buildings across northwest Ontario. These winds are going to bring with them high temperatures across the country and thunderstorms in many areas.

3. The U.S.
The country's heatwave is going to continue. Temperatures could rise to more than 100 degrees Fahrenheit by midday tomorrow. New York City's mayor is going to send out teams of workers to distribute 22,000 bottles of drinking water to local people. Meteorologists say that temperatures will continue to rise until the end of the week.

4. Mexico
Tropical storm Barbara is forming rapidly off the coast and will move towards land. Winds of 68 miles per hour are expected, and they could reach the popular resort of Acapulco over the next few days. Hotels and houses may have to be evacuated. Meteorologists say that the winds might even reach hurricane status.

5. South Africa
For the first time in 25 years forecasters in Johannesburg are predicting snow. Up to 4 inches could fall during the night, and this is causing much excitement throughout the city. SABC News is reporting that some parents are going to take their children to the local parks after midnight to play in the snow. Tambo International Airport may be affected.

CD2 6
1. I think it'll be a cold night tonight. Wear warm clothes if you go out.
2. I think I'll get a new computer. I want a laptop this time.
3. I think I'll take a cooking class. I can't even boil an egg.
4. I think you'll like the movie. It's a great story and really well cast.
5. I think we'll get to the airport in time. But we'd better get moving.
6. I think you'll get the job. You have all the right qualifications.

CD2 7
1. I don't think it'll be a cold night tonight. You won't need to take a jacket.
2. I don't think I'll get a new computer. It may seem old-fashioned to you, but it's OK for me.
3. I don't think I'll take a cooking class. I'll get lessons from my mom.
4. I don't think you'll like the movie. It's not really your kind of thing.

5. I don't think we'll get to the airport in time. There's too much traffic.
6. I don't think you'll get the job. You're too young, and you have no experience.

CD2 8 **Rocket man**

I = Interviewer   S = Steve

I   Steve Bennett's ambition was to be a rocket scientist. A few years ago, he almost won a $16 million prize, the X prize. Now Steve's building a rocket that will take him and two passengers up into space. He believes that space tourism is not really that far away.

S   Space tourism is just about to happen. There are a lot of people around the world who are actually putting a lot of money into space tourism. It's simply a question of *when*, not *if*. You know, just as the Internet made billionaires, well, space tourism is going to make trillionaires. And all the big names are at it—you have Jeff Bezos, he did Amazon.com, he's building his own spaceship; you have Richard Branson, even he is commissioning someone to build a spaceship for him. So it really is going to happen.

I   And what are you intending to take people into space in? What is your rocket?

S   A rocket that can carry three people into space. We're not going into orbit. It's going straight up and straight down, but it will go into space. It'll give you about three or four minutes of weightlessness, you'll see the blackness of space, the curvature of the earth, and you really will become an astronaut just like the early American astronauts.

I   And you are going to be one of the people who goes up, so it's going to be you and two space tourists. Have you been up in this exact rocket before, Steve?

S   No, we're still working on this one. We've launched about 16 big rockets to date but this actual space rocket, called *Thunderstar*, we're still working on it, we're still building it. I was influenced as a small child watching too many episodes of "Thunderbirds," I think.

I   Were you very much struck by the first moon landings as well?

S   Yup. I was about five years old when they landed on the moon. Um, my parents wouldn't let me stay up to watch the actual landing, which was a shame.

I   How mean!

S   Yeah … yeah. Well, they just didn't get it. "Oh, it's marvelous, but they should spend the money on something better" kind of attitude.

I   Lots of young boys will have had exactly that kind of experience themselves, but very few of them will now have a business that's making rockets and thinking about taking people up into space. Did you always feel you eventually would get to do it professionally?

S   I kept it pretty quiet. Ten, fifteen years ago you start talking about space tourism and people, they think you're nuts, so you keep that kind of thing to yourself.

I   Why do we really need to do that, though? I mean, is there actually any necessity to have more humans in space?

S   Well, that's pretty much where the human race needs to be in terms of expansion. You know, there's enough resources in space to allow the human race to grow and expand for the next 10 thousand years.

I   What kind of training do you have to do in order to go up in the rocket?

S   Actually, one of the most important things we do is skydiving training. We feel that if you don't have what it takes to jump out of an airplane with a parachute, you really shouldn't be strapping yourself to the top of a 17-ton rocket.

I   These two other people who've already booked their place on your *Thunderstar*, do you know who they are?

S   Absolutely. I've taken their money.

I   Right.

S   Well, it's a couple. It's two people who want to fly in space. They came to me a few years ago and basically they said, "Steve, we want to fly in the rocket. Here's the money." They gave me half a million dollars for it.

I   And how often do you consider the possibility that something might go wrong?

S   I think about it every day, you know? I've built a lot of rockets, most of them have worked really well. Some haven't, and I think about that every day.

CD2 9 **Spoken English**

1. A   Did your team win?
   B   No, but they did pretty well.
2. A   You haven't lost your cell phone again!
   B   No, no. I'm pretty sure it's in my bag somewhere.
3. A   Do you enjoy skiing?
   B   I do, but I'm pretty hopeless at it.
4. A   What do you think of my English?
   B   I think it's pretty good.

CD2 10   **see page 103**

CD2 11

1. Carlos and Diana don't get along at all. They disagree about everything.
2. Money does not always lead to happiness.
3. My aunt says today's kids are all rude and impolite.
4. Thanks for your advice, it was really helpful. I really appreciate your kindness.
5. My dad is useless at fixing his computer. I always have to help him.
6. Please don't misunderstand me. I didn't mean to be unkind. I'm really sorry.
7. Timmy fell off his bike and hit his head. He was unconscious for a few hours.
8. What was your wife's reaction when she heard you'd won the lottery?

CD2 12   **see page 40**

CD2 13

1. A   The doctors are going to operate on my grandma's knee.
   B   Oh, no!
   A   Don't worry, it's not a serious operation.
2. A   Did you explain the homework to Maria?
   B   I did, but I don't think she understood my explanation.
3. A   I couldn't find the book I wanted in the library.
   B   Did you ask the librarian? She'll tell you if they have it.
4. A   Can I have a copy of that photograph?
   B   Yes, of course. I'm not a great photographer, but this one's OK, isn't it?
   A   It is. Usually I can't stand photos of me.

CD2 14   **Arranging to meet**

G = Gary   M = Mike

G   Mike, it's me, Gary.
M   Gary! Long time no see. How are you doing?
G   Good, thanks. Listen, I'm coming up next weekend, and I was wondering if we could meet.
M   I'd love to, but this weekend of all weekends, I am *so* busy.
G   Look, you must have some free time.
M   Yeah, I'll get my calendar. Hold on … OK … shoot!
G   Right. What are you doing Friday evening?

M   Friday evening? Um … that's my Spanish class. Our company's going to do a lot of work in Mexico, so we're all learning Spanish. But I finish work early on Friday. I could meet you in the afternoon.
G   No, I'm afraid that's no good. My train doesn't get in until 7 o'clock. Do you have any free time on Saturday?
M   Um … let me see. What about Saturday afternoon? I'm having my hair cut in the morning and then I'm meeting my sister for lunch, but I'm free in the afternoon.
G   Oh, no, sorry, Saturday afternoon, I can't. I have an appointment with a real estate agent. I'm going to look at one of those amazing new apartments by the river. Didn't I tell you? I'm changing jobs and moving back to the big city.
M   Hey, great news, Gary. I knew small town life wasn't your thing!
G   So, what about Saturday evening? Is Saturday evening any good?
M   Sorry, the evening's out for me. I'm going to the theater with friends. We've had it booked forever. But … hold on, what time are you leaving on Sunday?
G   Late morning. I'm taking the 11:55 train.
M   Hey, I have a good idea. Why don't we meet at the station?
G   Good idea, we could have coffee together.
M   I have an even better idea. They make great pancakes at the cafe. Let's meet there for breakfast. How about ten o'clock?
G   Sounds good to me. But can you make it 10:30? It *is* Sunday.
M   Fine. 10:30 it is. I'll see you then. Bye, Gary! Hope you like the apartment.
G   Fingers crossed. Bye, Mike. See you Sunday.

CD2 15

1. I was wondering if we could meet.
2. I could meet you in the afternoon.
3. What about Saturday afternoon?
4. Is Saturday evening any good?
5. Why don't we meet at the station?
6. Let's meet there for breakfast.
7. How about ten o'clock?
8. Can you make it 10:30?

UNIT 6

CD2 16   **see page 42**

CD2 17   **Describing places**

1. What's your apartment like?
   It's modern, but it's cozy.
2. How big is it?
   About 850 square feet.
3. How many rooms are there?
   There are three rooms.
4. What size is the kitchen?
   Nine feet by eight.
5. Which floor is it on?
   The fourth.
6. Which part of town is it in?
   It's south of the river.
7. How far is it to the stores?
   Just five minutes.

CD2 18   **Describing things**

1. What brand is it?
   Sony.
2. How much does it weigh?
   3 pounds.
3. What's it made of?
   Carbon and titanium.

4. What's this button for?
   It turns it on.
5. How big is the screen?
   13.2 inches.
6. How long is the battery life?
   Eight hours.
7. What size is the hard disk?
   80 gigabytes.

CD2 19

1. What kind of bread do you have?
2. What flavor ice cream would you like?
3. Which way do we go?
4. What brand is your camera?
5. What kind of food do you like?
6. Whose top are you wearing?
7. How long does it take to get to the airport?
8. How far is your house from the beach?
9. How often do you go to the movies?
10. How many of you want coffee?
11. What size shoes do you wear?

CD2 20

fresh fruit
latest fashions
pretty woman
clear sky
fast food
crowded restaurant
casual clothes
close friend
handsome man
straight hair
cozy room
challenging job

CD2 21

1. Peter and I lived together in college.
2. He's a good student. He tries hard.
3. A Where's the town hall?
   B Go straight ahead.
4. Say that again. I didn't hear you.
5. Don't talk so loud! Everyone can hear you.
6. Why do you drive so fast? Slow down!
7. His wife's name is Mariana, not Maria! Get it right.
8. The vacation was a disaster. Everything went wrong.
9. This room is cool, even in summer.
10. A Are you ready?
    B Almost. Give me another five minutes.

CD2 22   My most treasured possession

1. Amy
I would have to save my photo albums. They have all the photos of my kids, when they were babies, their first steps, you know, when they walked for the first time, their birthday parties, their first day at school. And all the holidays we spent together. All those memories are irreplaceable.

2. Jack
I know it sounds a little sad, but I would have to save my computer. Not very sentimental, but very practical. It has all my work, all my e-mail contacts, several thousand photos, address books, work calendar for the next year. I just couldn't live without it.

3. Lucy
I have a matching hairbrush and hand mirror that belonged to my grandmother. She was given them as a wedding present, and she gave them to me before she died. I don't use them, but they're always on the shelf in my bedroom, and every time I see them I think of her. They're solid silver, and they're pretty heavy. They're not especially nice, but they have immense sentimental value.

CD2 23

Jen
The person that I'm closest to in my family is probably my mother. She's the kind of person you can talk to about anything. She's very open, my mother, and I can talk to her about boyfriends, stuff that's bothering me at work, friendships, anything. We have our ups and downs, of course, but basically we have an easy relationship. We go shopping together. What I like about her is her attitude. She's young at heart, like me, not old-fashioned or anything like that.

Brett
I'm closest to my grandmother. Um, my father I don't really get along with. We don't really see eye to eye on anything. My mother I hardly ever see. She's too busy. My grandmother and I like doing the same things. Um … we like watching TV and having lunch together. We love playing cards. And I think emotionally I'm closer to her than I am to my parents … because she and I have a similar attitude to life. I think we both like people. We're very outgoing, sociable, and open.

Julia
The person I'm closest to in my family, I think, would be my father. We stay up late listening to music and talking a lot. What I like about him is that he's interesting and interested. He has a curiosity about life. We can talk about anything and everything. We have the same sense of humor, the same love of life. My friends all love him because he's so funny. He doesn't care what people think of him, and I guess that's great. He's pretty cool, my dad.

Susan
I think the person that I'm probably closest to is my sister. The thing I love about her is the way everyone knows her. It doesn't matter where we go, everyone says, "Hi, Sarah! How you doin'?" I'm just her little sister. People call me "Baby Sarah," but that's fine. We're so different. We have big fights. She's so hyperactive and loud, she can't sit still, she has to have people around her, and everyone loves her. In many ways she drives me crazy. She just can't think straight. Me, I'm a lot quieter. I'm happy on my own. But we're so proud of each other.

Chris
I'm closest to my twin, Nick. Obviously, we have so much in common. The same friends. The same soccer team. The same music. We go everywhere together. But we have crazy arguments about everything. We're like oil and water. I'm like my Mom—calm and easygoing. Nick's like my Dad—very bad-tempered. They fight like cats and dogs. But things have changed now that we're older. We appreciate each other more. The biggest difference is probably interests. I'm into all things history and politics, and Nick's interested in science and nature. But of course we're a lot closer than just brothers and sisters. In a way we're like one. I would trust him like I would trust no one else.

CD2 24   In a department store

1. A Morning!
   B Hello. I'd like to try on these shoes, please.
   A Certainly, sir. What size do you wear?
   B Nine. That's 41, isn't it?
   A Uh, no, I think you'll find 43 would be more comfortable, sir.
2. A Do you have these soccer shorts for age 10-11?
   B I'm afraid that's all we have. We're sold out of that size.
   A Will you be getting any more in?
   B We should be getting a delivery by the end of the week.
3. A Do you have any sofas like this in stock?
   B No, we don't. They all have to be ordered.

A How long does delivery take?
B It all depends, but on average about eight weeks.
4. A Yes?
   B I'd like this fruit bowl, please.
   A Certainly. Is it a present?
   B Yes, it is.
   A Would you like me to gift wrap it?
   B Ooh, that would be great! Thank you so much!
5. A I like this.
   B How does it feel?
   A I love the color, but the size is wrong. It doesn't fit me. It's too tight.
   B Too bad. It really suits you. What's it made of?
   B Cashmere. It's so soft.
6. A Yes, sir?
   B I'll have this coffee maker, please.
   A Certainly. Do you have a store card?
   B No, just a debit card.
   A That's fine. Pin number, please. Keep your receipt. That's your warranty.
   B How long is the warranty for?
   A For a year.

UNIT 7

CD2 25   see page 51

CD2 26

1. Where and when was she born?
   She was born near Bristol, in England, in 1965.
2. When did she write her first story? What was it about?
   She wrote her first story when she was six. It was about a rabbit with measles.
3. What was she doing when she had the idea for Harry Potter?
   She was traveling by train between Manchester and London.
4. Where did she teach English?
   In Portugal.
5. When was the first Harry Potter book published?
   In 1997.
6. How long has she been writing the books?
   For nearly 20 years.
7. How many has she written?
   Seven.
8. How many children has she had?
   Three.
9. How many books have been sold?
   Over 300 million copies.
10. Which books have been made into movies?
    The first six.
11. How much money has she made?
    She's made over £600 million.
12. How many authors have become billionaires?
    Only one—her.

CD2 27

I = Interviewer   J = Jack

I So, Jack, I know you love Harry Potter. How long have you been a fan of the books?
J I think since I was about five, but I was so small I couldn't read yet and my mom read them to me.
I How many of the books have you read?
J I've read them all—well, not all, exactly.
I What do you mean?
J Well, I didn't like *Harry Potter and the Half-blood Prince*, so I didn't finish it.
I Which did you like best?
J I liked all the others but not that one. It was boring because it was just like the one before.
I Have you seen any of the Harry Potter movies?
J Yes, I have.

I Which have you seen?
J I've seen them all, every one.
I And did you like them all?
J Yes, I did. I thought they were fantastic, but my brother didn't, he got scared. He didn't like the Chamber of Secrets, the part where the Basilisk …
I The what?
J The Basilisk. It's kind of a huge snake, and it attacked Harry Potter.
I Oh, I bet a lot of children were frightened by it.
J I wasn't.
I Jack, do you have any idea how many Harry Potter books have been sold in the world?
J Um—I dunno. Um—millions, maybe 20 million.
I Um—not really. It's 300 million.
J 300 million. Wow! That's a lot of books.
I And what do you know about the author?
J I know it's J.K. Rowling, and she has two children. I wonder if they've read their mom's books.
I She has three children, actually. Have a lot of your friends read the books?
J Yes, every single one.
I What *all* your friends?
J Yeah, definitely—all of them.
I That's amazing. Now, I know that in addition to Harry Potter, you have another passion.
J Yeah, soccer.
I And how long have you been playing soccer?
J Since I could walk. I'd rather play soccer than do anything else in the world.
I So, if I asked you—what would you rather do this afternoon? Read Harry Potter or play soccer?
J You know the answer.

CD2 28 Discussing grammar

1. His plane took off a few minutes ago.
2. The president has resigned, and a new president has been elected.
3. I've been working in Dubai since last March. When did you arrive?
4. How many e-mails have you sent?
5. What have you been doing in the bathroom? You've been in there for ages.
6. A huge snowstorm has hit New York.

CD2 29

Calvin Klein – a passion for fashion
1. **A** How long has Calvin Klein been interested in fashion?
   B Since he was about 14. When he was a teenager he spent hours sketching women's suits and dresses.
2. **A** What different kinds of clothes has he designed in his career?
   B He's designed sportswear and underwear, but he is possibly most famous for his jeans, which always have his name on the back pocket.
3. **A** How many times has he been married and divorced?
   B He's been married twice and divorced twice. His first wife was Jayne Centre. He met her when they were both fashion students. His second wife was Kelly Rector—she was a rich New York socialite and photographer.
4. **A** How many children does he have?
   B Just one. A daughter, Marci, who is now a successful television producer.
5. **A** How many awards has he won?
   B He's won seven fashion awards altogether. He made history because he won awards for both men and women's fashions in the same year.
6. **A** How long has he been making his own perfumes?
   B He's been making Calvin Klein perfumes since the late 80s.
7. **A** What are they called?

B His first were called *Obsession* and *Eternity*; his most recent is called *Euphoria*. His others include *Truth* and *Crave*, which was designed for men.
8. **A** Which famous people has he worked with and designed for?
   B He's worked with the model Kate Moss and designed clothes for many stars, including Julia Roberts, Gwyneth Paltrow, and Helen Hunt. He's also worked with Brooke Shields, who, at the age of 15, modeled his jeans with the famous line "nothing comes between me and my Calvins."
9. **A** How long has he been selling cosmetics?
   B Since the 1990s. These are only sold in the best department stores such as Harrods in London, and Bloomingdale's in New York.

CD2 30

1. **A** How long are you here for?
   B Four more days. We came two days ago.
2. **A** How long have you been here?
   B Since Monday.
3. **A** How long are you here for?
   B Until Friday. We're leaving Friday morning.
4. **A** How long have you been here?
   B Over half an hour! Where have you been?
5. **A** How long are you here for?
   B We're staying a month altogether.

CD2 31

Things I am passionate about
Julia
I'm really passionate about playing tennis. I've been playing nearly 20 years. I was about 7 or 8 when I started taking lessons, and I had a fantastic teacher. I think that's why I still love it—she was passionate about the sport and that influenced me. I have played in competitions, mainly when I was at school. I still do sometimes. I enjoy it, I think, because it's a very psychological game. I mean, if you're playing badly, you have to push yourself to continue; it's a challenge not to give up. It's also a very sociable sport—I've made lots of friends playing doubles, and, it's a game that doesn't have to be expensive—anyone can play—all you need is a tennis racket. You don't need expensive clothing or equipment like you do for skiing, and it's a fantastic way to keep fit all year round—there's only about three months that you can't play. When I lived in Australia, I played every week of the year. I adored that, it was great.

Paul
My passion at the moment is horseback riding—it's strange to hear myself say that because I've only been doing it about a year and I never imagined I'd be so into it. It all happened because I was talking to someone who rode horses and I said that stupid thing people often say, "Oh, I've always wanted to do that," and she said, "Why don't you then?" And I thought, "Why not?" I've always liked horses, they're so big and powerful, but so beautiful when you see them racing around a field or on a track. It amazes me that they let people ride on their backs. Riding is very physically demanding because your body has to be in harmony … um, it has to move with the horse, but it keeps you fit. Of course, I have fallen off a few times, but it seems that the more you fall, the less it hurts. Also, you try and understand your horse. They have moods. You never quite know what a ride is going to be like—a horse you had a great ride on one week can be slow and miserable the next week. I really like that about horses—they have personalities.

Andrew
I'm passionate about poetry—I studied English Literature in college, but it wasn't until after I graduated that I really got into poetry and I started writing some myself. And I met some other people

who wrote poetry and I heard them read it aloud and that was amazing. I felt the power of the words—the thing I like so much about it is that you can say so much with just a few words. So little means a lot. Each word, each noun, adjective, preposition has to work hard. There's a poem by Simon Armitage called "To His Lost Lover"—it's a poem of regret, about not saying the things you should have said in a relationship. It has it all for me—poetry's all about saying what often goes unsaid, and with passion. It can be such a help in your life—if you feel tired or depressed, you can always find a poem that will help—it can be short or long, it doesn't matter.

James
The thing I'm passionate about, and this may surprise many people, is—um, Seattle weather. I know lots of people can't stand our weather—um, they complain about it all the time, but I love it. You see, when I was a child my family lived in California for five years and we had about 365 days of sunshine every year. It was so boring. I was ten when we came back to Seattle and I just loved all the changes in the weather. Here, you really appreciate the sunshine, and you notice the seasons. For me, one of nature's miracles is after a long hot, sunny day there's a thunderstorm or a downpour of rain and you go outside and you can smell the freshness in the air. The world has been washed clean and bright. It's magic. And you know it's a myth that it rains all the time; it doesn't. It rains less here than in New York or Atlanta!

Kim
Something I feel really passionately about is fishing. My father and uncles have always been into this sport and I started when I was about 6. We usually go fishing in Cape Cod, Massachusetts. We go out from about 5:30 in the morning, and we don't get back until late in the day. And the thing I love best about it is that you're away from everything and everyone, out in the water, just waiting, with nothing around you. In fishing, patience is the key to success. You have to keep quiet and still for hours on end until the fish bites the hook. But in my family we only catch, never kill the fish. Once we capture it, we carefully release it, and it's not harmed.

CD2 32 see page 57

CD2 33

Pleasure
That's great!
Wonderful!
Agreement
Definitely.
Fair enough.
Fine.
Surprise
You didn't!
You did what?
Sympathy
That's a shame.
That's too bad.
Bad luck.

CD2 34

A My grandfather hasn't been too well lately.
B Oh, no!
A He's 79. Don't you think at his age he should slow down a little?
B Absolutely.
A But he won't listen to me. He says he wants to enjoy his life to the fullest.
B Fair enough.
A Last summer he went on a two-week cycling trip in South America.
B You're kidding!

A We're going to give him a big party for his 80th birthday.
B That's great.
A But before that I'm going to have a word with him and tell him to take things easier.
B Good for you.

CD2 35

1. **A** My boyfriend just asked me to marry him.
   B Did he? Good for you! Did you say yes?
2. **A** Will spaghetti Bolognese be OK for dinner?
   B Of course. That's great. It's one of my favorites.
3. **A** There's a strike at the airport so my trip's been cancelled.
   B Oh, no! That's a shame. Will you get your money back?
4. **A** I failed my driving test again.
   B You didn't! That's too bad. Better luck next time.
5. **A** We're expecting a baby.
   B Are you? Congratulations! When is it due?
6. **A** So you think I should save to buy a car, not borrow the money?
   B Definitely. You already have too many debts.
7. **A** I told him I never wanted to see him again.
   B You're kidding! What a pity. I always thought the two of you were so good together.

UNIT 8

CD2 36 see pages 58-59

CD2 37

1. When we saw the photos we couldn't help feeling worried.
2. The photos made it look worse than it really was.
3. Your friends must promise to keep their room clean.
4. It's really kind of you to let them stay.
5. Did Victor help you escape from the crocodiles?
6. He warned us not to go swimming.
7. We couldn't help feeling a little scared.
8. Have you decided to come home yet?

CD2 38

M = Mom K = Kate

M Kate! It's so good to hear from you. Are you OK?
K Oh, Mom, I'm really sorry for worrying you so much. I really didn't mean to.
M We opened our e-mails, and we were so delighted to see all your photos, and then we saw that one.
K I didn't want my friends to post it on *Facebook*. I asked them not to.
M But, Kate, all those stitches, and you went to the hospital. We couldn't help feeling worried.
K I know, but honestly, Mom, my friends made me go to the hospital. I really didn't need to.
M How is your head now?
K Absolutely fine. Honestly. I'll e-mail you some more photos, and you can see for yourself.
M OK. Don't forget to.
K I'll call again soon, and I promise to text regularly. Bye.
M Bye. Take care!

CD2 39 Spoken English

1. **A** Did you mail my letter?
   B Oh, sorry, I forgot to.
2. **A** I can't go out with you this evening. Sorry.
   B Oh, but you promised to.
3. **A** Why did you e-mail your mother again?
   B Because she asked me to.

4. **A** Do you think you'll apply for that job?
   B Yes, I've definitely decided to.
5. **A** Are you taking your brother to the airport?
   B Well, I offered to, but he said he didn't want me to.

CD2 40 Fears and phobias

1. Jodie
I have a really unusual phobia. It began when I was a little girl. I was staying with my grandmother and she asked me to go upstairs and get her cardigan. I opened the cabinet and saw this big, dark green cardigan with huge, black buttons hanging there—I was terrified. I started screaming. My grandmother rushed upstairs and finally managed to calm me down, but from then on it was a problem. It was the buttons—all buttons made me feel uncomfortable. It's difficult for me to buy clothes—I try to find skirts and trousers with just belts and zippers, but it's not easy. About a year ago a button came off a colleague's jacket at work, and I had a panic attack. I've decided to see a therapist, but I'm embarrassed to say, "I'm scared of buttons." It sounds silly.

2. Dave
I'm not sure what first started my phobia, but my dad used to go fishing and afterwards I didn't like watching him cleaning the fish in the kitchen sink. Then, when I was about seven, I started feeling afraid when I saw him coming home with the fish. He had to stop catching it. As I grew up the problem got worse and worse. I couldn't go into supermarkets—the sight of fish made me feel sick. When I started going out with my wife, I had to ask her never to eat fish. I wouldn't go to restaurants because once I saw someone eating an oyster, and I had a panic attack. I can only eat in hamburger restaurants now. It makes life very difficult for my whole family. I've started to see a psychologist, but I haven't succeeded in conquering my phobia yet.

3. Melissa
I'm 13 years old and I've been terrified of balloons since I was five. I was trying to blow one up and it popped in my face. I can remember feeling the rubber on my skin—ugh, it was awful. My friends don't understand. They enjoy chasing me around with blown up balloons because they think it's fun to see me cry. Last time, we were in the school playground, and I had a panic attack. At first they refused to believe me and they didn't get the teacher, but then they saw how bad it was—I was having difficulty breathing and they got frightened. The worst thing is that I can't go to parties; if I do, I have to ask them not to have balloons. I can't imagine ever blowing one up. I can't even look at them on TV. I start to shake. I want to see somebody about it. My teacher says I have to.

CD2 41 The psychologist's view
Human beings are programed to be afraid of things that can hurt them. Show a baby a picture of a snake or a big, poisonous spider and the baby will show fear. It's in our DNA. We are all afraid of some things and that's good. But a phobia causes absolute terror, with physical symptoms such as a racing heart, sickness, and panic attacks. Phobias are usually the result of a bad experience, for example, a car crash can cause a fear of driving, but it's often just of ordinary things like balloons or a particular food. Some people are more likely to get phobias than others. It's in their genes. My job is to train people to conquer their phobia. First, we just talk about it, and help the patient relax. Then, we might show just a picture or cartoon of their phobia. After that, we sometimes show a movie, and finally, we ask them to touch the object. In this way, phobias can normally be treated in just three or four sessions.

CD2 42

1. The cat got up the tree easily enough, but I had to climb a ladder to get her down.
2. Daniel, stop staring out of the window, and get on with your work!
3. Since you whistled that tune I can't get it out of my head.
4. I hate it when my Aunt Mary hugs me close. She wears this disgusting perfume, and I smell like it afterwards.
5. Bob's hopeless at all sports. He can't even kick a soccer ball.
6. You better lick your ice cream—it's melting.
7. When I saw the penny on the floor, I kneeled down to pick it up. It's good luck!
8. I keep trying to stop biting my nails but I can't. It's a terrible habit.
9. I'm terrified of blowing up balloons in case they go "pop."
10. Don't scratch that insect bite. You'll get an infection.
11. By the end of the concert we were all clapping our hands in time with the music.
12. The tour guide pointed at a place on the map.
13. My dad's useless at doing things around the house. He can't even hit a nail with a hammer.
14. My two-year-old nephew is so cute. He loves marching up and down like a soldier.

CD2 43 see page 65

CD2 44 see page 65

CD2 45 A = Airline ticket agent
B = Passenger

A Good morning. Where are you flying to?
B Dubai.
A And how many bags do you want to check in?
B Just this one.
A Fine. Put it on the scales, please ... Oh, no.
B What's the matter?
A I'm afraid it's overweight. It's nearly 60 pounds, and you're only allowed 50.
B What can I do?
A Well, you can pay for excess baggage. The rate is $10 per pound.
B So, that's um …
A That's $100.
B Goodness. That's a fortune, but I'll just have to pay it.
A OK. And just the one piece of hand luggage?
B Yes, just this bag.
A That's fine. Here's your boarding pass. You're boarding from Gate 6 at 9:20. The gate will open 45 minutes before the flight. Have a good trip.
B Thank you.

CD2 46 A = Amtrak employee
B = Passenger

A Good morning. Amtrak. Can I help you?
B Oh, yes, I was trying to book train tickets online and it didn't work.
A That's OK. Where and when do you want to travel?
B I want to go from New York, Penn Station to Boston on the 13th of March.
A March 30th?
B No, no, March 13th. I want to go on the 13th and return on the 30th.
A OK, the 13th to the 30th—so you want a roundtrip ticket. And do you want to travel in the morning or the afternoon?
B Well, I want to travel up mid-morning if possible, but I'd like to come back on an evening train.
A Right. There's a train at 10:30 A.M., it arrives in Boston at 2:45 P.M.

B Sounds good. And returning?
A For the return there's one at 8:00 P.M., arrives back in New York just after midnight.
B Mmm … is there an earlier one?
A There's the 6:30. It arrives back in New York at 10:28.
B That sounds perfect. I'll take it. How much is that?
A It's $135. Is that OK?
B Fine.
A Can you give me your credit card details?
B Yes, it's a Visa card. The name on the card is K. Farnham. The number is 0494 7865 4562 1320.
A The expiration date?
B 05/12.
A And your address?
B 15 Wilson Road.
A Did you say 50 …?
B No, 15, one, five Wilson Road.

UNIT 9

CD3 2 Billy's story

1. I'd organize a school day which tried to educate everyone about bullying, and I'd invite social workers, police, and psychologists.
2. I'd get my dad to speak to them … if I was older, I'd speak to them myself!
3. I'd ask Billy to try to understand the bullies. I'd get all the parents to meet together.
4. I'd move so we could change his school and start again somewhere new.
5. I'd get really angry and yell at them.
6. I'd run away.

CD3 3 see page 67

CD3 4

1. If they'd understood, he wouldn't have run away.
2. If he'd gone to Kidcare, he could have talked about his problems.
3. If he hadn't left, Billy might have felt more secure.
4. If they hadn't threatened him, he wouldn't have run away.

CD3 5 You're an idiot!

1. "I went walking in the mountains for three days with no food or equipment."
   "You're an idiot! You could have died! You could have starved to death or died in the cold!"
2. "I didn't feel like going to work, so I called in sick. I went shopping instead."
   "You're such an idiot! Your boss might have seen you. You could have gotten fired."
3. "I had a temperature of 102, but I went out dancing all night."
   "That's so stupid! You could have been really sick. You should have gone to bed."
4. "I told Sandra I couldn't see her, then went out with Danielle."
   "That was a really dumb thing to do! Sandra might have seen you out with Danielle."
5. "I used to be really good at tennis—I was an under-14 champion—but then I gave it all up."
   "That's such a shame! You might have been a champion! You might even have won the U.S. Open."

CD3 6 A social conscience

1. I was in the bank the other day, and waiting in line. I'd just reached the front of the line when this guy jumped in front of me and said, "I just need to ask a quick question." I wasn't very happy and I hate making a scene, so I let him. But then it started taking forever. He looked back at me

and grinned. He was so pleased with himself, and I was just furious! What could I do? I said nothing.

2. I was in the park, right, and there was this woman with three kids. She'd obviously had a bad day, yeah, she'd just been shouting at the kids for messing around. One of the kids, the eldest boy, about eight, bumped into his little sister and knocked her over. The mother turned on this kid, the boy, and she hit him really hard. I went over to her and told her to stop. She told me to mind my own business, and said some very rude words and stormed off, screaming at this poor boy. He was just a kid!

3. My neighbor always lets his dog do his … you know … business in front of my front door, and I always clean it up, day after day, because it just stinks! So the other day I asked him if he could get his dog to do its business somewhere else, or could he pick it up because I didn't like it in front of my front door. He was absolutely awful and said he didn't care! So I suppose I'll just carry on picking it up. What else can I do?

4. I was on the bus the other day. There was just me and a couple of kids. These two kids had their feet on the seat in front of them, so I asked them to put their feet down. These kids, they must have been about sixteen or seventeen, came over to me, pushed me onto the floor, and started kicking me. I have bruises everywhere!

5. I was walking down the street coming home from work about ten at night, it was dark, and this guy jumped out of nowhere and said, "Gimme your wallet and phone!" He was a big guy and he had a knife. I didn't say anything. I was just terrified! I thought he was going to kill me. I just handed over both and he ran away. I was trembling for ten minutes. I couldn't move. I have never been so frightened in all my life.

CD3 7

1. Miwako isn't here. She just left.
2. I'm sorry I'm in a bad mood. I'm just tired, that's all.
3. I just love your new coat!
4. I just finished the most wonderful book! You have to read it!
5. I don't want any coffee. Just a glass of water, please.
6. John's so generous. I think he's just amazing!
7. "Who's coming tonight?" "Just me."
8. Hold on a minute. I'm just going to the restroom.

CD3 8 Dealing with money

1. **A** Here's your check.
   B Thank you. Is the tip included?
   A No, it isn't. I hope you enjoyed your meal.
2. **A** How much is a standard room?
   B $120 per night.
   A Does that include everything?
3. **A** I'll pay for the tickets with my MasterCard.
   B Can you give me your number?
4. **A** Could you give me the balance on my account?
   B Sure. Tell me your account number.
5. **A** Can I have a cappuccino and two bottles of water, please?
   B Sure. That's $14.50.
   A Thank you.
   B And here's your change. 50 cents.

CD3 9 Dealing with money

1. **A** Here's your check.
   B Thank you. Is the tip included?
   A No, it isn't. I hope you enjoyed your meal.
   B It was very nice, thank you.
   A Can you sign here? And here's your card and your receipt.

B Thanks. That's for you.
A That's very kind of you. I hope to see you again soon.
B Bye!

2. **A** How much is a standard room?
   B $120 per night.
   A Does that include everything?
   B That includes the room for two people, but it doesn't include breakfast.
   A Is that extra?
   B Yes, I'm afraid it is. But the $120 does include tax.

3. **A** I'll pay for the tickets with my MasterCard.
   B Can you give me your number?
   A 5484 6922 3171 2435.
   B What's the expiration date?
   A 09/12.
   B And the three-digit security number on the back?
   A 721.

4. **A** Could you give me the balance on my account?
   B Sure. Tell me your account number.
   A 4033 2614 7900.
   B Bear with me one moment. The current cleared balance on that account is $542.53 in credit.

5. **A** Can I have a cappuccino and two bottles of water, please?
   B Sure. That's $14.50.
   A Thank you.
   B And here's your change. 50 cents.
   A Thanks. Um … How much did I give you? I think you've made a mistake!
   B Sorry?
   A I think you must have made a mistake. I gave you $20, but you've given me change for $15.
   B No, I don't think so.
   A Well, I'm pretty sure I gave you a twenty dollar bill.
   B Oh, did you? Um … sorry about that. Here you are.
   A Thanks.

UNIT 10

CD3 10 The first computer

Charles Babbage (1791–1871) was a scientist and an engineer. He had the idea for the first programmable computer. He wanted to build a machine that could do calculations without making the mistakes that human "computers" made. He designed a machine called the Difference Engine, and the British government provided funds. The machine was never completed because Babbage ran out of money. In 1991, a team of engineers from the Science Museum in London built one of Babbage's machines using his original designs, and it worked perfectly.

CD3 11

1. Where did you have lunch today?
2. Where's your mother this morning?
3. Do you prefer tea or coffee?
4. What's the name of the river in Washington, D.C.?
5. Do you have a pet? What's its name?
6. What's your father's job?
7. How do you get to school?
8. What's the name of the book?
9. Who's sitting next to the window? Next to the teacher?
10. Where are you going after the class?

1. Living in New York has its disadvantages.
2. To start with, there's a lot of traffic.
3. New Yorkers like their parks and open spaces.
4. For them it's important to escape from busy city life.
5. New York's full of young people, and they're always on the move.
6. The elderly have their parts of town, and young people have theirs.

CD3 | 13

1. Tom
I go onto websites about sports. I'm into skateboarding, so I go onto skateboarding websites. I watch a lot of skateboarding videos on YouTube. I go on things like MySpace, where I can talk to friends from school.

Um … if I'm doing school work, I use Google and Wikipedia, which can be really useful.

I do a lot of shopping—clothes, shoes and stuff. I go to Amazon for DVDs, games, CDs. And eBay for all sorts of things. I'm trying to buy some tickets for a concerts on eBay. I'm also selling some of my old stuff on it.

2. Monica
I use the Internet mainly for Facebook. You post a photo and a profile of yourself. You can say what you want—biography, hobbies, interests, music, movies. You control who can see your profile. Other people search for friends, people who share common interests. When you identify someone on the site you'd like to meet, you can ask to become a friend.

I also use the Internet to look for jobs and apartments, and to see what's going on during the weekend.

3. Pedro
I use Internet banking. It's good because I can get my balance any time of the day or night. I can transfer money instantly. So I like paying bills online. I just log onto my bank and click on "Pay Now", and the bill is paid immediately. Easy!

I'm into baseball, so I watch live baseball games. And … what else? I book restaurants, movie tickets, vacations. I get traffic reports. Oh, yes! I do nearly all my shopping online. I do my weekly grocery shopping, and it's all delivered. Clothes, birthday presents, books, music—everything!

4. Daisy
I don't like reading onscreen, and I don't like watching DVDs, either, but I do use the Internet for three things. I e-mail a lot with Hotmail. I get the news every day on the CNN website. And I also check the weather every day. I get up in the morning, and get a weather forecast for my town for early morning, mid-morning, early afternoon, and evening. Then, and only then, I get dressed!

5. David
I went onto a website called Friends Reunited, and I met up with people from my school days. And I researched my family history, and traced my ancestors back over two hundred years. I'm retired, so I have time to do these things.

I like to keep up my languages, so I watch the news in Spanish and in French, too. And I download music onto my MP3 player. And I update my GPS system as well.

CD3 | 14   21st century city

a. It only rains for five days a year.
b. Shopaholics come to spend all their money in the forty-odd malls and souks.
c. The Dubai World Cup horserace has a $6 million prize.
d. Arabic nations have been traders for over five thousand years.

e. The country has invested more than $100 billion in new projects.
f. Companies are encouraged to locate in Dubai with the promise of zero percent taxes.
g. Dubai's 10 million tourists a year come for the beaches, but especially for the shops.
h. Temperatures outside can soar above 104°F.
i. Dubai has nearly 20% of the world's construction cranes.
j. The Burj Dubai tower has more than 200 floors.

CD3 | 15   see page 80

CD3 | 16   "I need one of those things …"

1. I need one of those things you use when you want to open a bottle. You know, you pull and it goes "pop."
2. I'm looking for some of that stuff you use when you want to clean between your teeth … It's like string. It's white.
3. They're long and thin, and the Chinese use them to pick up food.
4. It's made of plastic, and it's used for killing flies. SHPLAT! SHPLOUFF!
5. They're things you use when you're cooking and you want to pick up something that's hot.

CD3 | 17   see page 81

CD3 | 18

1. It's one of those things you use in the kitchen. You use it to do the dishes.
2. It's long and thin and sharp at one end. Usually you have two, one in each hand. You can make things out of wool with them.
3. It looks like a cell phone; it has buttons you push, but you use it to change channels on the TV.
4. It's the stuff you wash clothes with. You put it in the washing machine. It's a powder. It smells … aaaah!
5. It's used for sticking things on the wall, like pictures or posters. It's soft and sticky.
6. They're made of metal. You can also use them to stick things on the wall, but they're sharp. It makes a hole. You use them on a notice board.
7. It's a kind of ruler. You use it to measure things that are very long, like a room. It's made of metal, usually.
8. It's something you use when you're traveling. You put it on your suitcase so no one can get into it. You have a key to open it, to take it off.
9. You know! It has a round, metal part at one end, and the other end is made of glass. You put it in a lamp to make light.

CD3 | 19

1. It's one of those things you use in the kitchen.
2. It's long and thin and sharp at one end.
3. It looks like a cell phone.
4. It's the stuff you wash clothes with.
5. It's used for sticking things on the wall.
6. They're made of metal.
7. It's a kind of ruler.
8. It's something you use when you're traveling.
9. You know! It has a round, metal part at one end.

CD3 | 20

Conversation 1
A Yes. How can I help you?
B I'm looking for a thing you use in the house …
A Yes, now, what do you do with it exactly?
B Well, it's not one thing. It's two things. And they're usually made of plastic.
A Uh-huh.
B You know if you make a mess, like you drop bread or break a glass, and there are pieces all over the floor …?

A And you need to pick them up?
B Yes! You go like this … SHUP! SHUP!
A What you're talking about is …

Conversation 2
A Can I help you?
B Yes. I don't know how you say this in English. I'm looking for a thing you use in the kitchen …
A OK.
B It's like a thing with, you know, holes …
A Uh-huh. What's it for?
B Well, it's for cheese or vegetables like carrots.
A And what do you do with it?
B If you don't want a big piece of cheese, or a whole carrot, but you want little pieces, you can push … you can move … I don't know how you say it. Like this!
A Ah! OK! What you mean is …

UNIT 11

CD3 | 21   Optical illusions

A How many colors can you see?
B Um, three, if you don't include white—um green, pink, and red.
A No, look again. There's only two, pink and green. When the pink's next to the green it looks red.
B Really? I don't think so. They can't be the same color. Well—um, maybe. What about this one, the girl? That must be a candlestick in front of her face.
A Yes, you can see one girl behind a candlestick or two girls looking at each other.
B Oh, yes, amazing, three girls then! And that one, it looks like a man playing the saxophone.
A Or … another girl. Look, in the shadows.
B Yes, I can see her now—she's wearing a hat and lipstick.
A Do think so? Can you see any more people?
B Yes, that looks like someone wearing glasses and that one is an old lady, and, I'm not sure, but I think she might be wearing a feather in her hat.
A I can also see a young lady with a feather and a fur coat. And I can see the word "liar."
B Really? I can't see either of those.
A OK. Try this. Count the legs on that elephant.
B One, two, three—um, it can't have five legs. That's a clever drawing. So is that one, it could be a duck or a rabbit. It depends how you look at it.
A The square looks strange, don't you think?
B Yeah, it looks wobbly, like jelly.
A Hmmm, but the lines are all straight and parallel.
B No, they can't be.
A Well, they are. If you look line by line, you'll see.
B I suppose. The dots must be creating the illusion.
A And the last one. Which line's longer?
B Well, the one on the left must be longer.
A Get your ruler and measure.
B Um—They're the same size—of course. I should have known!
A Interesting, isn't it, the tricks your eyes can play?

CD3 | 22   Fact or fiction?

1. **Lightning never strikes in the same place twice.** This is completely untrue. Lightning often strikes in the same place over and over again—high trees, tall buildings, mountaintops. In fact the purpose of lightning conductors is to be struck time and time again.
2. **Hurricanes always have female names.** This used to be true. From 1953 to 1979 only female names were used, but now both men's and women's names are used. One name for each letter of the alphabet. The same lists are reused every six years. These are the first six names

for 2012: Alberto, Beryl, Chris, Debby, Ernesto, Florence.

3. **Women have a higher pain threshold than men.**
   Some research suggests the opposite, but most people still believe this to be true because women have to give birth. We will never know how men would cope with this experience.

4. **The sea is blue because it reflects the sky.**
   This is true in a way. The white light from the sun is a mixture of all the colors of the rainbow, but the air reflects blue light more than other colors so we see a blue sky. Then when the sky is brilliant blue, the sea is also, because the water reflects the blue of the sky.

5. **A penny dropped from a skyscraper can kill a person.**
   Not true. It might give you a cut or a bruise but it is not likely to kill you.

6. **Hair and nails continue to grow after death.**
   Not true. This is an optical illusion. After death the body quickly dehydrates and the skin shrinks, which gives the illusion that both nails and hair are still growing.

7. **Birds are bird-brained and stupid.**
   Not true. Some birds are the cleverest animals known to science. For example, crows are smarter than chimpanzees, and some parrots don't just mimic but understand human speech.

8. **No two snowflakes are the same.**
   This could be true. No one has yet found two identical snowflakes, but out of all the zillions that fall, it is likely that two may be the same.

9. **Bats are blind.**
   Not true. Bats have excellent eyesight. People think they must be blind because they have a sound radar, which means they can hunt insects at night. But it doesn't mean that they can't see.

CD3 23

1. A I think I lost my passport.
   B You must be very worried.
2. A Your phone's ringing!
   B It might be Jane.
3. A Paul's taking his umbrella.
   B It must be raining.
4. A Marcelo and Valeria never go on vacation.
   B They can't have much money.
5. A Hannah's not in class.
   B She could be in the coffee shop.
6. A Look! Three fire engines!
   B There must be a fire somewhere.
7. A Tom hasn't seen Zoe in a long time.
   B They can't be going out together anymore.
8. A Whose jacket is this?
   B It might be John's.
9. A You got the highest score in the class!
   B You must be joking!

CD3 24   **What are they talking about?**

1. A A cup of coffee and glass of water, please.
   B Tap or bottled?
   A Bottled, please.
   B Did you want ice and lemon with that?
   A Just ice, thanks. How much is that?
2. A I can't believe it. My screen's frozen again.
   B Unplug it and take the battery out. Then start it up again. That sometimes works for me.
   A OK. Here we go.
3. A So how did it go?
   B Not too bad, thanks.
   A Were you very nervous?
   B Yeah, but I tried not to show it.
   A When will you hear?
   B In a couple of days. They said they'd call me at the end of the week and let me know if I'd gotten it.

4. A Do you have any idea what to get them?
   B Not really, but it should be something special.
   A Yeah, 25 years is a long time.
   B It would be nice to get something silver.
   A Yeah. Why don't we get something from both of us, then we can afford something really nice.
   B Good idea. Mom and Dad would love that.
5. A Do you come here a lot?
   B What?
   A I said DO YOU COME HERE OFTEN?
   B Yeah, me and my friends come every Saturday night. This your first time?
   A Yeah, here. We usually go clubbing at the Zanzibah.
   B Wow—I've heard the Zanzibah's awesome.
   A Yeah, how'd you like to try it with me next Saturday?

CD3 25   **see page 84**

CD3 26

R = Rachel
C = Christina
R Hello.
C Rachel? It's me, Christina. Something awful has happened.
R Hi, Christina, what on earth's wrong? Tell me.
C My apartment's just been broken into.
R Oh, no! That's terrible. When?
C Well, I discovered it when I came in from work, two hours ago. The door was wide open.
R They must have known no one was at home. What did they take?
C My laptop, of course, with all my work and my photos on it.
R Did you save everything?
C Yes, fortunately. I'd put my work and most of my photos on a CD.
R Thank goodness. What else is missing?
C My camera, and a whole load of Lisa's jewelry and her new leather jacket.
R Not your camera! Well at least you still have your photos. Oh, but Lisa's expensive leather jacket! Does she know?
C No, she doesn't. She's not back from class yet.
R She's going to be so shocked when she gets back—and she has her final exams soon.
C I know, but at least she had her laptop with her so they didn't get that.
R Yeah, that's good. I know she always takes it with her to lectures. Have you called the police?
C Oh, yes, they're here now.
R Good. Do they have any idea who might have done it?
C Well, they say there have been many burglaries in the area and the apartment above me was also broken into.
R So, it wasn't just *your* apartment then. Is it messy? Did they turn the place upside down?
C The mess is terrible. Whoever did it emptied out all my drawers and my clothes are all over the bedroom floor.
R Oh, how awful! Your nice clothes. Did they take any of them?
C I don't know, I haven't checked. The police have told me not to touch anything.
R Yes, of course, and anyway, it must be really difficult to see exactly what's missing.
C Oh, it is. Oh, Rachel, it's just chaos here.
R Look, Christina, you're obviously really upset. I'm coming over. I'll help you clean up. I'll be there in 15 minutes.
C Oh, Rachel. You're a great friend. Thanks so much.

CD3 27   **see page 85**

CD3 28

1. A I can't carry all these shopping bags.
   B What on earth have you bought?
2. A Tom's broken his arm in three places.
   B How on earth did he do that?
3. A There's someone at the door!
   B Who on earth could it be at this time of night?
4. A My aunt left all her money to her cat.
   B Why on earth did she do that?
5. A I can't find my car keys.
   B Where on earth have you put them?

CD3 29   **see page 85**

CD3 30   **see page 85**

CD3 31

1. A I can't find my ticket.
   B You must have dropped it.
2. A John didn't come to school yesterday.
   B He must have been sick.
3. A Why is Isabel late for class?
   B She might have overslept.
4. A I can't find my notebook.
   B You must have left it at home.
5. A The teacher's checking Maria's exercise.
   B She can't have finished already!
6. A Why is Carl looking so happy?
   B He may have done well on the test.

CD3 32   **The Adventures of Sherlock Holmes**

SH = Sherlock Holmes   HS = Hilton Soames
G = Mr. Gilchrist   W = Dr. Watson   B = Bannister

HW Holmes, Watson! At last! Tell me. What have you found out? Can the Greek examination take place?
SH Absolutely, the mystery is solved.
HS Really? But who …? Which student …?
SH Dr. Watson, can you please ask Mr. Gilchrist to join us.
W Of course. Mr. Gilchrist, Mr. Gilchrist, can you join us, please?
G What is it? What's happened?
SH Close the door, Mr. Gilchrist. Now, sit down and tell me honestly, why did you do it? How did you do it?
G What! Oh, no! How did you find out? I'm sorry, so sorry.
SH Come, come, Mr. Gilchrist, perhaps it's easier if I speak. You see, when I learned that you were an athlete and a long jumper, I worked it out immediately.
HS How? I don't understand.
SH Let me continue. This is what must have happened. Yesterday afternoon, you, Mr. Gilchrist, were returning from practicing your sport. You were carrying your jumping shoes, which, as we all know, have spikes on their soles. You passed your tutor's window, and because you are over six feet tall, you could see into his room. You couldn't help notice the examination papers on his desk. As you passed the door, you tried it. Amazingly, it opened …
HS What! How …?
SH Yes, Bannister had forgotten to lock it. Is that not true, Bannister?
B Oh dear, Mr. Holmes. Mr. Soames, sir, I'm sorry, sir. Mr. Holmes could be right, I was in a hurry.
SH So, Gilchrist, you entered the room, put your shoes down on the desk, and moved to the window to copy the papers and watch for your tutor. Am I right so far?
G Yes, yes.
SH Suddenly, you heard your tutor coming in at the side door. Quickly, you picked up your shoes, scratching the top of the desk with the

spikes in your haste and leaving a lump of black mud. You ran into the bedroom. You didn't notice that another lump of mud fell to the floor from your shoes. This morning at 6:00 A.M., I went to the sports ground and collected a sample of mud. It was the same black mud.

W Brilliant, Holmes! Just brilliant.
SH Elementary, my dear Watson. Is this all correct, Mr. Gilchrist?
G Absolutely correct. I feel so bad, so guilty and ashamed. But can I just show you this, Mr. Soames?
HS What is it?
G It's a letter. I wrote it in the middle of the night. Read it, please. In it I say how sorry I am for what I did.
HS Ah, yes. And you say you are not going to take the examination. Oh, and you're going to leave the university and the country.
G Yes, I am. I'm going to work in Africa.
HS Gilchrist, I am really pleased to hear that.
B Oh, Mr. Soames. Mr. Gilchrist. It's all my fault. I'm so sorry.
G Absolutely not your fault, Bannister. I am the guilty one.
SH Well, Mr. Soames, Mr. Gilchrist, time for Watson and myself to have breakfast, I think. I hope the exams go well, Mr. Soames. Good luck in Africa, Mr. Gilchrist. Goodbye.
HS Thank you, Mr. Holmes. It was such a lucky chance that you were staying in town at this time.

CD3 33

1. You need to learn to relax. Why don't you take up yoga?
2. He's just come up with a brilliant plan to save the business.
3. There's no dessert until you've eaten up all your meat and vegetables.
4. Anne and Tony aren't talking to each other. They may even have broken up.
5. Did you hear the news? Three dangerous prisoners have broken out of the local prison.
6. You must learn to sort out your problems without your parents' help.
7. We saving up so we can buy a house.
8. Have you found out why you didn't get the job?

CD3 34

1. **A** I've just found out that I've won the lottery!
   B Congratulations!
2. **A** I never eat out because I can't really afford to.
   B Me neither.
3. **A** I can't figure out if I feel warm or cold today.
   B Yeah. It's one of those days.
4. **A** I'm saving up to take my grandma on vacation.
   B That's nice.
5. **A** I need to sort out my life. I have problems at work and I have problems with my girlfriend …
   B Poor you. Come on, let's go out for a walk. Take your mind off things.
6. **A** I've just come up with a fantastic idea.
   B Uh! I'll believe it when I hear it.
7. **A** It's important to make up after an argument.
   B Yeah, kiss and make up. Never let the sun go down on an argument.

CD3 35 see page 89

CD3 36

"Did you hear about Marcos? You know, the guy who works in my office. Well … apparently, he is going to be promoted. To be honest, I don't understand why. Personally, I think he's hopeless at his job. He never does any work. In fact, all he does all day is talk to his friend on the phone and drink coffee. Unfortunately, his desk is next to mine. Presumably, he'll move to another office now, so hopefully I won't have to work with him anymore. Anyway, enough about me. How's your work going? Are you still enjoying it?"

CD3 37

1. **A** Hi! You're Emily, aren't you?
   B Actually, no, I'm not. Emily's over there talking to Robert.
2. **A** What did you think of the movie? Great, wasn't it?
   B Personally, I thought it was terrible. I just don't like all that blood and fighting.
3. **A** What's the latest gossip about Kate and her boyfriend?
   B Apparently, she's going to dump him. She met someone else.
4. **A** What's the weather like in spring?
   B Generally, it's warm during the day, but you still need to wear a jacket or sweater in the evening.
5. **A** What time will we arrive?
   B Hopefully, in the next hour, unless there's another traffic jam.
6. **A** I've called and left messages for them but no reply.
   B Presumably, they're away on vacation. Try them on their cell.
7. **A** What did you do when you saw the accident?
   B Obviously, we called 911 immediately. Then went to see if we could do anything to help.
8. **A** How did you feel when they offered you the job?
   B To be honest, I was amazed. I didn't expect to get it, but of course I was delighted. It'll be a challenge.

UNIT 12

CD3 38 I read it in the papers …

A three-year-old boy used his mother's computer to buy a $15,000 car on the Internet auction site eBay.

Jack Neal's parents only discovered their son's successful bid when they received a message from the website.
The message said they had bought a pink Nissan Figaro.
Mrs. Neal, 36, said that they couldn't understand it. She had been on the Internet the day before but hadn't bought anything.

"Jack kept telling us that he was so happy, and that we would soon get a big surprise."

Mrs. Neal, from Houston, Texas, thought Jack was joking. He often used the computer, and she was pretty sure that he knew her password.
Her husband, John, 37, called the seller of the car, and explained that there had been a mistake.

"Fortunately, he saw the funny side and said he would advertise the car again."

Mr. Neal has told Jack to be more careful, and he has asked his wife to change her password.

CD3 39

1. Mrs. Neal said her son was very clever.
2. She told me he usually played computer games.
3. His father explained that he had bought the computer for his work.
4. Mrs. Neal decided that she wouldn't use eBay anymore.
5. Jack said he didn't know how it had happened.
6. He told reporters that he had always liked computers.
7. His mother asked Jack to clean up his room.
8. His father told him to go and play soccer.

CD3 40 Man throws away $30,000 in town center

A mystery man started a riot in a busy town center yesterday by hurling $30,000 into the air.
Traffic was stopped at 11:00 A.M. as money rained down from the sky.
Local store clerk Anthony Jones, 55, said, "I couldn't understand it, so I asked my neighbor what was happening." They saw people on their hands and knees grabbing money. "No one knew where the money came from," he said. "They were just stuffing it in their pockets."
Passerby Eleanor Morris said, "I wondered if there had been an accident, because the traffic was at a complete standstill."
Florist Jane Thomas saw the man, who was wearing a red shirt. "I asked him why he was giving away all his money, but he didn't answer. He just laughed."
Police asked Jane if she knew the man. "I told him I'd never seen him before. He certainly wasn't from around here."
The police confirmed that a local forty-year-old man had been questioned. "He refused to tell us why he'd done it," a spokesman said, "so it's a complete mystery. He wanted to know if we were going to arrest him, but giving away money isn't against the law."

CD3 41

A I was coming home from the gym the other night and I was stopped by the police.
B Were you? Did they ask you a lot of questions?
A They certainly did. They asked me where I was going and where I'd been, and they wanted to know if I lived in the area.
B Were you scared?
A You bet!
B What else did they ask?
A Well, they wondered how old I was, and they wanted to know if I'd been with friends.
B Huh! I'm glad I wasn't with you.
A They also asked if I could remember when I'd left home.
B Do you know why they were asking all this?
A No idea. They wouldn't tell me.

CD3 42 But you said … !

1. **A** Bill's coming to the party tonight.
   B Really? I thought you said he wasn't feeling well.
2. **A** I'm making dinner for Joe tonight.
   B I didn't know you could cook!
3. **A** Oh, no! I spilled ketchup on my white shirt!
   B I told you to be careful. I knew you'd do that.
4. **A** Did you get me something to eat?
   B Sorry. I didn't realize you were here. What would you like?
5. **A** I'm 25 today!
   B Are you? I didn't know it was your birthday. Hope you have a great day!
6. **A** Oh, no! It's raining!
   B Really? But the weather forecast said it was going to be a nice day.
7. **A** You left the doors and windows of the apartment open this morning.
   B I'm sorry. I was pretty sure I'd closed all the doors and windows.
8. **A** Where did Tom go last night?
   B I have no idea where he went.

CD3 43 The interview

They wanted to know how old I was.
They asked me what I was doing at the moment.
They asked me how much I was earning.
They asked where I'd worked before.
They asked me if I liked working in a team.
They wanted to know when I could start!

1. She asked me to help her.
2. He reminded her to mail the letter.
3. She promised to study hard for her exams.
4. He invited me to his party.
5. She encouraged me to travel.
6. He offered to give me a lift to the airport.
7. He persuaded me to apply for the job.
8. She explained that she'd been very busy.

CD3 45

1. **Merinda calling Jenny**
   A Can I speak to Jenny, please?
   B I'm afraid she isn't here right now. Who's calling?
   A This is Merinda, from work. Could you give her a message?
   B Sure.
   A Can you ask her to call me as soon as she's back? It's very important.
   B I'll give her your message.

2. **Peter is talking to his boss**
   A Currently, we can offer you the job as Assistant Manager. I hope that's acceptable. The salary is $50,000 a year.
   B That's fine. I'll take the job.
   A There's a possibility of promotion in the next six months, if everything works out.
   B Great!

3. **Caroline is talking to her son, Ben**
   A Now, Ben, you can play on the bike for a bit, but then you have to let Mike have a turn. OK? You have to learn to share your toys.
   B OK, Mom.

4. **Sue leaving a message for James**
   This is a message for James. It's Sue here. I got movie tickets for 8:00, so I'll see you inside the theater at about 7:45. Hope that's OK. See you later.

5. **Tom is talking to Sue**
   A I'll look at your computer for you, but I can't promise to fix it. I'm not an expert.
   B Will you charge me for it?
   A Don't be silly. Of course not. I'll do it for nothing.

CD3 46 **What the papers say**

An interview with Jamie Seabrook

Part 1

A And now for my final guest. He's a singer and songwriter who's been in the music business for twenty years. He still performs sell-out concerts in front of fifty thousand people. But his life hasn't all been easy. He's had problems with his family, and he's been in trouble with the law. And he's just completed a month's rehab in a clinic in Texas. He's never out of the headlines … Please welcome Jamie Seabrook!
J Hello, good evening.
A Now, Jamie, you are in the newspapers and magazines every day. You are photographed wherever you go. Tell me, what do you think of the press?
J Well, it's kind of nice to have people want to know all about me. Sometimes it gets to be too much, but most of the time I don't mind the media attention. I'm sure there are some reporters who really try to tell the truth, but I'm afraid that most of them make up stories to sell their newspapers.
A Are you saying that the stories aren't true at all?
J That's right! They're completely invented!
A Can you give us an example?
J Sure I can! I can give you hundreds!

Part 2

J Two years ago, reporters said my career was finished, and that I'd never sing again. Some friends, who are now ex-friends, said that my marriage was breaking up, and that my brother and I argued about money and weren't speaking to each other. Not one word of that was true!
A And, in fact, your career is on a high …
J I just recorded a new album, and my marriage is fine. Sally and I just celebrated our fifteenth wedding anniversary … and my brother and I get along just fine.
A But things haven't all been easy for you. You spent a month in rehab because police officers said that you had a nervous breakdown …
J All that's just lies! I've never had a nervous breakdown. I was driving home from the recording studio and it was two o'clock in the morning and I'd been working all day and I was exhausted! I fell asleep at the wheel and police officers asked me to stop the car. I checked into a clinic for a month because I was suffering from exhaustion.
A Now, you had another legal problem recently. Your personal assistant, Barbara James, said you hadn't paid her for six months, and you made her work seven days a week without a break. Is that true?
J It broke my heart when Barbara, my PA, said those things about me. I treated her like my own family. When I met her she was nothing, and I gave her everything. None of what she says is true.

Part 3

A I read that you have become a Buddhist, that you have stopped eating meat, that you spend four hours a day meditating, and that you are going to give half your future income to charity. Is this true?
J Yes, it is. I've decided that life is too short, and I'm getting old. I don't care what people think. I made up my mind to do something useful with my life.
A Now, when this story broke a few days ago, the news anchor on MBC's *Morning News* refused to read the story, saying that there were much more serious stories that deserved attention, and that you were just a celebrity. What do you say to that?
J I can't control what the press says about me. I have to be true to myself. I live my life as honestly as I can. I try to be nice to everyone around me. If you're in the public eye, then you have to be prepared to have some pretty terrible things said about you. I know what's true about me and what's a lie, but I can't change what is said about me in the newspapers and on television.
A Well, sadly, our time has run out and we've come to the end of the show. A big thank you to my guest, Jamie Seabrook, and good luck with the new album!
J Thank you. It's been a pleasure.

CD3 47 see page 97

Grammar Reference

UNIT 1

1.1 Tenses

Unit 1 aims to review what you know. It has examples of the Present Simple and Continuous, the Past Simple and Continuous, and the Present Perfect. There are also examples of the passive voice.
All these forms are covered again in later units.

Present tenses	Unit 2
Past tenses	Unit 3
Present Perfect	Unit 7
Passive	Units 2, 3, 7

1.2 Verbs

1. There are three classes of verbs in English.

   Auxiliary verbs *do, be,* and *have*
   These are used to form tenses, and to show forms such as questions and negatives.

   Modal auxiliary verbs
   Must, can, should, might, will, and *would* are examples of modal auxiliary verbs. They "help" other verbs, but unlike *do, be,* and *have,* they have their own meanings. For example, *must* expresses obligation; *can* expresses ability. (See Units 4, 5, 9, 11.)

   Full verbs
   These are **all** the other verbs in the language, for example, *play, run, help, think, want, go, see, eat, enjoy, live, die, swim,* etc.

2. *Do, be,* and *have* can also be used as full verbs with their own meanings.

   do
   I **do** *my laundry on Saturdays.*
   *She **does** a lot of business in Latin America.*

   be
   *We **are** in class at the moment.*
   *They **were** at home yesterday.*

   have
   *He **has** a lot of problems.*
   *They **have** three children.*

3. There are two forms of *have* in the present.

   ***have* as a full verb**
   *I **have** a job.*
   *Do you **have** an apartment?*
   *He doesn't **have** a car.*

1.3 Auxiliary verbs and tenses

1 *be* and the continuous forms

Be + verb + *-ing* is used to make continuous verb forms which describe activities in progress and temporary activities.
*He's **washing** his hair.* (Present Continuous)
*They **were going** to work.* (Past Continuous)
*I've **been learning** English for two years.* (Present Perfect Continuous)
*I'd like **to be lying** on the beach right now.* (Continuous infinitive)

2 *be* and the passive voice

Be + past participle is used to form the passive.
*Paper **is made** from wood.* (Present Simple passive)
*My car **was stolen** yesterday.* (Past Simple passive)

*The house **has been** redecorated.* (Present Perfect passive)
*This homework needs **to be done** tonight.* (Passive infinitive)
There is an introduction to the passive on page 131.

3 *have* and the perfect forms

Have + past participle is used to make perfect verb forms.
*He **has worked** in seven different countries.* (Present Perfect)
*She was crying because she **had had** some bad news.* (Past Perfect)
*I'd like **to have met** Napoleon.* (Perfect infinitive)
Perfect means "completed before," so Present Perfect means "completed before now." Past Perfect means "completed before a time in the past."

1.4 Auxiliary verbs and negatives

1. To make a negative, add *-n't* to the auxiliary verb. If there is no auxiliary verb, use *don't/doesn't/didn't.*

Positive	Negative
He's working.	*He **isn't** working.*
I was thinking.	*I **wasn't** thinking.*
We've seen the play.	*We **haven't** seen the play.*
She works in a bank.	*She **doesn't** work in a bank.*
They like skiing.	*They **don't** like skiing.*
He went on vacation.	*He **didn't** go on vacation.*

2. It is possible to contract the auxiliaries *be* and *have* and use the uncontracted *not.*
   *He's **not** playing today.* (= He *isn't* playing today.)
   *We're **not** going to Italy after all.* (= We *aren't* going to Italy …)
   *I've **not** read that book yet.* (= I *haven't* read that book yet.)
   BUT   *I'm **not** working.*   NOT   ~~I amn't working~~.

1.5 Auxiliary verbs and questions

1. To make a question, invert the subject and the auxiliary verb. If there is no auxiliary verb, use *do/does/did.*

Question	
She's wearing jeans.	*What **is she** wearing?*
You were born in Mexico.	*Where **were you** born?*
Peter's been to China.	***Has Peter** been to China?*
I know you.	***Do I** know you?*
He wants ice cream.	*What **does he** want?*
They didn't go out.	*Why **didn't they** go out?*

2. There is usually no *do/does/did* in subject questions.

Who wants ice cream?	*What flavor ice cream **do** you want?*
What happened to your eye?	*What **did** you do to your eye?*
Who broke the window?	*How **did** you break the window?*

1.6 Auxiliary verbs and short answers

Short answers are very common in spoken English. If you just say *Yes* or *No,* it can sound rude. To make a short answer, repeat the auxiliary verb. In the Present and Past Simple, use *do/does/did.*

Short answer	
Are you coming with us?	***Yes,** I **am.***
Have you had breakfast?	***No,** I **haven't.***
Does she like walking?	***No,** she **doesn't.***
Did Mary call?	***Yes,** she **did.***

UNIT 2

2.1 Present Simple

Form

The form is the same for *I/we/you/they*.

*I **work** from 9–5 P.M.*
*They **don't work** full time.*
*Where **do** you **work**?*

He/She/It: add *-s* or *-es*, and use *does/doesn't* in questions and short answers.

*He **doesn't work** on weekends.*
*Where **does** she **live**?*

Short answer

Do you live in Chicago?	*Yes, **we do**.*
Does he have a car?	*No, **he doesn't**.*

Use

The Present Simple is used to express:

1. an action that happens again and again (a habit).
   *I **go** to work by car.*
   *She **drinks** ten cups of coffee a day.*

2. a fact that is always true.
   *Ronaldo **comes** from Brazil.*
   *My daughter **has** brown eyes.*

3. a fact that is true for a long time (a state).
   *He **works** in a bank.*
   *I **live** in an apartment near downtown.*

Spelling of *he/she/it* forms

1. Most verbs add *-s* to the base form of the verb.
   wants   eats   helps   drives

2. Add *-es* to verbs that end in *-ss, -sh, -ch, -x*, and *-o*.
   kisses   washes   watches   fixes   goes

3. Verbs that end in a consonant + *-y* change the *-y* to *-ies*.
   carries   flies   worries   tries
   But verbs that end in a vowel + *-y* only add *-s*.
   buys   says   plays   enjoys

2.2 Adverbs of frequency

1. We often use adverbs of frequency with the Present Simple.

0%			50%				100%
never	rarely	hardly ever	not often	sometimes	often	usually	always

2. They go before the main verb, but after the verb *to be*.

*I **usually** start at 9:00.*	*They're **usually** here by now.*
*I **rarely** see Peter these days.*	*We're **rarely** home on weekends.*

3. *Sometimes* and *usually* can also go at the beginning or the end.

***Sometimes** we play cards.*	*We play cards **sometimes**.*
***Usually** I go shopping with friends.*	*I go shopping with friends **usually**.*

2.3 Present Continuous

Form

am/is/are + verb + **-ing**

*I'm **playing** tennis.*
*He's **cooking** lunch.*

*I'm **not enjoying** my new job.*
*They **aren't working** today.*

*What's he **doing**?*
*Where **are** you **living**?*

Short answer

Are you going by train?	**Yes, I am.**/No, I'm **not**.

Use

The Present Continuous is used to express:

1. an activity that is happening now.
   *Don't turn the TV off. I'm **watching** it.*
   *You can't speak to Lisa. She's **taking** a bath.*

2. an activity that is not necessarily happening at the moment of speaking but is happening around now.
   *Don't take that book. Jane's **reading** it.*
   *I'm **taking** a Spanish evening class this year.*

3. a temporary activity.
   *Peter is a student, but he's **working** as a waiter during the summer.*
   *I'm **living** with friends until I find a place of my own.*

4. a planned future arrangement.
   *I'm **having** lunch with Glenda tomorrow.*
   *We're **meeting** at 1:00 outside the restaurant.*

Spelling of verb + *-ing*

1. Most verbs add *-ing* to the base form of the verb.
   going   wearing   visiting   eating

2. Verbs that end in one *-e* lose the *-e*.
   smoking   coming   hoping   writing
   BUT *lie → lying*
   Verbs that end in *-ee* don't drop an *-e*.
   agreeing   seeing

3. Verbs of one syllable, with one vowel and one consonant, double the consonant.
   stopping   getting   running   planning   jogging
   If the final consonant is *-y* or *-w*, it is not doubled.
   playing   showing

2.4 State verbs

1. There are certain groups of verbs that are usually only used in the Present Simple. Their meanings are related to states or conditions that are facts, not activities.

Verbs of thinking and opinions

believe	think	understand	suppose	expect	agree
doubt	know	remember	forget	promise	mean
imagine	realize	deserve	guess		

*I **believe** you.*
*Do you **understand** what I mean?*
*I **know** his face, but I **forget** his name.*

Verbs of emotions and feelings

like	love	hate	care	hope
wish	want	prefer	adore	dislike

*I **like** black coffee.*
*Do you **want** to go out?*
*I **don't care**.*

Verbs of having and being

belong	own	have	possess	contain	cost	seem
matter	need	depend	weigh	resemble	fit	involve

*This book **belongs** to Jane.*
*How much **does** it **cost**?*
*He **has** a lot of money.*

Verbs of the senses

look	hear	taste	smell	feel	sound

*The food **smells** good.*
*My hair **feels** soft.*

We often use *can* when the subject is a person.
*I **can** hear someone crying.*
***Can** you smell something burning?*

2. Some of these verbs can be used in the Present Continuous, but with a change of meaning. In the continuous, the verb expresses an activity, not a state. Compare:

*I **think** you're right.*	*We're **thinking** of going to the movies.*
(opinion)	(mental activity)
*He **has** a lot of money.*	*She's **having** a bad day.*
(possession)	(activity)
*I **see** what you mean.*	*Are you **seeing** Dan tomorrow?*
(= understand)	(activity)
*The soup **tastes** awful.*	*I'm **tasting** the soup to see if it needs salt.*
(state)	(activity)

2.5 THE PASSIVE

Form

***to be** + past participle*
The tense of the verb *to be* changes to give different tenses in the passive.
***Are** you **being served**?* (Present Continuous)
*My car **is insured** with ASM.* (Present Simple)
***Were** you **taken** to visit the museum?* (Past Simple)
*I've **been invited** to a wedding.* (Present Perfect)
*I'd love **to be introduced** to a movie star.* (Passive infinitive)

Use

1. Passive sentences move the focus from the subject to the object of active sentences.

    *Shakespeare **wrote** Hamlet in 1601 while he was living in London.*
    *Hamlet, the most famous play in English literature, **was written** by William Shakespeare.*

    The passive is not another way of expressing the same sentence in the active. We choose the active or the passive depending on what we are more interested in.

2. *By* and the agent are often omitted in passive sentences if …
    … the agent is not known:
    *I **was robbed** last night.*
    … the agent is not important:
    *This bridge **was built** in 1886.*
    … the agent is obvious:
    *I **was fined** $100 for speeding.*

3. The passive is associated with an impersonal, formal style. It is often used in notices and announcements.

    *Customers **are requested** to refrain from eating in the store.*
    *It **has been noticed** that reference books **have been removed** from the library.*

4. In informal language, we often use *you, we,* and *they* to refer to people in general or to no person in particular. In this way, we can avoid using the passive.

    ***You can buy** stamps in many places, not just post offices.*
    ***They're building** a new department store downtown.*
    ***We speak** English in this shop.*

❶ Many past participles are used as adjectives.
*I'm very **interested** in modern art.*
*We were extremely **worried** about you.*
*I'm **exhausted**! I've been working hard all day.*

2.6 Present Simple and Present Continuous passive

Form

Present Simple Passive (*am/is/are* + past participle)
*Most workers **are paid** monthly.*
***Is** the tip **included** in the check?*

Present Continuous Passive (*am/is/are being* + past participle)
*This road **is being widened**.*
***Are** you **being served**?*

Use

The uses are the same in the passive as in the active.
*My car **is serviced** every six months.* (habit)
*Computers **are used** everywhere.* (fact that is always true)
*The house **is being redecorated** right now.* (activity happening now)

UNIT 3

3.1 PAST TENSES

We use different past tenses to describe moments and periods of time in the past.
Look at the diagram. Read the sentences.
When Andrea arrived at work at 9:00 …

———— 8:30 ———— | 9:00 | ———— 9:30 ———— 10:00 ————

… her secretary had opened the mail.

… her secretary was opening the mail.

… her secretary opened the mail.

3.2 Past Simple

Form

The form of the Past Simple is the same for all persons.
*He **left** at three o'clock.*
*They **arrived** three weeks ago.*

*She **didn't finish** on time yesterday.*
*I **didn't visit** my parents last weekend.*

*When **did** he **finish** the report?*
*What time **did** his train **leave**?*

Short answer
Did you enjoy the meal?   **Yes**, we **did**./**No**, we **didn't**.

Use

The Past Simple is used to express:

1. a finished action in the past.
    *We **met** in 2000.*
    *I **went** to Boston last week.*
    *John **left** two minutes ago.*

2. actions that follow each other in a story.
    *Mary **walked** into the room and **stopped**. She **listened** carefully. She **heard** a noise coming from behind the curtain. She **threw** the curtain open, and then she **saw** …*

3. a past situation or habit.
    *When I **was** a child, we lived in a small house by the sea. Every day I **walked** for miles on the beach with my dog.*
    This use is often expressed with *used to*. See 3.5 on page 132.
    *We **used to** live in a small house … I **used to** walk for miles …*

Spelling of verb + -ed

1. Most regular verbs add -ed to the base form of the verb.
   worked wanted helped washed

2. When the verb ends in -e, add -d.
   liked used hated cared

3. If the verb has only one syllable, with one vowel + one consonant, double the consonant before adding -ed.
   stopped planned robbed
   But we write *cooked, seated,* and *moaned* because there are two vowels.

4. The consonant is not doubled if it is -y or -w.
   played showed

5. In most two-syllable verbs, the end consonant is doubled if the stress is on the second syllable.
   pre'ferred ad'mitted
   But we write *'entered* and *'visited* because the stress is on the first syllable.

6. Verbs that end in a consonant + -y change the -y to -ied.
   carried hurried buried
   But we write *enjoyed*, because it ends in a vowel + -y.

There are many common irregular verbs.

▶▶ **Irregular verbs page 155**

Past Simple and time expressions

Look at the time expressions that are common with the Past Simple.

I met her	last night.
	two days ago.
	yesterday morning.
	in 2001.
	in the summer.
	when I was young.

3.3 Past Continuous

Form

was/were + verb + -ing
I was learning Japanese.
They were driving to Tokyo.

We weren't waiting for a long time.

What were they doing?
Where was he studying?

Short answer

Were you looking for me?   **Yes, I was./No, I wasn't.**
Were they waiting outside?   **Yes, they were./No, they weren't.**

Use

The Past Continuous is used:

1. to express activities in progress before, and probably after, a particular time in the past.
   At seven o'clock this morning I was having my breakfast.
   You made a lot of noise last night. What were you doing?

2. for descriptions.
   Jan looked beautiful. She was wearing a green cotton dress. Her eyes were shining in the light of the candles that were burning nearby.

3. to express an interrupted past activity.
   When the phone rang, I was taking a shower.
   While we were playing tennis, it started to rain.

4. to express an incomplete activity.
   I was reading a book during the flight. (I didn't finish it.)
   I watched a movie during the flight. (the whole movie)

3.4 Past Simple or Past Continuous?

1. Sometimes both tenses are possible. The Past Simple focuses on past actions as complete facts. The Past Continuous focuses on the duration of past activities. Compare:
   A *I didn't see you at the party last night.*
   B *No. I **stayed** at home and **watched** the game.*
   A *I didn't see you at the party last night.*
   B *No, I **was watching** the game at home.*

2. Questions in the Past Simple and Past Continuous refer to different time periods. The Past Continuous asks about activities before; the Past Simple asks about what happened after.
   A *What **were** you **doing** when the accident happened?*
   B *I **was shopping**.*
   A *What **did** you **do** when you saw the accident?*
   B *I **called** the police.*

3.5 used to

Used to expresses a habit or state in the past that is now finished.
*I **used to** read comics when I was a kid. (but I don't now)*
*My dad and I **used to** play basketball together. (but we don't now)*
***Did** you **use to** read comics when you were a child?*
*This town **didn't use to** be a nice place to live, but then it changed.*

3.6 Past Perfect

Perfect means "completed before." The Past Perfect refers to an action in the past that was completed before another action in the past.

Form

The form of the Past Perfect is the same for all persons.

Positive and negative

I	'd (had)	seen him before.
You	hadn't	finished work at six o'clock.
We		

Question

| Where had | you she they | been before? |

Short answer

Had he already left?   **Yes**, he **had./No**, he **hadn't**.

Use

1. The Past Perfect is used to make clear that one action in the past happened *before* another action in the past.
   *When I got home, I found that someone **had broken** into my apartment and **had stolen** my DVD player.*
   *I didn't go to the movie theater because I'd **seen** the movie before.*

2. The Past Simple tells a story in chronological order.
   Sue met Pete in college. They dated for six years. They got married last month.

   The Past Perfect can be used to tell a story in a different order.
   Sue and Pete got married last month. They'd met in college and had dated for six years.

3. Notice the difference between these sentences.
   *When I got to the party, Peter **went** home.*
   (= First I arrived, then Peter left.)
   *When I got to the party, Peter **had gone** home.*
   (= First Peter left, then I arrived.)

4. The Past Perfect Continuous refers to longer actions or repeated activities.

*We were exhausted because we'd **been driving** all day.*

3.7 Past tenses in the passive

Form

Past Simple Passive: *was/were* + past participle
*The museum **was opened** in 1987.*
*We **were robbed** last night.*

Past Continuous Passive: *was/were being* + past participle
*The vase **was being restored**.*

Past Perfect Passive: *had been* + past participle
*The house **had been redecorated**.*

Use

The uses are the same in the passive as in the active.
*The bridge **was built** in 1876.* (finished action in the past)
*The bomb **was being defused** when it exploded.* (interrupted past activity)
*The letter didn't arrive because it **had been sent** to my old address.* (one action before another action in the past)

UNIT 4

4.1 *have to*

Form

has/have + to + infinitive
*You **have to go** to school.*
*She **has to study** hard.*

*He **doesn't have to wear** a uniform.*
*We **don't have to take** exams.*

***Does** she **have to study** math?*
***Do** they **have to leave** now?*

Use

1. *Have to* expresses strong obligation.
   *You **have to** work hard if you want to succeed.*
2. *Have to* expresses a general obligation based on a law or rule, or based on the authority of another person.
   *Children **have to** go to school until they are 16.*
   *Mom says you **have to** clean your room before you go out.*
3. *Have to* is impersonal. It doesn't necessarily express the opinion of the speaker.
   *The doctor says I **have to** lose weight.*
   *People all over the world **have to** learn English.*
4. *Have to* has all verb forms. *Must* doesn't.
   *I **had to** work last night.* (Past)
   *You'll **have to** study hard.* (Future)
   *She's rich. She's never **had to** do any work.* (Present Perfect)
   *I hate **having** to get up on winter mornings.* (*-ing* form)

4.2 *have got to*

1. *Have got to* is common in spoken English. It is more informal than *have to*.
   *I've **got to** go now. See you!*
   *We've **got to** get up early tomorrow.*

2. *Have got to* expresses an obligation now, or on a particular occasion soon.
   *I've **got to** stop eating ice cream! It's too yummy!*
   *You've **got to** pay me back tomorrow.*

3. *Have to* expresses a general repeated obligation.
   *I always **have to** tell my parents where I'm going.*
   *Teachers **have to** prepare lessons and correct homework.*

4.3 MODAL AND RELATED VERBS

These are the modal verbs:
can, could, may, might, will, would, should, must, ought to.
They are used before other verbs and add meanings, such as certainty, possibility, obligation, ability, and permission.
*You **must** be exhausted.*
*I **can** swim.*
*It **might** rain.*

Form

1. There is no *-s* in the third person singular.
   *She **can** ski.   He **must** be tired.   It **might** rain.*
2. There is no *do/does/don't/doesn't* in the question or negative.
   *What **should** I do?   **Can** I help you?   You **mustn't** steal!*
   *He **can't** dance.   I **won't** be a minute.*
3. Modal auxiliary verbs are followed by the infinitive without *to*. The exception is *ought to*.
   *You **must** go.   I'll **help** you.   You **ought to** see a doctor.*
4. They have no infinitives and no *-ing* forms. Other expressions are used instead.
   *I'd love to **be able to** ski.*
   *I hate **having to** get up on cold winter mornings.*
5. They don't usually have past forms. Instead, we use them with Perfect infinitives.
   *You **should have told** me that you can't swim. You **might have drowned**!*
   Or we use other expressions.
   *I **had to** study hard in school.*
6. *Could* is used with a past meaning to talk about a general ability.
   *I **could** swim when I was six.* (= general ability)
   To talk about ability on one specific occasion, we use *was able to/managed to*.
   *The prisoner **was able to/managed to** escape by climbing onto the roof of the prison.*

Use

1. Modal verbs express our attitudes, opinions, and judgments of events. Compare:
   "Who's that knocking on the door?"
   "It's John." (This is a fact.)
   "Who's that knocking on the door?"
   *"It **could/may/might/must/should/can't/'ll** be John."* (These all express our attitude or opinion.)
2. Each modal verb has at least two meanings. One use of all of them is to express possibility or probability. (See Units 5 and 11.)
   *I **must** mail this letter!* (= obligation)
   *You **must** be tired!* (= deduction, probability)
   ***Could** you help me?* (= request)
   *We **could** go to Thailand for our vacation.* (= possibility)
   *You **may** go home now.* (= permission)
   *"Where's Anna?"   "I'm not sure. She **may** be at work."* (= possibility)

4.4 Obligation: *should*, *ought to*, and *must*

Should, *ought to*, and *must* are modal verbs. See 4.3 on page 133 for form.

Use

1. *Should* and *ought to* express mild obligation, suggestions, or advice. They express what, in the speaker's opinion, is the right or best thing to do. We often use them with *I think/don't think …*

   *You're always asking me for money. I think you **should** spend less.*
   *You **shouldn't** sit so close to the television! It's bad for your eyes.*
   *You **ought to** be more careful with your money.*

2. We often use *Do you think …?* in the question.

   ***Do you think** I should see a doctor?*
   *What **do you think** I should wear to the party?*

3. *Must*, like *have to*, expresses strong obligation. *Must* can express an obligation that involves the speaker's opinion. It is personal.

   *I **must** pass the exam to graduate.*
   *The government **must** do something about the environment.*

4. *Must* is also associated with a formal, written style.

   *All visitors **must** show proper ID.*
   *Books **must** be returned on or before the due date.*

have to and must

1. *Have to* and *must* are sometimes interchangeable.

   *I **must** be home by midnight.*
   *I **have to** be home by midnight.*

2. There is sometimes a difference in meaning. *Must* usually expresses the feelings and wishes of the speaker.

   *I **must** buy my mother a birthday card.*
   *Tommy, you **must** look after your toys.*

   Have to often expresses an obligation that comes from somewhere else.

   *You **have to** work hard in this life.*
   *Visitors **have to** report to reception.*

   It is for this reason that you need to be careful when you say *You must …*, because you can sound authoritarian.

   Have to is used more than *must*. If you don't know which to use, use *have to*.

3. Question forms with *have to* are more common.

   *Do I **have to** do what you say?*
   ***Must** I …?* is unusual.

❶ Remember, *have to* has all verb forms. *Must* can only refer to present or future time when used to express obligation.

don't have to

1. *Don't have to* expresses absence of obligation — you can, but it isn't necessary.

   *Some people iron their socks, but you **don't have to**. I think it's a waste of time.*
   *When you go into a store, you **don't have to** buy something. You can just look.*

4.5 Permission: *can* and *be allowed to*

Can is a modal verb. See 4.3 on page 133 for form.

Use

The main use of *can* is to express ability.

*I **can** swim.*

Can and *be allowed to* express permission. *Can* is more informal and usually spoken.

*You **can** borrow my bike, but you **can't** have the car. I need it.*
*They **can't** come in here with those muddy shoes!*

*You're **allowed to** get married when you're 18.*
*Are we **allowed to** use a dictionary for this test?*

4.6 Making requests: *can*, *could*, *will*, and *would*

1. There are many ways of making requests in English.

   ***Can** I speak to you, please?*
   ***Could** I ask you a question?*

   ***Will** you help me, please?*
   ***Would** you pass me the salt?*

   ***Would you mind** passing me the water?*
   ***Do you mind if** I open the window?*
   ***Would you mind if** I closed the window?*
   Can, could, will, and *would* are all modal verbs.

2. *Could* is a little more formal; *can* is a little more familiar. *Could I …?* and *Could you …?* are very useful because they can be used in many different situations.

   ***Could** I try on this sweater?*
   ***Could** you tell me the time?*

3. Here are some ways of responding to requests:

   A *Excuse me! Could you help me?*
   B *Sure./Of course./Well, I'm afraid I'm a little busy right now.*

   A *Would you mind if I opened the window?*
   B *No, not at all./No, that's fine./Well, I'm a little cold, actually.*

4.7 Making offers: *will* and *should*

1. The contracted form of *will* is used to express an intention, decision, or offer.

   *Come over after work. **I'll** cook dinner.*
   *"It's Jane's birthday today."   "Is it? **I'll** buy her some flowers."*
   *Dave**'ll** give you a lift.*
   *Give it back or we**'ll** call the police!*

2. We use *should* to make an informal suggestion.

   *"What **should** we have for dinner?"*
   *"Where **should we** go?"*

UNIT 5

5.1 FUTURE FORMS

1. There is no future tense in English. Instead, English has several forms that can refer to the future.

   *I'll **see** you later.* (*will*)
   *We're **going to see** a movie tonight.* (*going to*)
   *I'm **seeing** the doctor tomorrow.* (Present Continuous)
   *If the traffic's bad, I **might be** late.* (*might*)
   *Who knows? You **may win**!* (*may*)
   *Take an umbrella. It **could rain** later.* (*could*)

2. The difference between them is not about near or distant future, or certainty. The speaker chooses a future form depending on how he/she sees the future event. Is it a plan, a decision, an intention, an offer, an arrangement, or a prediction?

5.2 *will/going to* and the Present Continuous

Form

Positive and negative

*I'll **see** you later.*
*I **won't be** late.*
*We're **going to stay** in a hotel.*
*We **aren't going to rent** a beach house.*
*I'm **meeting** Jan for lunch.*
*I'm **not seeing** her till 2:00.*

Question

*When **will** you **be** back?*
*Where **are** you **going to stay**?*
*What time **are** you **seeing** Jan?*

❶ We avoid saying *going to come* or *going to go*.

*We're **coming** tomorrow.*
*When **are** you **going** home?*

Facts and predictions

will

1. The most common use of *will* is as an auxiliary verb to show future time. It expresses a future fact or prediction. It is called the pure future or the Future Simple.

   *We'll **be** away for two weeks.*
   *Those flowers **won't grow** under the tree. It's too dark.*
   *Our love **will last** forever.*
   *You'll **be** sick if you eat all those sweets!*

2. *Will* for a prediction can be based more on an opinion than a fact.

   *I don't think Laura **will do** very well on her exam. She doesn't do any work.*
   *I am convinced that inflation **will fall** to three per cent next year.*

going to

1. *Going to* can also express a prediction, especially when it is based on a present fact. There is evidence now that something is certain to happen.

   *She's **going to have** a baby.*
   (We can see she's pregnant.)
   *Our team **is going to win** the game.*
   (It's the fourth quarter, and there are only five minutes left to play.)
   *It **isn't going to rain** today.*
   (Look at that beautiful blue sky.)

2. Sometimes there is no difference between *will* and *going to*.

   *This government **will ruin** the country.*
   *This government **is going to ruin** the country.*

Plans, decisions, intentions, and arrangements

will

Will is used to express a decision, intention, or offer made at the moment of speaking.

*I'll **have** the steak, please.*	NOT	*I have the steak …*
*Give me a call. We'll **go** out for coffee.*	NOT	*We go …*
*There's the phone! I'll **get** it.*	NOT	*I get …*

going to

Going to is used to express a future plan, decision, or intention made before the moment of speaking.

*When I grow up, I'm **going to be** a doctor.*
*Jane and Peter **are going to get married** after they graduate.*
*We're **going to paint** this room blue.*

Arrangements

1. The Present Continuous can be used to express a future arrangement between people. It usually refers to the near future.

   *We're **going** out with Jeremy tonight.*
   *I'm **having** my hair cut tomorrow.*
   *What **are** we **having** for lunch?*

2. Think of the things you put in your calendar to remind you of what you are doing over the next few days and weeks. These are the kinds of events that are expressed by the Present Continuous for the future. There is often movement or activity.

   *I'm **meeting** Peter tonight.*
   *The Taylors **are coming** for dinner.*
   *I'm **seeing** the doctor in the morning.*

3. You can't use the Present Simple for this use.

*We're **going** to a party on Saturday night.*	NOT	*We go …*
*I'm **having** lunch with Sarah.*	NOT	*I have …*
*What are you **doing** this evening?*	NOT	*What do you do …*

4. Sometimes there is no difference between an arrangement and an intention.

   *We're **going to get** married in the spring.*
   *We're **getting** married in the spring.*

5.3 Future possibility: *may/might/could*

Form

May, *might*, and *could* are modal verbs.

Positive and negative

I	may might could	see you later.

I	may not might not	get the job.

Question

Questions about future possibility are often asked with *Do you think … will …?*

***Do you think** you'll get the job?*

Use

1. *May*, *might*, and *could* all express a future possibility.

It	may might could	rain later.

2. *May* can be more formal.

   *The government **may** increase income tax.*

3. *Could* suggests something less definite.

   *I **could** be a champion if I trained hard.*
   *The house is nice, but it **could** be beautiful.*

UNIT 6

6.1 Information questions

1. *What* and *which* can be followed by a noun.
   What color *are your eyes?*
   What size *shoes do you wear?*
   What sort *of music do you like?*
   Which part *of town do you live in?*
   Which way *do we go?*
   Which one *do you want?*

   We use *which* when there is a limited choice.
   Which one *do you want, the red one or the blue one?*
   Which restaurant *should we go to?*

   We use *what* when there is (almost) unlimited choice.
   What language *do they speak in Brazil?*
   What car *do you drive?*

   Sometimes there is no difference.
   What/Which newspaper *do you read?*
   What/Which channel *is the game on?*

2. *Whose* can be followed by a noun.
   Whose book *is this?*
   Whose *is this book?*

3. *How* can be followed by an adjective or an adverb.
   How tall *are you?*
   How big *is the memory?*
   How far *is it to the station?*
   How often *do you go to the movies?*
   How long *does it take you to get ready?*

4. *How* can be followed by *much* or *many*.
   How many *rooms are there?*
   How much *money do you have?*

6.2 *What ... like? How ...?*

1. *What ... like?* asks about the permanent nature of people and things. It asks for a general description.
   What's Mexican food like?   *Really tasty.*
   What's Pete like?   *He's a great guy.*

2. *How ...?* asks about the present condition of something. This condition can change.
   How's work these days?   *It's better than last year.*
   How was the traffic this morning?   *It was worse than usual.*

   To ask about the weather, we can use both questions.
   How's the weather
   What's the weather like | where you are?

3. *How ...?* asks about people's health and happiness.
   How's Peter?   *He's fine.*

4. *How ...?* asks about people's reactions and feelings.
   How's your meal?
   How's your new job?

6.3 Relative clauses

1. Relative clauses identify which person or thing we are talking about. They make it possible to give more information about the person or thing.
   The boy went to the beach. (Which boy?)
   The boy **who lives next door** *went to the beach.*

   The book is very good. (Which book?)
   The book **that I bought yesterday** *is very good.*

   There is a photo of the hotel. (Which hotel?)
   There is a photo of the hotel **where we stayed.**

2. We use *who/that* to refer to people, and *which/that* to refer to things.
   This book is about a girl **who marries a millionaire.**
   What was the name of the horse **that won the race?**

3. When *who* or *that* is the object of a relative clause, it can be left out.
   The person **you need to talk to** *is on vacation.*
   The movie **I watched last night** *was very good.*

   But when *who* or *that* is the subject of a relative clause it must be included.
   I like people **who are kind and considerate.**
   I want a computer **that's easy to use.**

4. *Which* can be used to refer to the whole previous sentence or idea.
   I passed my driving test on the first attempt, **which was a surprise.**
   Jane can't come to the party, **which is a shame.**

5. We use *whose* to refer to someone's possessions.
   That's the man **whose wife won the lottery.**
   That's the woman **whose dog ran away.**

6. We can use *where* to refer to places.
   The hotel **where we stayed** *was right on the beach.*
   We went back to the place **where we first met.**

6.4 Participles

Participles after a noun define and identify in the same way as relative clauses.
That woman **driving** *the red Porsche is my aunt.*
The men **seen** *outside were probably the thieves.*

UNIT 7

7.1 THE PRESENT PERFECT

1. The same form (*have* + past participle) exists in many European languages, but the uses in English are different. In English, the Present Perfect links past and present. It expresses the effect of the past on the present.

PAST   PRESENT PERFECT   PRESENT

2. Present Perfect means "completed before now." The Present Perfect does not express when an action happened. If we say the exact time, we use the Past Simple.
   In my life, I **have traveled** *to all seven continents.*
   I **traveled** *around Africa in 1998.*

7.2 Present Perfect

Form

***has/have* + past participle**
I've **lived** *in Seoul.*
She's **lived** *in New York.*
He **hasn't lived** *here long.*
They **haven't bought** *their apartment.*
How long **have** *they* **known** *Peter?*
How long **has** *she* **been married?**

Short answer
Have you always lived in Peru?   **Yes, I have./No, I haven't.**

Use

There are three main uses of the Present Perfect.

1 Unfinished past

The Present Perfect expresses an action that began in the past and still continues.

*We've **lived** in the same house for 25 years.*
*How long **have** you **known** each other?*
*They've **been** married for 20 years.*

❗ Be careful! Many languages express this idea with a present tense, but in English this is wrong.

*Jan **has been** a nurse for ten years.* NOT ~~Jan is a nurse for ten years.~~

Time expressions

Notice the time expressions that are common with this use.

for	two years a month a few minutes half an hour ages	since	1970 August 8:00 I was a child the summer

We use *for* with a period of time and *since* with a point in time.

2 Experience

The Present Perfect expresses an experience that happened at some time in one's life. The action is finished, but the effects of the action are still felt.

*I've **been** to the United States.* (I still remember.)
*Have you ever **had** an operation?* (at any time in your life)
*How many times **has** he **been** married?* (in his life)

Exactly *when* the action happened is not important. Questions and answers about definite times are expressed in the Past Simple.

*When **did** you **go** to the United States?*
*I **broke** my leg once.*

Time expressions

The adverbs *ever*, *never*, and *before* are common with this use.

*Have you **ever** been to Australia?*
*I've **never** tried bungee jumping.*
*I haven't tried sushi **before**.*

3 Present result

The Present Perfect expresses a past action that has a present result. The action is usually in the recent past.

*The taxi **hasn't arrived** yet.* (We're still waiting for it.)
*What **have** you **done** to your lip?* (It's bleeding.)

We often announce news in the Present Perfect.

*Have you **heard**? The Prime Minister **has resigned**.*
*Susan's **had** her baby!*

Details will be in the Past Simple.

*She **resigned** because she **lost** a vote of no confidence.*
*It's a boy. He **weighed** seven pounds.*

Time expressions

The adverbs *yet*, *already*, and *just* are common with this use.

*I haven't done my homework **yet**.* (negative)
*Has the mailman come **yet**?* (question)
*I've **already** done my homework.*
*She's **just** had some good news.*

❗ Be careful with *been* and *gone*.

*He's **been** to the United States.* (experience — he isn't there now)
*She's **gone** to the United States.* (present result — she's there now)

7.3 Present Perfect or Past Simple?

1. The Present Perfect can express unfinished actions. The Past Simple expresses completed actions.

Present Perfect	Past Simple
I've lived in Texas for six years. (I still live there.)	*I lived in Texas for six years.* (Now I live somewhere else.)
I've written several books. (I can still write some more.)	*Shakespeare wrote 30 plays.* (He can't write any more.)

2. The Present Perfect refers to indefinite time. The Past Simple refers to definite time. Notice the time expressions used with the two tenses.

Present Perfect – indefinite		Past Simple – definite	
I've done it	for a long time. since July. before. recently.	I did it	yesterday. last week. two days ago. at 8:00. in 1987.
*I've **already** done it.* *I **haven't** done it **yet**.*			when I was young. for a long time.

❗ Be careful with *this morning/afternoon*, etc.

*Have you **seen** Amy this morning?* (It's still morning.)
*Did you **see** Amy this morning?* (It's the afternoon or evening.)

7.4 Present Perfect Simple passive

Form

has/have been + past participle

It They	has been have been	sold.

Use

The uses are the same in the passive as in the active.

*Two million cars **have been produced** so far this year.* (unfinished past)
*Has she ever **been fired**?* (past experience)
*"Have you heard? Two hundred homes **have been washed away** by a tidal wave!"* (present importance)

7.5 Present Perfect Continuous

Form

has/have + been + -ing

*She's **been studying** for three years.*
*They **haven't been working** here long.*
*How long **have** they **been living** there?*

Use

The Present Perfect Continuous expresses:

1. an activity that began in the past and is continuing now.

*I've **been studying** English for three years.*
*How long **have** you **been working** here?*

Sometimes there is no difference between the simple and the continuous.

*I've **played** the piano since I was a boy.*
*I've **been playing** the piano since I was a boy.*

The continuous can express a temporary activity, while the simple expresses a permanent state.

*I've **been living** in this house for the past few months.* (temporary)
*I've **lived** here all my life.* (permanent)

❗ Remember: State verbs are rarely used in the continuous (see 2.4 page 130).

*I've **had** this book for ages.*
*I've always **loved** sunny days.*

2. a past activity that has caused a present result.
I've been working all day. (I'm tired now.)
Have you been crying? (Your eyes are red.)
Roger's been cutting the grass. (I can smell it.)

The past activity might be finished or it might not. The context usually makes this clear.
Look out the window! It's been snowing!
(It has stopped snowing now.)
I've been writing this book for two years. (It still isn't finished.)
I'm covered in paint because I've been decorating the bathroom.
(It might be finished or it might not. We don't know.)

7.6 Present Perfect Simple or Continuous?

1. The simple expresses a completed action.
I've painted the kitchen, and now I'm doing the bathroom.
The continuous expresses an activity over a period of time.
I have got paint in my hair because I've been decorating.

We use the simple if the sentence has a number or quantity, because the simple expresses completion. The continuous isn't possible.
I've been reading all day. I've read ten chapters.
She's been eating ever since she arrived. She's eaten ten cookies already.

2. Some verbs have the idea of a long time, for example, *wait, work, play, try, learn, rain.* These verbs are often found in the continuous.
I've cut my finger. (One short action.)
I've been cutting firewood. (Perhaps over several hours.)

Some verbs don't have the idea of a long time, for example, *find, start, buy, die, lose, break, stop.* These verbs are more usually found in the simple.
I've lost my passport.
Have you started your holiday shopping yet?

UNIT 8

Verb patterns
The infinitive

1. The infinitive is used after some verbs.
We've decided to move abroad.
I want to go home.
I'm trying to call Pete.
She'd love to meet you.

2. Some verbs are followed by a person + the infinitive.
They asked me to help them.
I want you to try harder.
He told me to apply for the job.

3. *Make* and *let* are followed by a person + the infinitive without *to.*
She'll make you feel welcome.
I'll let you know when I'm coming.

4. The infinitive is used after some adjectives.
It's impossible to save money.
It's great to see you.
Pleased to meet you.
It was good to hear your news.

The -ing form

1. The -ing form is used after some verbs.
I enjoy reading history books.
He's finished washing the car.
I don't mind helping you.
We like walking.
He goes fishing on weekends.

2. Some verbs are followed by an object + -ing.
I hate people telling me what to do.
You can't stop me doing what I want.
I can hear someone calling.

3. The -ing form is used after prepositions.
I'm good at finding things.
He's afraid of being mugged.
We're thinking of going to Sweden.
I'm looking forward to meeting you.

▶▶ Verb patterns page 154

UNIT 9

9.1 CONDITIONALS

There are many different ways of making sentences with *if.* It is important to understand the difference between sentences that express:
    possible conditions = first conditional
    improbable conditions = second conditional
    impossible conditions = third conditional
    no condition = zero conditional

Possible conditions
If I see Dave, I'll tell him to call you.
This is a sentence about reality.

If I see Dave …	= a real possibility
… I'll tell him to call you.	= the result of a possible situation

Improbable conditions
If I had the money, I'd buy a Mercedes.
This is a sentence that is contrary to reality.

If I had the money …	= not impossible. The reality is I don't have the money.
… I'd buy a Mercedes.	= the result of an improbable situation

Impossible conditions
If I'd known you were coming, I'd have cooked you a meal.
This is a sentence about an impossible situation. It didn't happen, and now it's too late to change the result.

If I had known …	= impossible, because I didn't know.
I'd have cooked …	= the result of an impossible situation.

No conditions
If I get a headache, I take an aspirin.
If metal is heated, it expands.
These are sentences that are always true. They refer to "all time," and are called zero conditionals. *If* means *when* or *whenever.*

9.2 Second conditional: improbable conditions
Form
if + Past Simple, *would* + verb

Positive
If I won some money, I'd go around the world.
My father would kill me if he could see me now.

Negative
I'd give up my job if I didn't like it.
If I saw a ghost, I wouldn't talk to it.

Question
What would you do if you saw someone shoplifting?
If you needed help, who would you ask?

❗ *Was* can change to *were* in the condition clause.

If I If he	were rich,	I he	wouldn't have to work.

Other modal verbs are possible in the result clause.
I **could** buy some new clothes if I had some money.
If I saved a little every week, I **might** be able to buy a car.

Use

1. We use the second conditional to express an unreal situation and its probable result. The situation or condition is improbable, impossible, imaginary, or contrary to known facts.
   If I **were** *the president of my country, I'd* **increase** *taxes.* (But it's not very likely that I will ever be the president.)
   If my mother **was** *still alive, she'd be very proud.* (But she's dead.)
   If Ted **needed** *money, I'd* **lend** *it to him.* (But he doesn't need it.)

2. *If I were you, I'd …* is used to give advice.
   If I were you, I'd *apologize to her.*
   I'd take it easy for a while **if I were you.**

3. When the condition is understood, it is common to find the result clause on its own.
   What would you do if you had lots of money?
   I'd **travel.**
   I'd **give** *it all* **away.**
   I'd **buy** *my mom and dad a nice house. They'd* **love** *that!*
   You'd **give away** *your last penny!*

4. *Would* can express preference.
   I'd love a cup of coffee.
   Where **would** *you like to sit?*
   I'd rather have coffee, please.
   I'd rather not tell you, if that's all right.
   What **would** *you rather do, stay in or go out?*

5. *Would* can express a request.
   Would *you open the door for me?*
   Would *you mind lending me a hand?*

9.3 First or second conditional?

Both conditionals refer to the present and future. The difference is about probability, not time. It is usually clear which conditional to use. First conditional sentences are real and possible. Second conditional sentences express situations that will probably never happen.
If I **lose** *my job, I'll …* (My company is doing badly. There is a strong possibility of being fired.)
If I **lost** *my job, I'd …* (I probably won't lose my job. I'm just speculating.)
If there **is** *a nuclear war, we'll all …* (Said by a pessimist.)
If there **was** *a nuclear war, we'd …* (But I don't think it will happen.)

9.4 Third conditional: impossible conditions

Form
if + Past Perfect, would + have + past participle

Positive
If I'd **(had)** *worked harder, I'd* **(would)** *have made more money.*
They'd **(would)** *have been here hours ago if they'd* **(had)** *followed my directions.*

Negative
If I hadn't seen it with my own eyes, I **wouldn't have believed** *it.*
If you'd **listened** *to me, you* **wouldn't have gotten** *lost.*

Question
What **would** *you* **have done** *if you'd* **been** *me?*
If the hotel **had been** *full, where* **would** *you* **have stayed?**

Use
We use the third conditional to express an impossible situation in the past and its probable result. It is too late! These things didn't happen.
If **she'd known** *he was cruel,* **she wouldn't have** *married him.*
My parents **wouldn't have met** *if they* **hadn't** *studied at Oxford University.*

9.5 might/could have done

Use

Might have done and *could have done* express possibilities in the past that didn't happen.
Thank goodness you went to hospital. You **might have died.**
She **could have married** *anyone she wanted.*

They are found in the result clauses of third conditional sentences.
If I'd told him I had no money, he **might have given** *me some.*
If I'd really wanted, I **could have been** *a professional golfer.*

Might have done and *could have done* can express criticism.
You **might have told** *me it was her birthday!*
She **could have helped** *clean the apartment instead of going out!*

9.6 should have done

Use

Should have done expresses advice for a past situation, but the advice is too late!
You **should have apologized.** *He wouldn't have been so angry.*
You **shouldn't have said** *she looked old. She really didn't like it.*

Should have done can express criticism.
You **should have asked** *me before you borrowed my car.*

UNIT 10

10.1 NOUN PHRASES

A noun phrase is a group of words before and/or after a noun.

$$book = \textbf{noun}$$

> *a book*
> *my book*
> *this book*
> *some books*
> *the book that I was reading*
> *my favorite book*

= **noun phrases**

Grammatically speaking, these words are:
articles – *the, a/an*
possessives – *my, your, his, her …*
demonstratives – *this, that, these, those*
determiners – *some, any, all, each, every …*
relative pronouns – *who, that, which …*
compound nouns – *notebook, address book …*

10.2 Articles

Indefinite articles
The indefinite articles *a/an* are used:

1. to say what something or somebody is.
   This is **a** *book.*   *I'm* **an** *optimist.*
   Jane's **a** *teacher.*   *He's* **an** *idiot.*

2. to refer to a thing or a person for the first time.
   She lives in **a** *farmhouse.*   *Can you lend me* **a** *pen?*
   He's going out with **a** *model.*   *Would you like* **a** *cookie?*
   I bought **a** *pair of shoes today.*

Definite article

The definite article *the* is used:

1. to refer to a person or a thing known to the speaker and the listener.
   *Do you have **the** car keys?*
   *The children are in **the** garden.*

2. to refer to a person or a thing for the second time.
   *I got **a** book and **a** computer for my birthday. **The** book is about modern art. I haven't unpacked **the** computer yet.*

3. when it is clear which one(s) we mean.
   *I'm going to **the** mall. Do you want anything?*
   *Dave's in **the** kitchen.*
   *Did you enjoy **the** party?*
   *What's **the** score?*
   *Have you heard **the** news?*
   *We went to **the** same school.*
   *I'll meet you on **the** corner.*

4. to refer to the only one there is.
   ***The** sky is very gray today.*
   ***The** earth is older than we think.*
   ***The** government in this country is awful.*
   ***The** French like bicycle races.*

5. to refer to things in our physical environment that we all know.
   *I love walking in **the country**.*
   *People always talk about **the weather**.*
   *We can see **the sea** from our house.*
   *We're going to **the movies** tonight.*

6. with superlatives.
   *You're **the best** teacher.*
   *He was **the first** boy I kissed.*

7. with some place names.
   ***the** United States of America*
   ***the** Eiffel Tower*
   ***the** Pyramids*
   ***the** British Museum*
   ***the** Empire State Building*

Zero article

No article (–) is used:

1. to refer to things or people in general.
   I like (–) cheese.
   (–) Doctors earn more than (–) teachers.
   I'm afraid of (–) dogs.
   (–) English is spoken all over the world.
   (–) Life is hard.

2. in some common expressions.
   places
   He's at (–) work. She's at (–) home in (–) bed.
   He's at (–) school. She's in (–) college.
   travel
   I travel by (–) car/bus/train …
   meals
   We had (–) lunch at 12:00.
   What do you want for (–) dinner?
   time
   I'll do it (–) next week.
   I saw her (–) last year.
   academic subjects
   I'm no good at (–) math.
   games
   I like (–) chess.

3. in some place names.
   I've traveled a lot in (–) Europe and (–) South America.
   I live on (–) Station Road.
   She studied at (–) Oxford University.
   We walked in (–) Central Park.
   We had lunch in (–) Carluccio's Restaurant.
   The plane left from (–) LaGuardia Airport.
   I'll meet you at (–) Penn Station.
   I climbed (–) Mount Everest.

10.3 Possessives

Possessive adjectives and pronouns

1. Possessive adjectives are used with a noun.
   *This is **my** brother.*
   *You should come and see **our** new house.*
   ***Their** teacher is new.*

2. The possessive pronouns are:

mine	yours	his	hers	ours	theirs

   They are used on their own.
   *Don't touch that! It's **mine**.*
   *Take it. It's **yours**.*
   *Can you bring those books? They're **ours**.*

Apostrophe *'s* and *s'*

1. *'s* is used with singular nouns.
   Lorna's dog
   Harry's girlfriend
   the boy's father (= one boy)
   "Whose is this?"   "It's my brother's."
   I have a week's vacation.

2. *s'* is used with regular plural nouns.
   my parents' house
   the boys' father (= more than one boy)
   For irregular plurals we use *'s*.
   the children's room
   Notice we use *'s* with two people.
   We were at Alan and Carol's house last night.

10.4 *all* and *every*

all

All can be used in different ways:

1. *all* + noun
   ***All** men are born equal.*
   *I like **all** kinds of music.*
   *I invited **all** the students in my class.*
   *I've loved the Beatles **all** my life.*

2. *all* + *of* + noun
   *I invited **all of** the students in my class.*
   *"How much did you eat?"   "**All of** it."*
   *"Who did she invite?"   "**All of** us."*

3. *all* + adjective/adverb/preposition
   *I'm **all wet**.*
   *She lives **all alone**.*
   *Tell me **all about** your vacation.*

4. pronoun + *all*
   *The sweets are for everyone. Don't eat **them all**.*
   *She loves **us all**.*

5. *all* + verb

We **all support** the team.
They have **all been** to college.
My friends **all love** you.

every

Every is used with a singular noun.
Every student in the class passed the exam.
I've been to **every country** in Asia.

all and *every*

1. *All* is not usually used to mean everybody/everything.
   All the people came to the party.   NOT   ~~All came …~~
   Everybody came to the party.
   She lost **all** her possessions in the fire.   NOT   ~~She lost all in …~~
   She lost **everything** in the fire.

2. *All* can mean everything, but only in relative clauses.
   All I want for breakfast is coffee.
   That's **all** I need.
   I've told you **all** I know.
   Love is **all** you need.

10.5 *themselves* and *each other*

Reflexive pronouns

1. Reflexive pronouns are:

myself	yourself	himself	herself
itself	ourselves	yourselves	themselves

2. We use reflexive pronouns when the subject and object are the same.
   I cut **myself** shaving.
   You could hurt **yourself**.
   I'm going to buy **myself** something nice.
   Make **yourselves** at home.
   I hope you're enjoying **yourself**.

3. They are used after prepositions.
   You should be ashamed **of yourself**.
   She looked **at herself** in the mirror.
   I live **by myself**.
   Selfish people only think **of themselves**.
   I can look **after myself**.

4. We use reflexive pronouns for emphasis.
   Do you like the cake? I made it **myself**.
   My daughter can dress **herself** now.
   The manager **himself** interviewed me.

each other

Each other expresses the idea of one to another.
They looked at **each other**.
We send **each other** birthday cards.
They hate **each other**.
We've known **each other** since childhood.

MODAL VERBS OF PROBABILITY

Modal auxiliary verbs can express ability, obligation, permission, and requests. They can also express probability, or how certain a situation is. There is an introduction to modal auxiliary verbs on page 133.

11.1 Probability in the present and future

1. *Must* and *can't* express the logical conclusion of a situation.
   must = logically probable
   can't = logically improbable
   We don't have all the facts, so we are not absolutely sure, but we are pretty certain.
   He **must** be exhausted. He hasn't slept for 24 hours!
   Sue **can't** have a ten-year-old daughter! She's only 24!
   He's in great shape, even though he **must** be at least 60!
   A walk in this weather! You **must** be joking!
   Aren't they answering? They **must** be in bed. They **can't** be out this late!

2. *May/might/could* express probability in the present or future. *May/might* + *not* is the negative. *Couldn't* is rare in this use.
   He **might** be lost.
   They **may** be stuck in traffic.
   You **could** win the lottery this week. Who knows?
   Dave and Beth aren't at home. They **could** be at the concert, I suppose.
   We **may** go to Greece for our vacation. We haven't decided yet.
   Take your umbrella. It **might** rain later.
   I **might not** be able to come tonight. I **might** have to work late.
   They **may not** know where we are.

3. The continuous infinitive is formed with *be* + *-ing*.
   You **must be joking**!
   They **can't** still **be eating**!
   Peter **might be working** late.
   They **may be coming** on a later train.
   I **could be sitting** on a beach right now.

11.2 Asking about possibilities

Question forms with modal verbs of probability are unusual. To ask about possibility/probability we usually use *Do you think …?*
"**Do you think** she's married?"
"She can't be."

"Where **do you think** he's from?"
"He might be Brazilian."

"**Do you think** they've arrived yet?"
"They may have. Or they might have gotten stuck in the traffic."

11.3 Probability in the past

1. The perfect infinitive is formed with *have* + past participle.
   He **must have caught** a later train.
   They **might have lost** our phone number.

2. These forms express degrees of probability in the past.
   He **must have been** exhausted.
   She **couldn't have told** him about us yet.
   The letter **may have gotten lost** in the mail.
   He **might have changed** his mind.
   They **could have moved**.

3. The continuous infinitive is formed with *have* + *been* + *-ing*.
   She must **have been joking**.
   They couldn't **have been trying** very hard.
   He could **have been lying** to you.

UNIT 12

12.1 Reported speech and thought

1. It is usual for the verb in the reported clause to move "one tense back" if the reporting verb is in the past tense (e.g. *said, told*).

   Present → Past
   Present Perfect → Past Perfect
   Past → Past Perfect
   will → *would*

   "**I'm going**." *He said he **was going**.*
   "**She's passed** her test." *He told me she **had passed** her test.*
   "My father **died** when I was six." *She said her father **had died** when she was six.*
   "I'll **see** you later." *She **said she'd** see me later.*

   The verb also moves "one tense back" when we are reporting thoughts and feelings.
   *I thought she **was** married, but she isn't.*
   *I didn't know he **was** a teacher. I thought he **worked** in a bank.*
   *I forgot you **were coming**. Never mind. Come in.*
   *I didn't realize you **were** here.*
   *I hoped you **would** call.*

2. There is no tense change if …

   … the reporting verb is in the present tense (*says*).
   "The train **will be** late." *He says the train **will be** late.*
   "I **come** from Korea." *She says she **comes** from Korea.*

   … the reported speech is about something that is still true.
   "Rain forests **are being destroyed**."
   *She told him that rain forests **are being destroyed**.*
   "I **hate** football."
   *I told him I **hate** football.*

3. Some modal verbs change.
   can → *could*
   will → *would*
   may → *might*

   "She **can** type well." *He told me she **could** type well.*
   "**I'll** help you." *She said she'd help me.*
   "I **may** come." *She said she **might** come.*

   Other modal verbs don't change.
   "You **should** go to bed." *He told me I **should** go to bed.*
   "It **might** rain." *She said she thought it **might** rain.*

   Must stays as *must*, or changes to *had to*.
   "I **must** go!" *He said he **must/had to** go.*

12.2 Reporting verbs

1. We rarely use *say* with an indirect object.
   She said she was going. NOT ~~She said to me …~~

2. *Tell* is always used with an indirect object in reported speech.

She told	me the doctor us her husband	the news.

3. We can use *that* after *say* and *tell*.
   *He told her (**that**) he would be home late.*
   *She said (**that**) sales were down from last year.*

4. Many verbs are more descriptive than *say* and *tell*, for example:

explain	promise	invite	insist	admit
complain	warn	offer	refuse	

   Sometimes we report the idea, rather than the actual words.
   "I'll lend you some money." *He offered to lend me some money.*
   "I won't help you." *She refused to help me.*

5. There are different verb patterns.
   verb + *sb* + infinitive
   *He **told me to go** away.*
   *They **asked me to teach** them English.*
   *I **invited her to come**.*
   *We **encouraged him to apply** for the job.*
   *She **reminded me to mail** her letter.*

   verb + infinitive
   *She **promised to help**.*
   *They **offered to lend** me some money.*

   verb + *that* + clause
   *He **explained that** he would be home late.*
   *She **complained that** she never had any free time.*
   *They **admitted that** sales were down that year.*
   *I **agreed that** it would be best to stop trying.*

6. We use *tell* for reported statements and reported commands, but the form is different.

   Reported statements
   *He **told** me **that** he was going.*
   *She **told** them **what** had been happening.*

   Reported commands
   *He **told** me **to** keep still.*
   *The police **told** people **to** move on.*

7. We use *ask* for reported commands and reported questions, but the form is different.

   Reported commands
   *He **asked** me **to** open my suitcase.*
   *She **asked** me **to** leave.*

   Reported questions
   *He **asked** me **what** I did for a living.*
   *She **asked** me **why** I had come.*

8. For negative commands, use *not* before *to*.
   *He told me **not to** tell anyone.*
   *The police warned people **not to** go out.*

12.3 Reported questions

1. The word order in questions is different in reported speech. There is no inversion of subject and auxiliary verb and there is no *do/does/did*.
   "Why have you come here?" *I asked her **why she had come** here.*
   "What time is it?" *He wants to know **what time it is**.*
   "Where do you live?" *She asked me **where I lived**.*

2. If there is no question word (*What, Who, Why, Where,* …), use *if* or *whether*.

She wants to know	if whether	she should wear a dress.

3. The rules are the same when we report questions that are thoughts.
   I didn't know what was happening.
   I wondered where she'd bought her dress.
   We couldn't understand what they were saying.

Extra Materials

EVERYDAY ENGLISH
Role play

4 Work with a partner. Act out the situations.

1. You are with an American friend when you meet another friend. Introduce them to each other.

2. You are in a coffee shop. You asked for a latte and a muffin, but the waiter has brought you an espresso and a piece of chocolate cake.

3. You are in a hotel. You call reception because the television in your room isn't working.

4. You are at the airport and you can't find the check-in desk for your flight to Bangkok. Ask at the information desk.

5. You are cooking for some friends. They're all hanging out in the living room and chatting. You want them to come to the table and help themselves to the food.

CD1 13 Listen and compare.

UNIT 2 *page 13*

4 Work in small groups. Look at the chart. Compare the correct answers with your ideas.

Which salaries do you think are unfair? Are any surprising?

Who earns how much in the U.S.?	
Doctor	$140,000
Basketball player	$1 million
Senior Director	$750,000
Nurse	$25,000
Supermarket cashier	$20,000
Pilot	$65,000
Police officer	$30,000
Teacher	$40,000
Lawyer	$200,000
Farmer	$48,000

READING – A Shakespearean tragedy

5 Read Shakespeare's lines from *Romeo and Juliet* in more modern English.

Romeo AND Juliet

1   **Tybalt**   Peace? I hate the word peace like I hate hell, all Montagues, and you.

2   **Romeo**   Did my heart ever love before now? Because I never saw true beauty before tonight.

       Juliet   The only man I love is the son of the only man I hate!

3   **Juliet**   Oh, Romeo, Romeo, why are you a Montague? Forget your father and give up your name. … What's a Montague anyway? … A rose would smell just as sweet if it was called any other name.

4   **Romeo**   I have fallen in love with the beautiful daughter of rich Capulet.

       Friar Laurence   This marriage may be lucky enough to turn the hatred between your families into pure love.

5   **Romeo**   Now, Tybalt, … Mercutio's soul is above our heads. Either you, or I, or both of us have to join him.

       Tybalt   You, wretched boy, are going with him now.

6   **Friar Laurence**   Take this small bottle and drink the liquid. No pulse or breath will show you are alive for forty-two hours.

       Juliet   Give it to me! Love will give me strength.

7   **Juliet**   Romeo, Romeo, Romeo! Here's a drink. I drink to you.

       Nurse   Oh, hateful day! There has never been so black a day as today. Oh, painful day!

8   **Romeo**   Eyes, look for the last time! Arms, make your last embrace! … Here's to my love! Oh, honest pharmacist! Your drugs work quickly. So I die with a kiss.

9   **Juliet**   What's this here? A cup, closed in my true love's hand? Poison, I see … I will kiss your lips. Some poison is still on your lips. Your lips are warm. Oh, happy dagger! Let me die!

10   **Prince**   There never was a more tragic story than the story of Juliet and her Romeo.

MODERN DILEMMAS

Readers ask, readers reply

2 Read the readers' questions and the complete replies.

1 A reader asks

How should I deal with my difficult and disagreeable neighbor? He is in the habit of dumping his garden waste along the public sidewalk between our two houses.

Jim T. via e-mail

(d) A reader replies

You have to act with self-control in a situation like this. I don't think you should confront him. Arguments between neighbors can get out of hand. If I were you, I'd quietly clean up his mess and keep the peace.

2 A reader asks

Is it OK to greet people with a "How are you?" In California (my home) it's considered friendly, but here in New York some people react with a cold look. Should I be less friendly in my greetings?

Erica Fleckberg, New York

(c) A reader replies

You don't have to be like New Yorkers just because you're in New York. Be yourself. Be warm. Be Californian.

3 A reader asks

My new PC automatically picks up wireless networks to gain access to the Internet. This includes the one belonging to my neighbor. Is it right for me to use it?

Richard Dalton, via e-mail

(g) A reader replies

You can stop others from accessing your wireless network if you use a password. You must tell your neighbor this. It's the only right thing to do.

4 A reader asks

My stepfather's driver's license was suspended for six months for speeding, but we have learned that he still drives over the speed limit all the time. Should we keep quiet or inform the police?

Stella Milne, Connecticut

(a) A reader replies

Your stepfather is not allowed to drive by law. He is a danger to himself and everyone else on the road. You must call "Crimestoppers" and report him. You don't have to give your name.

5 A reader asks

I am a medical student. After I graduate in June, I have one month before my first house job starts. My fiancée says that I am not allowed to claim unemployment benefits for this month. I disagree, because I'll be unemployed. The benefits are for all those who are out of work. What do you think?

J. R. Collin, via e-mail

(b) A reader replies

Your fiancée's right. You aren't allowed to claim unemployment benefits, but I think you are allowed other benefits. You should check online. Perhaps you should claim these benefits and give the money to charity, if you don't need it.

6 A reader asks

Is it wrong for me to record CDs borrowed from my local library? I am not denying anyone the money, as I wouldn't buy the CD anyway.

Pete Rodriguez, via e-mail

(e) A reader replies

It's not only wrong, it's illegal. You are not allowed to do this. You should buy the CD.

7 A reader asks

Is it ever permissible to lie to children? I lied to my two-year-old granddaughter to remove her from a fairground ride without a tantrum. I said: "You must get off now because the man is going to get his dinner." She got down without a fuss. But I'm worried that if she remembers this, she won't trust me in the future.

Barbara Hope, Philadelphia

(f) A reader replies

Not only should you lie sometimes, you often have to. Children should be treated with respect, but you don't have to explain everything. Also, it's a good way to learn that we often have to tell "white lies," such as when asked, "What do you think of my new boyfriend?" "Um—very nice."

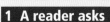

LISTENING AND SPEAKING
Rules for life

4 Work with a partner. Read the song and discuss which word fits best in each of the blanks.

I Believe
by Ian Dury & the Blockheads

I believe in _____ _____   **bottle banks / Citibank*
And beauty from within
I believe in saying _____   *hello / thanks*
And fresh _____ on the skin   *hair / air*

I believe in healthy _____   *walks / thoughts*
As tonic for the feet
I believe in serious talks
And _____ _____ to eat   *just enough / a lot*

Chorus
That's what I believe
Surprising as it seems
I believe that happiness
Is well within our dreams

I believe in being _____   *nice / polite*
In spite of what you think
I believe in good _____   *manners / advice*
And not too much to _____   *eat / drink*

I believe in being _____   *faithful / true*
In everything you try to _____   *do / say*
I believe in me and you
I hope you share my _____   *point of view / opinion*

Chorus

I believe in being _____   *generous / kind*
Especially when it's hard
I believe an open _____   *mind / door*
Can show a fine regard

I believe that _____ make   *manners / kindness*
A person good to know
I believe in birthday _____   *presents / cake*
And going _____   *in the snow / with the flow*

Chorus

That's what I believe
Although it seems naïve
I believe that _____   *happiness / peace and love*
Are there to be achieved
That's what I believe . . .

                  *Recycling bin

CD1 46 Listen and check.

WRITING – Telling a story

7 Compare your stories with the story below.

THE TROJAN HORSE

The Greeks and the Trojans had been at war for ten years.

The exhausted Greek army was camped outside the city of Troy when the Greek king Odysseus suddenly had a good idea. He knew that horses were sacred animals to the Trojans, so he decided to build a huge, hollow, wooden horse on wheels, a horse big enough for some of his soldiers to hide inside.

The horse was properly built and some of the soldiers climbed inside. The others set fire to the camp and pretended they were going to sail back home to Greece, defeated. In fact they hid nearby.

The Trojans, delighted that the Greeks had left, immediately came out of the city gates and found the horse. They were very curious indeed. As part of the plan, the Greeks had left behind one soldier hiding near the horse. The Trojans soon found him and asked him about the horse. He said it was an offering to the goddess Athena.

EVERYDAY ENGLISH — Objects

4 **CD3 18** Listen again. Which objects are being described?

1 ___ 2 ___ 3 ___ 4 ___ 5 ___ 6 ___ 7 ___ 8 ___ 9 ___

The Trojans tried to pull the huge horse into the city. However, it was so big that they had to tear down part of the city wall to get it in. They took it to the temple of Athena and had a big party to celebrate victory over the Greeks and the end of the war.

Finally, everyone was exhausted from all the festivities, and they fell asleep. Now the Greek soldiers crept out of the horse. They killed all the guards on the walls and then signaled to the Greeks on the other side to attack Troy.

There was a bloody battle, and the Greeks won easily. All the Trojan men were killed, and the women and children were taken back to Greece as slaves.

6 Work with a partner. Take turns describing some of the other objects. Point to what your partner describes.

They're made of metal. They're small. You use them to ...

Word List

Here is a list of most of the new words in the units of *American Headway* **Student Book 3.**

adj = **adjective**	*pl* = **plural**
adv = **adverb**	*prep* = **preposition**
conj = **conjunction**	*pron* = **pronoun**
coll = **colloquial**	*pp* = **past participle**
n = **noun**	*v* = **verb**
opp = **opposite**	

UNIT 1

archaeology *n* /arki'alədʒi/
area *n* /'ɛriə/
background *n* /'bækgraʊnd/
barrel *n* /'bærəl/
Basque *adj* /bæsk/
beat *v* /bit/
bilingual *adj* /ˌbaɪ'lɪŋgwəl/
block *n* /blak/
brief *v* /brif/
bright *adj* /braɪt/
cancellation *n* /ˌkænsə'leɪʃn/
cherish *v* /'tʃɛrɪʃ/
client *n* /'klaɪənt/
close-knit *adj* /kloʊsnɪt/
communal *adj* /kə'myunl/
community *n* /kə'myunəti/
cosmopolitan *adj* /ˌkazmə'palətn/
cracked *adj* /krækd/
culture *n* /'kʌltʃər/
daylight *n* /'deɪlaɪt/
demolition *n* /ˌdɛmə'lɪʃn/
destroy *v* /dɪ'strɔɪ/
dressmaker *n* /'drɛsmeɪkər/
earthquake *n* /'ərθkweɪk/
elderly *adj* /'ɛldərli/
end up *v* /ˌɛnd ʌp/
equator *n* /ɪ'kweɪtər/
extended family *n* /ɪk'stɛndɪd fæmli/
extinct *adj* /ɪk'stɪŋkt/
fee *n* /fi/
filling *n* /'fɪlɪŋ/
for good /fər gʊd/
forbid *v* /fər'bɪd/
frail *adj* /freɪl/
frugally *adv* /'frugəli/
global warming *n* /gloʊbl wɔrmɪŋ/
(not) go far /goʊ far/
go live *v* /goʊ lɪv/
go on about *v* /goʊ an ə'baʊt/
a great deal /eɪ greɪt dil/
headquarters *n* /'hɛdkwɔrtərz/
heritage *n* /'hɛrətɪdʒ/
hold *v* /hoʊld/
hopefully *adv* /'hoʊpfli/
hospitality *n* /ˌhaspə'tæləti/
iceberg *n* /'aɪsbərg/
immediate family *n* /ɪ'midiət fæmli/
kit *n* /kɪt/
life expectancy *v n* /laɪf ɪk'spɛktənsi/

make *v* /meɪk/
means *n* /minz/
motto *n* /'matoʊ/
muffin *n* /'mʌfən/
municipal *adj* /my'nɪsəpl/
neutral *adj* /'nutrəl/
nonsense *n* /'nansɛns/
noticeable *adj* /'noʊtəsəbl/
on the clock *n* /an ðə klak/
operator *n* /'apəreɪtər/
performance *n* /pə'fɔːməns/
pin number *n* /'pɪn nʌmbər/
policy *n* /'paləsi/
preschool *n* /'priskul/
prestigious *adj* /prɛ'stɪdʒəs/
presumably *adv* /prɪ'zuməbli/
profile *n* /'proʊfaɪl/
propaganda *n* /prapə'gændə/
provide *v* /prə'vaɪd/
pyjamas *n* /pə'dʒæməz/
raise *v* /reɪz/
reach *v* /ritʃ/
regret *n* /rɪ'grɛt/
research *n* /'risərtʃ/
settle down *v* /'sɛtl daʊn/
shortly *adv* /'ʃɔrtli/
similarity *n* /ˌsɪmə'lærəti/
slum *n* /slʌm/
storey *n* /'stɔri/
stressed *adj* /strɛst/
structure *n* /'strʌktʃər/
stuck *adj* /stʌk/
suburb *n* /'sʌbərb/
survey *n* /sər'veɪ/
take home *v* /teɪk hoʊm/
take out *v* /teɪk aʊt/
tricky *adj* /'trɪki/
ultimately *adv* /'ʌltəmətli/
urgent *adj* /'ərdʒənt/
vote *n/v* /voʊt/
well-balanced *adj* /wɛl'bælənst/
widely *adv* /'waɪdli/

UNIT 2

accomplish *v* /ə'kamplɪʃ/
actually *adv* /'æktʃuəli/
amazing *adj* /ə'meɪzɪŋ/
ambassador *n* /æm'bæsədər/
annual *adj* /'ænyuəl/
attend *v* /ə'tɛnd/
bake *v* /beɪk/
baking dish *n* /beɪkɪŋ dɪʃ/

banking *n* /'bæŋkɪŋ/
bargain *n* /'bargən/
be in touch /bi ɪn tʌtʃ/
(surf)board *n* /sərfbɔrd/
boarding school *n* /bɔrdɪŋ skul/
boil *v* /bɔɪl/
broadcaster *n* /'brɔdkæstər/
budget *n* /'bʌdʒət/
butler *n* /'bʌtlər/
buzz *n* /bʌz/
cash flow *n* /'kæʃ floʊ/
cashier *n* /kæ'ʃɪər/
catch up on *phr v* /kætʃ ʌp an/
challenging *adj* /'tʃæləndʒɪŋ/
charity *n* /'tʃærəti/
charming *adj* /'tʃarmɪŋ/
check *n* /tʃɛk/
chop *v* /tʃap/
concentrate *v* /'kansntreɪt/
concerned *adj* /kən'sərnd/
conservative *adj* /kən'sərvətɪv/
convenient *adj* /kən'vinyənt/
cope *v* /koʊp/
day off *n* /deɪ ɔf/
decent *adj* /'disənt/
deputy *n* /'dɛpyəti/
documentary *n* /ˌdakyə'mɛntəri/
drill *n* /drɪl/
dutiful *adj* /'dutɪfl/
duty *n* /'duti/
earn a living /ˌərn eɪ 'lɪvɪŋ/
earner *n* /'ərnər/
eccentric *adj* /ɪk'sɛntrɪk/
employee *n* /ɛm'plɔɪi/
engagement *n* /ɪn'geɪdʒmənt/
enormous *adj* /ɪ'nɔrməs/
expand *v* /ɪk'spænd/
extensively *adv* /ɪk'stɛnsɪvli/
extravagantly *adv* /ɪk'strævəgəntli/
ferry *n* /'fɛri/
fly by *v* /'flaɪ ˌbaɪ/
food processor *n* /ˌfud 'prasɛsər/
frustration *n* /frʌ'streɪʃn/
fry *v* /fraɪ/
get away from it all *v* /ˌgɛt ə'weɪ frəm ɪt ɔl/
goods *pl n* /gʊdz/
ground beef *n* /ˌgraʊnd bif/
handyman *n* /'hændimæn/
hardware *n* /'hardwɛr/
hard-working *adj* /ˌhard 'wərkɪŋ/
head of state *n* /ˌhɛd əv 'steɪt/
heir *n* /ɛr/
helmet *n* /'hɛlmət/

herb *n* /ərb/
honey *n* /'hʌni/
host *v* /hoʊst/
housekeeper *n* /'haʊskipər/
huge *adj* /hyudʒ/
human resources *n* /ˌhyumən 'risɔrsɪz/
hunting *n* /'hʌntɪŋ/
in charge /ɪn tʃardʒ/
in response to /ɪn rɪ'spans tə/
include *v* /ɪn'klud/
inconvenience *adj* /ˌɪnkən'vinyəns/
industry *n* /'ɪndəstri/
invoice *n* /'ɪnˌvɔɪs/
involve *v* /ɪn'valv/
land *v* /lænd/
laptop *n* /'læptap/
lavish *adj* /'lævɪʃ/
lifeguard *n* /'laɪfgard/
lifetime *n* /'laɪftaɪm/
lively *adj* /'laɪvli/
madly *adv* /'mædli/
maid *n* /meɪd/
managing director *n* /ˌmænɪdʒɪŋ də'rɛktər/
manufacture *v* /ˌmænyə'fæktʃər/
meditate *v* /'mɛdəteɪt/
memo *n* /'mɛmoʊ/
mild *adj* /maɪld/
mix *v* /mɪks/
modernize *v* /'madərnaɪz/
monarch *n* /'manərk/
negotiate *v* /nə'goʊʃieɪt/
occupy *v* /'akyəpaɪ/
organic *adj* /ɔr'gænɪk/
payment *n* /'peɪmənt/
peel *v* /pil/
personnel *n* /ˌpərsə'nɛl/
plant *v* /plænt/
politician *n* /palə'tɪʃn/
porter *n* /'pɔrtər/
portray *v* /pɔr'treɪ/
praise *v* /preɪz/
product *n* /'pradʌkt/
promote *v* /prə'moʊt/
qualification *n* /ˌkwaləfə'keɪʃn/
racket *n* /'rækət/
reception *n* /rɪ'sɛpʃn/
reckon *v* /'rɛkən/
recruit *v* /rɪ'krut/
redecorate *v* /ri'dɛkəreɪt/
ridiculous *adj* /rɪ'dɪkyələs/
roast *v* /roʊst/
sales *pl n* /seɪlz/
screwdriver *n* /'skrudraɪvər/
serve an ace *v* /sərv ən 'eɪs/
shift *n* /ʃɪft/
shooting *n* /'ʃutɪŋ/
situate *v* /sɪtʃueɪt/
sketch *v* /skɛtʃ/
small talk *n* /'smɔl tɔk/
soap *n* /soʊp/

socializer n /'soʊʃlaɪzər/
stay fit v /steɪ fɪt/
squeeze v /skwiz/
state n /steɪt/
stiff adj /stɪf/
support n /sə'pɔrt/
sweat v /swɛt/
sweetheart n /'swithɑrt/
tackle v /'tækl/
tantrum n /'tæntrəm/
tax n /tæks/
tell off v /ˌtɛl ɔf/
throne n /θroʊn/
trade n /treɪd/
training n /'treɪnɪŋ/
understanding n /ˌʌndər'stændɪŋ/
valet n /væ'leɪ/
VIP n /vi aɪ pi/
weed v /wid/
weigh v /weɪ/
well intentioned adj /wɛl ɪn'tɛnʃnd/
workforce n /'wərkfɔrs/
zoom n /zum/

UNIT 3

according to prep /ə'kɔrdɪŋ tə/
alliance n /ə'laɪəns/
apothecary n /ə'paθɪkɛri/
art dealer n /ɑrt 'dilər/
asylum n /ə'saɪləm/
ban v /bæn/
banish v /'bænɪʃ/
beg v /bɛg/
beloved adj /bɪ'lʌvd/
blind adj /blaɪnd/
bury v /'bɛri/
cemetery n /'sɛmətɛri/
clumsy adj /'klʌmzi/
collection n /kə'lɛkʃn/
comfort n /'kʌmfərt/
commit v /kə'mɪt/
dagger n /'dægər/
dawn n /dɔn/
declare v /dɪ'klɛr/
decline v /dɪ'klaɪn/
depression n /dɪ'prɛʃn/
despite prep /dɪ'spaɪt/
dismiss v /dɪs'mɪs/
donate v /'doʊneɪt/
dynasty n /'daɪnəsti/
electric adj /ɪ'lɛktrɪk/
embrace n /ɪm'breɪs/
enemy n /'ɛnəmi/
entire adj /ɪn'taɪər/
eternal adj /ɪ'tərnl/
exile v /'ɛksaɪl/
explode v /ɪk'sploʊd/
fair adj /fɛr/
fair enough adj /fɛr ɪ'nʌf/
fall in love v /fɔl ɪn lʌv/
farewell n /fɛr'wɛl/
fellow adj /'fɛloʊ/
feud n /fyud/
fiercely adv /'fɪrsli/

friar n /fraɪər/
funny adj /'fʌni/
genius n /'dʒinyəs/
glad adj /glæd/
go out v /goʊ 'aʊt/
go weak at the knees /goʊ wik ət θə niz/
grief n /grif/
hateful adj /'heɪtfll/
hatred n /'heɪtrəd/
(fall) head over heels /hɛd oʊvər 'hilz/
heavily adv /'hɛvɪli/
horrible adj /'hɔrəbl/
horrified adj /'hɔrəfaɪd/
identify v /aɪ'dɛntəfaɪ/
insane adj /ɪn'seɪn/
lifeless adj /'laɪfləs/
liquor n /'lɪkə(r)/
madness n /'mædnəs/
move v /muv/
nature n /'neɪtʃər/
nightmare n /'naɪtmɛr/
nobleman n /noʊblmən/
on the mend /ɑn ðə mɛnd/
overwhelmed adj /oʊvər'wɛlmd/
pay attention /ˌpeɪ ə'tɛnʃn/
peace n /pis/
pleasurable adj /'plɛʒərəbl/
poison n /'pɔɪzn/
porcelain n /'pɔrsələn/
precious adj /'prɛʃəs/
pretend v /prɪ'tɛnd/
priceless adj /'praɪsləs/
psychiatrist n /saɪ'kaɪətrɪst/
psychology n /saɪ'kɑlədʒi/
publish v /'pʌblɪʃ/
pulse n /pʌls/
quarrel n /'kwɔrəl/
rancour n /'ræŋkə(r)/
razor blade n /'reɪzər ˌbleɪd/
reciprocated adj /rɪ'sɪprəkeɪtɪd/
recognize v /'rɛkəgnaɪz/
regrettable adj /rɪ'grɛtəbl/
reject v /rɪ'dʒɛkt/
rescue v /'rɛskyu/
sense of humor n /sɛns əv 'hyumər/
a shame /eɪ ʃeɪm/
shiny adj /'ʃaɪni/
slip v /slɪp/
slow motion n /sloʊ moʊʃn/
soul n /soʊl/
stab v /stæb/
stuff n /stʌf/
stunned adj /stʌnd/
suicide n /'suəsaɪd/
swear v /swɛr/
tension n /'tɛnʃn/
testify v /'tɛstəfaɪ/
tight adj /taɪt/
tomb n /tum/
tragedy n /'trædʒədi/
tragic adj /'trædʒɪk/
treasure n /'trɛʒər/
unfortunate adj /ʌn'fɔrtʃənət/
uninvited adj /ˌʌnɪn'vaɪtəd/

unite v /yu'naɪt/
unrecognized adj /ʌn'rɛkəgnaɪzd/
upside down adj /ˌʌpsaɪd daʊn/
valuable adj /'vælyəbl/
vase n /veɪs/
vial n /vaɪəl/
voluntarily adv /'vɑləntɛrɪli/
warring adj /'wɔrɪŋ/
wed v /wɛd/
weep v /wip/
windowsill n /'wɪndoʊsɪl/
woe n /woʊ/
wretched adj /'rɛtʃəd/
yoga n /yoʊgə/

UNIT 4

access n /'æksɛs/
accessory n /ək'sɛsəri/
adjust v /ə'dʒʌst/
apparently adv /ə'pærəntli/
appreciate v /ə'priʃieɪt/
bargain n /'bɑrgən/
battered adj /'bætərd/
benefit n /'bɛnəfɪt/
borrow v /'bɑroʊ/
bottle bank n /'bɑtl bæŋk/
bring up v /ˌbrɪŋ 'ʌp/
chore n /tʃɔr/
claim v /kleɪm/
code n /koʊd/
confront v /kən'frʌnt/
consider v /kən'sɪdər/
council house n /'kaʊnsl ˌhaʊs/
cut off v /ˌkʌt 'ɔf/
deal with v /dil wɪð/
decorate v /'dɛkəreɪt/
demand n /dɪ'mænd/
dig v /dɪg/
dilemma n /də'lɛmə/
disagreeable adj /'dɪsə'griəbl/
discipline n /'dɪsəplɪn/
disqualify v /dɪs'kwɑləfaɪ/
domestic adj /də'mɛstɪk/
dump v /dʌmp/
electronic adj /ɪlɛk'trɑnɪk/
enter v /'ɛntər/
equipment n /ɪ'kwɪpmənt/
era n /'ɪrə/
fair adj /fɛr/
fiancée n /fi'ɑnseɪ/
freeze v /friz/
gadget n /'gædʒət/
gain v /geɪn/
get through v /ˌgɛt θru/
gift-wrap v /gɪft-ræp/
give in v /ˌgɪv 'ɪn/
go with the flow /goʊ wɪð ðə floʊ/
great-grandmother n /greɪt grænmʌðər/
greet v /grit/
hi-tech adj /haɪ-tɛk/
in spite of prep /ɪn'spaɪt əv/
iron v /aɪərn/
keep quiet v /kip kwaɪət/
lift n /lɪft/

make n /meɪk/
match n /mætʃ/
medical adj /'mɛdɪkl/
menace n /'mɛnəs/
military service n /'mɪlətɛri 'sərvəs/
missionary n /'mɪʃənɛri/
morals pl n /'mɔrəlz/
naïve adj /nɑ'iv/
open adj /'oʊpən/
optimist n /'ɑptəmɪst/
out of work /ˌaʊt əv 'wərk/
permissible adj /pər'mɪsəbl/
pessimist n /'pɛsəmɪst/
pick up v /ˌpɪk 'ʌp/
point of view n /ˌpɔɪnt əv vyu/
pump n /pʌmp/
punk n /pʌŋk/
push up v /poʊʃ ʌp/
put up with v /poʊt ʌp wɪð/
qualify v /'kwɑləfaɪ/
react v /ri'ækt/
regard n /rɪ'gɑrd/
remove v /rɪ'muv/
retell v /ˌri'tɛl/
row n /raʊ/
scary adj /'skɛri/
set an example /ˌsɛt ɪg'zæmpl/
set up v /ˌsɛt ʌp/
share v /ʃɛr/
spread v /sprɛd/
space station n /'speɪs ˌsteɪʃn/
stepfather n /'stɛpfɑðər/
strict adj /strɪkt/
strip v /strɪp/
stuck adj /stʌk/
suit v /sut/
take after v /ˌteɪk 'æftər/
take up v /ˌteɪk 'ʌp/
tear n /tɪr/
thrift n /θrɪft/
token n /'toʊkən/
tonic n /'tɑnɪk/
transform v /træns'fɔrm/
transport v /træn'spɔrt/
treat n /trit/
valuable adj /'vælyəbl/
Victorian adj /vɪk'tɔriən/
wardrobe n /'wɔrdroʊb/
wireless adj /'waɪərləs/
woodwork n /'wʊdwərk/

UNIT 5

addiction n /ə'dɪkʃn/
advance n /əd'væns/
alien n /'eɪliən/
amateur adj /'æmətʃər/
astronaut n /'æstrənɔt/
attitude n /'ætətud/
awareness n /ə'wɛrnəs/
beyond your wildest dreams /bɪ'yɑnd yər ˌwaɪldɪst 'drimz/
blackness n /'blæknɛs/
breakthrough n /'breɪkθru/
cause for concern /kɔz fər kən'sərn/
cell n /sɛl/

centenarian *n* /sɛntɪˈnɛriən/
confidently *adv* /ˈkanfədəntli/
confirmation *n* /kanfərˈmeɪʃn/
consciousness *n* /ˈkanʃəsnəs/
controversial *adj* /kantrəˈvərʃl/
cooking *n* /ˈkʊkɪŋ/
current *adj* /ˈkərənt/
curvature *n* /kərvətʃər/
cyber- /ˈsaɪbər/
damage *n* /ˈdæmɪdʒ/
diseased *adj* /dɪˈzizd/
disorder *n* /dɪsˈordər/
distribute *v* /dɪˈstrɪbyut/
drought *n* /draʊt/
emotion *n* /ɪˈmoʊʃn/
evacuate *v* /ɪˈvækyueɪt/
evidence *n* /ˈɛvədəns/
existence *n* /ɪgˈzɪstəns/
expand *v* /ɪkˈspænd/
expect (a baby) *v* /ɪkˈspɛkt/
expense *n* /ɪkˈspɛns/
extend *v* /ɪkˈstɛnd/
fiction *n* /ˈfɪkʃn/
fingers crossed /ˈfɪŋgərz krɔst/
flood *n* /flʌd/
forecast *n* /ˈfɔrkæst/
form *v* /fɔrm/
galaxy *n* /ˈgæləksi/
generate *v* /ˈdʒɛnəreɪt/
generation *n* /dʒɛnəˈreɪʃn/
get in *v* /ˌgɛt ˈɪn/
give birth *v* /ˌgɪv ˈbərθ/
glow *v* /gloʊ/
half-time *n* /ˌhæf ˈtaɪm/
heatwave *n* /hitweɪv/
hopeless *adj* /ˈhoʊpləs/
hurricane *n* /ˈhərəkən/
infinite *adj* /ˈɪnfənət/
injection *n* /ɪnˈdʒɛkʃn/
knowledge *n* /ˈnalɪdʒ/
laboratory *n* /ˈlæbrətori/
limb *n* /lɪm/
major *adj* /ˈmeɪdʒər/
mammal *n* /ˈmæml/
mankind *n* /mænˈkaɪnd/
marvel *n* /ˈmarvl/
melt *v* /mɛlt/
meteorologist *n* /mitiəˈra--lədʒɪst/
mission *n* /ˈmɪʃn/
nuclear energy *n* /ˈnukliər ˈɛnərdʒi/
orbit *n* /ˈorbət/
organ *n* /ˈorgən/
parallel *adj* /ˈpærəlɛl/
permafrost *n* /ˈpərməfrɔst/
pill *n* /pɪl/
presence *n* /ˈprɛzns/
primate *n* /ˈpraɪmeɪt/
prove *v* /pruv/
quote *n* /kwoʊt/
rainfall *n* /ˈreɪnfɔl/
rapidly *adv* /ˈræpədli/
realist *n* /ˈriəlɪst/
reassure *v* /riəˈʃur/
reduce *v* /rɪˈdus/
regenerate *v* /rɪˈdʒɛnəreɪt/
regrow *v* /rɪˈgroʊ/
replace *v* /rɪˈpleɪs/

research *v* /rɪˈsərtʃ/
resource *n* /ˈrisɔrs/
revulsion *n* /rɪˈvʌlʃn/
science fiction *n* /ˈsaɪəns fɪkʃn/
sensational *adj* /sɛnˈseɪʃnl/
sensor *n* /ˈsɛnsər/
sink into *v* /ˌsɪŋk ˈɪntu/
skydiving *n* /ˈskaɪdaɪvɪŋ/
snowstorm *n* /ˈsnoʊstorm/
spine *n* /spaɪn/
status *n* /ˈstætəs/
study *n* /ˈstʌdi/
suitable *adj* /ˈsutəbl/
supply *n* /səˈplaɪ/
take for granted /ˌteɪk fər ˈgræntəd/
task *n* /tæsk/
technical *adj* /ˈtɛknɪkl/
the norm *n* /ðə norm/
throughout *prep* /θruˈaʊt/
thunderstorm *n* /ˈθʌndərstorm/
transplantation *n* /ˌtrænsplænteɪʃn/
tropical *adj* /ˈtrapɪkl/
universe *n* /ˈyunəvers/
vertebrate *n* /ˈvərtəbrət/
vigorous *adj* /ˈvɪgərus/
virtual *adj* /ˈvərtʃuəl/
weightlessness *n* /ˈweɪtləsnɛs/

UNIT 6

appliance *n* /əˈplaɪəns/
associate *v* /əˈsoʊʃieɪt/
astronomy *n* /əˈstranəmi/
attractive *adj* /əˈtræktɪv/
badly behaved *adj* /bædli bɪˈheɪvd/
basement *n* /ˈbeɪsmənt/
battery *n* /ˈbætəri/
bomb *n* /bam/
bother *v* /ˈbaðər/
brightly *adv* /ˈbraɪtli/
button *n* /ˈbʌtn/
cashmere *n* /kæʒˈmɪr/
casual *adj* /ˈkæʒuəl/
cattle *n* /ˈkætl/
celebration *n* /sɛləˈbreɪʃn/
china *n* /ˈtʃaɪnə/
clearance *n* /ˈklɪrəns/
coach *n* /koʊtʃ/
consume *v* /kənˈsum/
cosmetics *pl n* /kazˈmɛtɪkz/
cozy *adj* /ˈkoʊzi/
cottage *n* /ˈkatɪdʒ/
crumble *v* /ˈkrʌmbl/
curiosity *n* /kyʊriˈasəti/
curly *adj* /ˈkərli/
dome *n* /doʊm/
dominant *adj* /ˈdamənənt/
drive sb crazy /ˌdraɪv sʌmbʌdi ˈkreɪzi/
emigrate *v* /ˈɛməgreɪt/
equipped *adj* /ɪˈkwɪpd/
file *n* /faɪl/
fluently *adv* /ˈfluəntli/
full-time *adj* /ˌfʊlˈtaɪm/
fully *adv* /ˈfʊli/
garlic *n* /ˈgarlɪk/
get together *v* /gɛt təˈgɛðər/
gigabyte *n* /ˈgɪgəbaɪt/
glassware *n* /ˈglæswɛr/
good-looking *adj* /ˌgʊdˈlʊkɪŋ/
gravitate *v* /ˈgrævəteɪt/
guarantee *n* /ˌgærənˈti/
handmade *adj* /ˌhændˈmeɪd/
handy *adj* /ˈhændi/
hard disk *n* /ˌhard ˈdɪsk/
hard-working *adj* /ˌhard ˈwɜːkɪŋ/
homecomings *n* /ˈhoʊmkʌmɪŋz/
housewife *n* /ˈhaʊswaɪf/
hut *n* /hʌt/
hyperactive *adj* /ˌhaɪpərˈæktɪv/
immense *adj* /ɪˈmɛns/
in tune with /ˌɪn ˈtun wɪð/
independent *adj* /ɪndɪˈpɛndənt/
ingredient *n* /ɪnˈgridiənt/
insecure *adj* /ɪnsəˈkyʊr/
irreplaceable *adj* /ˌɪrɪˈpleɪsəbl/
kitchenware *n* /ˈkɪtʃənwɛr/
lentils *pl n* /ˈlɛntlz/
like oil and vinegar /laɪk ɔɪl ənd ˈvɪnɪgər/
linen *n* /ˈlɪnɪn/
long-lasting *adj* /lɔŋˈlæstɪŋ/
low-fat *adj* /loʊ ˈfæt/
loyalty *n* /ˈlɔɪəlti/
massage *n* /məˈsɑʒ/

medium height *n* /ˈmidiəm ˌhaɪt/
mud *n* /mʌd/
nightlife *n* /ˈnaɪtlaɪf/
orchard *n* /ˈortʃərd/
painkiller *n* /ˈpeɪnkɪlə(r)/
panoramic *adj* /ˌpænəˈræmɪk/
paradise *n* /ˈpærədaɪs/
practical *adj* /ˈpræktɪkl/
premises *pl n* /ˈprɛməsəz/
pre-packed *adj* /ˌpriˈpækt/
prosecute *v* /ˈprasəkyut/
purchase *v* /ˈpərtʃəs/
rabbit *n* /ˈræbət/
remind *v* /rɪˈmaɪnd/
responsible *adj* /rɪˈspansəbl/
restore *v* /rɪˈstor/
safety *n* /ˈseɪfti/
seek *v* /sik/
sell out *v* /ˌsɛl ˈaʊt/
sentimental *adj* /sɛntəˈmɛntl/
shelter *n* /ˈʃɛltər/
simply *adv* /ˈsɪmpli/
sociable *adj* /ˈsoʊʃəbl/
solid *adj* /ˈsaləd/
staff *n* /stæf/
stationery *n* /ˈsteɪʃnɛri/
stone *n* /stoʊn/
subscribe *v* /səbˈskraɪb/
take-out *adj* /ˈteɪk-aʊt/
tempting *adj* /ˈtɛmptɪŋ/
terrace *n* /ˈtɛrəs/
think straight /ˈθɪŋk ˌstreɪt/
tiny *adj* /ˈtaɪni/
toiletries *pl n* /ˈtɔɪlətriz/
top floor *n* /tap ˌflor/
treasure *v* /ˈtrɛʒər/
turmeric *n* /ˈtʊrmərɪk/
wavy *adj* /ˈweɪvi/
wear *n* /wɛr/
wedding *n* /ˈwɛdɪŋ/
well behaved *adj* /ˌwɛl bɪˈheɪvd/
well dressed *adj* /ˌwɛl ˈdrɛst/
whisper *v* /ˈwɪspər/
young at heart /ˌyʌŋ ət hart/

UNIT 7

accustomed *adj* /əˈkʌstəmd/
agreement *n* /əˈgrimənt/
apply for *v* /əˈplaɪ fər/
be fond of *v* /bi ˈfand əv/
best-selling *adj* /bɛstˈsɛlɪŋ/
chamber *n* /ˈtʃeɪmbər/
chaos *n* /ˈkeɪas/
common *adj* /ˈkamən/
contact *v* /ˈkantækt/
continent *n* /ˈkantənənt/
copy *n* /ˈkapi/
countless *adj* /ˈkaʊntləs/
create *v* /kriˈeɪt/
deathly *adj* /ˈdɛθli/
decade *n* /ˈdɛkeɪd/
demanding *adj* /dɪˈmændɪŋ/
dominate *v* /ˈdaməneɪt/
don't mind *v* /ˌdoʊnt ˈmaɪnd/
doubles *pl n* /ˈdʌblz/
downpour *n* /ˈdaʊnpɔr/
due *adj* /du/
elect *v* /ɪˈlɛkt/
enthusiastic *adj* /ɪnθuziˈæstɪk/
eternity *n* /ɪˈtərnəti /
euphoria *n* /yuˈfɔriə/
fail *v* /feɪl/
fan *n* /fæn/
female *n* /ˈfimeɪl/
fine *adj* /faɪn/
gifted *adj* /ˈgɪftəd/
goblet *n* /ˈgablɪt/
ground *n* /graʊnd/
hallow *n* /ˈhæloʊ/
harmony *n* /ˈharməni/
have a *word* *v* /həv eɪ wərd/
heated *adj* /ˈhitəd/
hero *n* /ˈhiroʊ/
horseback riding *n* /ˈhɔrsbæk
  raɪdɪŋ/
image *n* /ˈɪmɪdʒ/
infectious *adj* /ɪnˈfɛkʃəs/
institute *n* /ˈɪnstətut/
introduce *v* /ɪntrəˈdus/
invest *v* /ɪnˈvɛst/
launch *v* /lɔːntʃ/
lifestyle *n* /ˈlaɪfstaɪl/
loathe *v* /loʊð/
longhand *n* /ˈlɔŋhænd/
make your mark *v* /ˌmeɪk yər
  mark/
male *n* /meɪl/
measles *n* /ˈmizlz/
medieval *adj* /mɛdˈivl/
mob *n* /mab/
musical *n* /ˈmyuzɪkl/
myth *n* /mɪθ/
name *v* /neɪm/
numerous *adj* /ˈnumərəs/
obsession *n* /əbˈsɛʃn/
once and for all /ˌwʌns ənd fər ˈɔl/
orphan *n* /ˈɔrfən/
passionate *adj* /ˈpæʃnət/
philosopher *n* /fəˈlasəfər/
phoenix *n* /ˈfiːnɪks/
poverty *n* /ˈpavərti/

producer *n* /prəˈdusər/
psychological *adj* /saɪkəˈladʒɪkl/
public school *n* /ˌpʌblɪk ˈskul/
regular *adj* /ˈrɛgyələr/
resign *v* /rɪˈzaɪn/
respond *v* /rɪˈspand/
rivalry *n* /ˈraɪvlri/
slow down *v* /sloʊ ˈdaʊn/
snap up *v* /ˌsnæp ˈʌp/
soccer *n* /ˈsakər/
socialite *n* /ˈsoʊʃəlaɪt/
sort out *v* /ˌsɔrt ˈaʊt/
stage *n* /steɪdʒ/
statistics *n pl* /stəˈtɪstɪks/
strike *n* /straɪk/
sympathy *n* /ˈsɪmpəθi/
talent *n* /ˈtælənt/
tattoo *n* /tæˈtu/
the big time /ðə ˈbɪg ˌtaɪm/
to the fullest /tə ðə ˈfʊlɛst/
totally *adv* /ˈtoʊtli/
track *n* /træk/
trademark *n* /ˈtreɪdmark/
try one's luck /traɪ wʌnz ˈlʌk/
underwear *n* /ˈʌndərwɛr/
video game *n* /ˈvɪdioʊ ˌgeɪm/
violent *adj* /ˈvaɪələnt/
wizard *n* /ˈwɪzərd/

UNIT 8

approach *v* /əˈproʊtʃ/
ascent *n* /əˈsɛnt/
base *n* /beɪs/
battle *n* /ˈbætl/
bite *v* /baɪt/
blow *v* /bloʊ/
blow up *v* /ˌbloʊ ˈʌp/
body language *n* /ˈbadi læŋgwɪdʒ/
bold *adj* /boʊld/
bunk bed *n* /ˌbʌŋk ˈbɛd/
canoe *n* /kəˈnu/
catapult *v* /ˈkætəpʌlt/
clap *v* /klæp/
cliff *n* /klɪf/
conquer *v* /ˈkaŋkər/
crew *n* /kru/
cross *v* /krɔs/
crossing *n* /ˈkrɔsɪŋ/
cure *v* /kyʊr/
dare *v* /dɛr/
daring *adj* /ˈdɛrɪŋ/
declare *v* /dɪˈklɛr/
defeat *v* /dɪˈfit/
defeat *n* /dɪˈfit/
DIY *n* /ˌdi aɪ ˈwaɪ/
DNA *n* /ˌdi ɛn ˈeɪ/
empire *n* /ˈɛmpaɪər/
face *v* /feɪs/
fearless *adj* /ˈfɪrləs/
ferry *v* /ˈfɛri/
fighter *n* /ˈfaɪtər/
force *v* /fɔrs/
found *v* /faʊnd/
freak out *v* /frik aʊt/
gene *n* /dʒin/
get out of hand *v* /gɛt aʊt əv
  ˈhænd/
go over someone's head *v*
  /goʊ oʊvər ... hɛd/
have a sweet tooth *v* /hæv eɪ
  ˌswit ˈtuθ/
hit a snag *v* /ˌhɪt eɪ snæg/
hollow *adj* /ˈhaloʊ/
hug *v* /hʌg/
iceberg *n* /ˈaɪsbərg/
illiterate *adj* /ɪˈlɪtərət/
infection *n* /ɪnˈfɛkʃn/
initially *adv* /ɪˈnɪʃli/
innocent *adj* /ˈɪnəsnt/
install *v* /ɪnˈstɔl/
kneel *v* /nil/
lack *n* /læk/
ladder *n* /ˈlædər/
leadership *n* /ˈlidərʃɪp/
lick *v* /lɪk/
lifeboats *n* /ˈlaɪfboʊts/
lower *v* /ˈloʊər/
maiden voyage *n* /ˌmeɪdn ˈvɔɪɪdʒ/
manpower *n* /ˈmænpaʊər/
military *adj* /ˈmɪlətɛri/
nail *n* /neɪl/
numerous *adj* /ˈnumərəs/
overcome *v* /oʊvərˈkʌm/
overweight *adj* /oʊvərˈweɪt/
oxygen *n* /ˈaksɪdʒən/

oyster *n* /ˈɔɪstər/
panic *v* /ˈpænɪk/
pass *n* /pæs/
perish *v* /ˈpɛrɪʃ/
phobia *n* /ˈfoʊbiə/
pitch-black *adj* /ˌpɪtʃ ˈblæk/
plain *n* /pleɪn/
playground *n* /ˈpleɪgraʊnd/
poisonous *adj* /ˈpɔɪznəs/
pray *v* /preɪ/
program *n* /ˈproʊgræm/
prosperous *adj* /ˈpraspərəs/
province *n* /ˈpravəns/
psychotherapist *n*
  /saɪkoʊˈθɛrəpɪst/
pull someone's leg *v* /ˌpʊl ... ˈlɛg/
put up *v* /ˌpʊt ˈʌp/
raft *n* /ræft/
recognize *v* /ˈrɛkəgnaɪz/
reduce *v* /rɪˈdus/
remain *v* /rɪˈmeɪn/
remarkable *adj* /rɪˈmarkəbl/
remote *adj* /rɪˈmoʊt/
revolutionary *adj* /ˌrɛvəˈluʃənɛri/
rule *v* /rul/
scar *n* /skar/
scratch *v* /skrætʃ/
see eye to eye *v* /si ˌaɪ tu ˈaɪ/
set off *v* /set ˈɔf/
sickness *n* /ˈsɪknəs/
silly *adj* /ˈsɪli/
slide *v* /slaɪd/
slip *v* /slɪp/
snorkel *n* /ˈsnɔrkl/
soldier *n* /ˈsoʊldʒər/
stack *n* /stæk/
stare *v* /stɛr/
steerage *n* /ˈstɪrɪdʒ/
struggle *v* /ˈstrʌgl/
suffer *v* /ˈsʌfər/
sumptuous *adj* /ˈsʌmptʃuəs/
superior *adj* /səˈpɪriər/
swallow *v* /ˈswaloʊ/
sweaty *adj* /ˈswɛti/
symptom *n* /ˈsɪmptəm/
tear down *phr v* /tɪr ˈdaʊn/
terrified *adj* /ˈtɛrəfaɪd/
terror *n* /ˈtɛrər/
threaten *v* /ˈθrɛtn/
trek *n* /trɛk/
tribesmen *n pl* /ˈtraɪbzmɛn/
tune *n* /tun/
unbelievable *adj* /ˌʌnbɪˈliːvəbl/
unsinkable *adj* /ʌnˈsɪŋkəbl/
waste your breath *v* /ˌweɪst yər
  brɛθ/
whistle *v* /ˈwɪsl/

UNIT 9

action-packed *adj* /'ækʃn pækt/
ages *pl n* /'eɪdʒɪz/
arrest *v* /ə'rɛst/
ashamed *adj* /ə'ʃeɪmd/
balance *n* /'bæləns/
bear with *v* /'bɛr wɪð/
blood *n* /blʌd/
bother *v* /'baðər/
brainstorm *v* /'breɪnstɔrm/
buddy *n* /'bʌdi/
bully *v* /'bʊli/
bump into *v* /ˌbʌmp 'ɪntu/
burglary *n* /'bərgləri/
clean up *v* /ˌkliːn 'ʌp/
clear *v* /klɪr/
convict *v* /kən'vɪkt/
counselor *n* /'kaʊnsələr/
curious *adj* /'kyʊriəs/
determined *adj* /dɪ'tərmənd/
digit *n* /'dɪdʒɪt/
dozen *n* /'dʌzn/
dysfunctional *adj* /dɪs'fʌŋkʃənl/
economize *v* /ɪ'kɑnəmaɪz/
effective *adj* /ɪ'fɛktɪv/
eldest *adj* /'ɛldəst/
encounter *n* /ɪn'kaʊntər/
enter *v* /'ɛntər/
explode *v* /ɪk'sploʊd/
faceless *adj* /'feɪsləs/
find fault *v* /ˌfaɪnd 'fɔlt/
fraud *n* /frɔd/
get through to *v* /ˌgɛt 'θru tu/
grin *v* /grɪn/
gym *n* /dʒɪm/
hand over *v* /ˌhænd oʊvər/
head teacher *n* /ˌhɛd 'titʃər/
heroin *n* /'hɛroʊən/
hit rock bottom /hɪt ˌrɑk bɑtəm/
homeless *adj* /'hoʊmləs/
imprisonment *n* /ɪm'prɪznmənt/
in touch /ɪn 'tʌtʃ/
jail *v* /dʒeɪl/
knock over *v* /nɑk oʊvər/
letter box *n* /lɛtər bɑks/
light *v* /laɪt/
limit *n* /'lɪmət/
litter bin *n* /'lɪtər bɪn/
locate *v* /loʊkeɪt/
make a scene *v* /ˌmeɪk ə 'sin/
mind your own business /ˌmaɪnd
  yər oʊn 'bɪznəs/
ordinary *adj* /'ɔrdnɛri/
outburst *n* /'aʊtbərst/
overdrawn *adj* /ˌoʊvər 'drɔn/
passer-by *n* /pæsərbaɪ/
penniless *adj* /'pɛnɪləs/
phone in *v* /ˌfoʊn 'ɪn/
prison *n* /'prɪzn/
protect *v* /prə'tɛkt/
punishment *n* /'pʌnɪʃmənt/
purpose *n* /'pərpəs/
pursue *v* /pər'su/
receipt *n* /rɪ'sit/
register *v* /'rɛdʒəstər/
rehabilitate *v* /riə'bɪləteɪt/
release *v* /rɪ'lis/
relieved *adj* /rɪ'livd/
restorative justice *n* /rɪˌstɔrətɪv
  dʒʌstəs/
rude *adj* /rud/
scruffy *adj* /'skrʌfi/
shop-lift *v* /'ʃɑplɪft/
social worker *n* /soʊʃl wərkər/
stitch *n* /stɪtʃ/
stop dead *v* /stɑp dɛd/
storm off *v* /stɔrm ɔf/
stuff *v* /stʌf/
stunned *adj* /stʌnd/
suspect *n* /sə'spɛkt/
temperature *n* /'tɛmprətʃər/
theft *n* /θɛft/
timid *adj* /'tɪməd/
tremble *v* /'trɛmbl/
urban *adj* /'ərbən/
VAT *n* /ˌvi: eɪ 'ti:/
victim *n* /'vɪktəm/
violence *n* /'vaɪələns/

UNIT 10

amenity *n* /ə'mɛnəti/
ancestor *n* /'æncɛstər/
appear *v* /ə'pɪr/
arch *n* /ɑrtʃ/
basically *adv* /'beɪsɪkli/
bronze *adj* /brɑnz/
calculation *n* /kælkyə'leɪʃn/
capacity *n* /kə'pæsəti/
censorship *n* /'sɛnsərʃɪp/
chairman *n* /'tʃɛrmən/
code *n* /koʊd/
commerce *n* /'kɑmərs/
complex *adj* /'kəm'plɛks/
crystal *adj* /'krɪstl/
daily *adv* /'deɪli/
decoration *n* /dɛkə'reɪʃn/
democracy *n* /dɪ'mɑkrəsi/
depict *v* /dɪ'pɪkt/
device *n* /dɪ'vaɪs/
diagnose *v* /daɪəg'noʊs/
digital *adj* /'dɪdʒətl/
distinctive *adj* /dɪs'tɪŋktɪv/
district *n* /'dɪstrɪkt/
efficient *adj* /ɪ'fɪʃnt/
error *n* /'ɛrər/
ethnic group *n* /ɛθnɪk grup/
facilities *pl n* /fə'sɪlətiz/
feat *n* /fit/
feature *n* /'fitʃər/
float *v* /floʊt/
found *v* /faʊnd/
gig *n* /gɪg/
glide *v* /glaɪd/
haircut *n* /'hɛrkʌt/
halt *n* /hɔlt/
handcuffs *pl n* /'hændkʌfs/
headlight *n* /'hɛdlaɪt/
headphones *pl n* /'hɛdfoʊnz/
headquarters *pl n* /'hɛdkwɔrtərz/
headway *n* /'hɛdweɪ/
homemade *adj* /hoʊm'meɪd/
influence *n* /'ɪnfluəns/
instantly *adv* /'ɪnstəntli/
laundry *n* /'lɔndri/
log onto *v* /lɔg ɑntə/
major *adj* /'meɪdʒə(r)/
motorcycle *n* /'moʊtərsaɪkl/
mouth (of a river) *n* /maʊθ əv
  eɪ rɪvər/
newsagent *n* /nuzeɪdʒənt/
nickname *n* /'nɪkneɪm/
online dating *n* /ɑn'laɪn 'deɪtɪŋ/
onscreen *n* /ɑnskrin/
operate *v* /'ɑpəreɪt/
outdated *adj* /ˌaʊt'deɪtɪd/
penthouse *n* /'pɛnthaʊs/
perfectly *adv* /'pərfɪktli/
plumbing *n* /'plʌmɪŋ/
poster *n* /'poʊstər/
print *v* /prɪnt/
programmable *adj* /'proʊgræməbl/
real estate agent *n* /ril ɪ'steɪt
  'eɪdʒənt/
remote *n* /rɪ'moʊt/
sharp *adj* /ʃɑrp/

silicon *n* /'sɪlɪkən/
skateboarding *n* /skeɪtbɔrdɪŋ/
skyline *n* /'skaɪlaɪn/
social networking *n* /soʊʃl
  nɛtwərkɪŋ/
span *n* /spæn/
stick *v* /stɪk/
sticky *adj* /'stɪki/
storage *n* /'stɔrɪdʒ/
supply *v* /sə'plaɪ/
surface *n* /'sərfəs/
surgeon *n* /'sərdʒən/
switch *v* /swɪtʃ/
trace *v* /treɪs/
traffic jam *n* /'træfɪk ˌdʒæm/
traffic lights *pl n* /'træfɪk ˌlaɪts/
transfer *v* /trænsfər/
transistor *n* /træn'zɪstər/
treat *v* /trit/
undivided *adj* /ˌʌndɪ'vaɪdɪd/
wallpaper *n* /'wɔlpeɪpər/
wool *n* /wʊl/
wrapping paper *n* /'ræpɪŋ ˌpeɪpər/

UNIT 11

acquaintance *n* /əˈkweɪntns/
afford *v* /əˈfɔrd/
agitated *adj* /ˈædʒəteɪtəd/
anniversary *n* /ˌænɪˈvərsəri/
apparently *adv* /əˈpærəntli/
available *adj* /əˈveɪləbl/
battery *n* /ˈbætəri/
bird-brained *adj* /ˈbərd-breɪnd/
break out of *v* /ˌbreɪk ˈaʊt əv/
break up *v* /ˌbreɪk ˈʌp/
bruise *n* /bruz/
candlestick *n* /ˈkændlstɪk/
chimpanzee *n* /ˌtʃɪmpænˈzi/
clue *n* /klu/
come up with *v* /kʌm ˈʌp wɪð/
cricket *n* /ˈkrɪkət/
crow *n* /kroʊ/
culprit *n* /ˈkʌlprət/
dehydrate *v* /ˌdihaɪˈdreɪt/
dot *n* /dat/
dump *v* /dʌmp/
eat out *v* /ˌit ˈaʊt/
eat up *v* /ˌit ˈʌp/
elementary *adj* /ˌɛləˈmɛntəri/
eyesight *n* /ˈaɪsaɪt/
fall out *v* /ˌfɔl ˈaʊt/
feather *n* /ˈfɛðər/
gamble *v* /ˈgæmbl/
have around *v* /həv əˈraʊnd/
hopefully *adv* /ˈhoʊpfli/
identical *adj* /aɪˈdɛntɪkl/
impatiently *adv* /ɪmˈpeɪʃntli/
intruder *n* /ɪnˈtrudər/
investigation *n* /ɪnˌvɛstəˈgeɪʃn/
irritably *adv* /ˈɪrətəbli/
jelly *n* /ˈdʒɛli/
lecture *n* /ˈlɛktʃər/
liar *n* /ˈlaɪə(r)/
lightning *n* /ˈlaɪtnɪŋ/
lightning conductor *n* /ˈlaɪtnɪŋ
  kənˈdʌktər/
long jump *n* /ˈlɔŋ dʒʌmp/
look like *v* /ˈlʊk ˌlaɪk/
lottery *n* /ˈlatəri/
lump *n* /lʌmp/
make sth up *v* /ˌmeɪk ... ʌp/
make up (w sb) *v* /ˌmeɪk ʌp .../
mimic *v* /ˈmɪmɪk/
motive *n* /ˈmoʊtɪv/
naturally *adv* /ˈnætʃrəli/
No kidding! /ˌnoʊ ˈkɪdɪŋ/
obviously *adv* /ˈabviəsli/
on tiptoe /an ˈtɪptoʊ/
optical illusion *n* /ˈaptɪkl ɪˈluʒn/
oversleep *v* /ˌoʊvərˈslip/
parrot *n* /ˈpærət/
personally *adv* /ˈpərsənəli/
presumably *adv* /prɪˈzuməbli/
promote *v* /prəˈmoʊt/
radar *n* /ˈreɪdɑr/
really *adv* /ˈrili/
reflect *v* /rɪˈflɛkt/
refuse *v* /rɪˈfyuz/
responsible *adj* /rɪˈspansəbl/
save up *v* /ˌseɪv ˈʌp/

scandal *n* /ˈskændl/
shrink *v* /ʃrɪŋk/
skyscraper *n* /ˈskaɪskreɪpər/
snowflake *n* /ˈsnoʊfleɪk/
sole *n* /soʊl/
solve *v* /salv/
sort out *v* /sɔrt ˈaʊt/
spare *v* /spɛr/
spike *n* /spaɪk/
strike *v* /straɪk/
suspicious *adj* /səˈspɪʃəs/
take up *v* /ˌteɪk ˈʌp/
threshold *n* /ˈθrɛʃhoʊld/
to be honest /tə bi anəst/
translation *n* /trænzˈleɪʃn/
trick *n* /trɪk/
tutor *n* /tutər/
undoubtedly *adv* /ʌnˈdaʊtədli/
unplug *v* /ˌʌnˈplʌg/
work out *v* /ˌwərk ˈaʊt/
work sth out *v* /ˌwərk .... ˈaʊt/
wobbly *adj* /ˈwabli/
zillions *pl n* /ˈzɪlyənz/

UNIT 12

abandon *v* /əˈbændən/
absurd *adj* /əbˈsərd/
accuse *v* /əˈkyuz/
adapt *v* /əˈdæpt/
adolescent *adj* /ˌædəˈlɛsnt/
agnostic *n* /ægˈnastɪk/
alienate *v* /ˈeɪlyəneɪt/
angle *n* /ˈæŋgl/
auction *n* /ˈɔkʃn/
bid *n* /bɪd/
bulk *n* /bʌlk/
chain *v* /tʃeɪn/
charge *v* /tʃardʒ/
clinic *n* /ˈklɪnɪk/
concept *n* /ˈkansɛpt/
conditions *pl n* /kənˈdɪʃnz/
contradict *v* /ˌkantrəˈdɪkt/
contrary to *adj* /ˈkantrɛri tu/
descended from *v* /dɪˈsɛndɪd frəm/
disorder *n* /dɪsˈɔrdər/
encourage *v* /ɪnˈkərɪdʒ/
equality *n* /ɪˈkwaləti/
evolve *v* /ɪˈvalv/
ex- /ɛks/
existence *n* /ɪgˈzɪstəns/
expert *n* /ˈɛkspərt/
force-feeding *n* /ˌfɔrs ˈfidɪŋ/
gossip *v* /ˈgasəp/
healer *n* /ˈhilər/
heresy *n* /ˈhɛrəsi/
heretical *adj* /hɛˈrɛtɪkl/
highs and lows *pl n* /ˌhaɪz ənd
  loʊz /
hip *n* /hɪp/
hunger strike *n* /ˈhʌŋgərˌstraɪk/
hurl *v* /hərl/
hysterical *adj* /hɪˈstɛrɪkl/
in the public eye /ɪn ðə ˌpʌblɪk ˈaɪ/
incapable *adj* /ɪnˈkeɪpəbl/
indifferent *adj* /ɪnˈdɪfrənt/
individually *adv* /ˌɪndəˈvɪdʒuəli/
influential *adj* /ˌɪnfluˈɛnʃl/
insoluble *adj* /ɪnˈsalyəbl/
irresponsible *adj* /ˌɪrɪˈspansəbl/
ketchup *n* /ˈkɛtʃəp/
law-breaker *n* /ˈlɔw-breɪkər/
mediocre *adj* /ˌmidiˈoʊkər/
meditate *v* /ˈmɛdəteɪt/
mesmerize *v* /ˈmɛzməraɪz/
method *n* /ˈmɛθəd/
migraine *n* /ˈmaɪgreɪn/
militant *adj* /ˈmɪlətənt/
motivation *n* /ˌmoʊtəˈveɪʃn/
natural selection *n* /ˌnætʃərəl
  səˈlɛkʃn/
notion *n* /ˈnoʊʃn/
observe *v* /əbˈzərv/
opponent *n* /əˈpoʊnənt/
originate *v* /əˈrɪdʒəneɪt/
password *n* /ˈpæswərd/
persuade *v* /pərˈsweɪd/
planet *n* /ˈplænət/
presenter *n* /prɛˈzɛntər/
process *n* /ˈprasɛs/
promotion *n* /prəˈmoʊʃn/

protest *v* /proʊtɛst/
put forward *v* /ˌpʊt ˈfɔrwərd/
railings *pl n* /ˈreɪlɪŋz/
rain down *v* /ˌreɪn ˈdaʊn/
rational *adj* /ˈræʃənl/
recommend *v* /rɛkəˈmɛnd/
recording studio *n* /rɪˈkɔrdɪŋ
  studioʊ/
remind *v* /rɪˈmaɪnd/
reputation *n* /rɛpyəˈteɪʃn/
reverse *v* /rɪˈvərs/
rhythm *n* /ˈrɪðəm/
right *n* /raɪt/
right-wing *adj* /ˌraɪtˈwɪŋ/
riot *n* /ˈraɪət/
rotate *v* /roʊteɪt/
sell-out *n* /ˈsɛl-aʊt/
sensational *adj* /sɛnˈseɪʃnl/
shake *v* /ʃeɪk/
significance *n* /sɪgˈnɪfəkəns/
simply *adv* /ˈsɪmpli/
slash *v* /slæʃ/
species *n* /ˈspiʃiz/
spill *v* /spɪl/
standstill *n* /ˈstændstɪl/
struggle *n* /ˈstrʌgl/
suffragette *n* /sʌfrəˈdʒɛt/
suffragist *n* /ˈsʌfrədʒɪst/
tactic *n* /ˈtæktɪk/
telescope *n* /ˈtɛləskoʊp/
theory *n* /ˈθiri/
threat *n* /θrɛt/
unaware *adj* /ʌnəˈwɛr/
undermine *v* /ˈʌndərmaɪn/
unverifiable *adj* /ʌnˈvɛrɪfaɪəbl/

Verb Patterns

Verbs + -ing

adore	
can't stand	
don't mind	doing
enjoy	swimming
finish	cooking
imagine	
loathe	

Note

We often use the verb *go* + *-ing* for sports and activities.

> I **go swimming** *every day.*
> I **go shopping** *on weekends.*

Verbs + preposition + -ing

give up	
look forward to	
succeed in	doing
think of	

Verbs + to + infinitive

afford	
agree	
choose	
dare	
decide	
expect	
forget	
help	
hope	
learn	
manage	to do
mean	to come
need	to cook
offer	
plan	
promise	
refuse	
seem	
want	
would hate	
would like	
would love	
would prefer	

Notes

1. *Help* and *dare* can be used without *to*.
   > We **helped clean up** *the kitchen.*
   > They didn't **dare disagree** *with him.*
2. *Have to* for obligation.
   > I **have to wear** *a uniform.*
3. *Used to* for past habits.
   > I **used to exercise**, *but I don't anymore.*

Verbs + sb + to + infinitive

advise		
allow		
ask		
beg		
encourage		
expect		
force		
help	me	to do
invite	him	to go
need	them	to come
order	someone	
persuade		
remind		
tell		
want		
warn		
would like		

Note

Help can be used without *to*.
> I **helped** *him* **do** *the dishes.*

Verbs + sb + infinitive (no to)

help		
let	her	do
make	us	

Notes

1. *To* is used with *make* in the passive.
   > We were **made to work** *hard.*
2. *Let* cannot be used in the passive. *Allowed to* is used instead.
   > She was **allowed to leave**.

Verbs + -ing or to + infinitive
(with little or no change in meaning)

begin	
continue	
hate	
like	doing
love	to do
prefer	
start	

Verbs + -ing or to + infinitive
(with a change in meaning)

remember	
stop	doing
try	to do

Notes

1. I **remember mailing** *the letter.*
   > (= I have a memory now of a past action: mailing the letter.)

   I **remembered to mail** *the letter.*
   > (= I reminded myself to mail the letter. I didn't forget.)
2. I **stopped drinking** *coffee.*
   > (= I gave up the habit.)

   I **stopped to drink** *a coffee.*
   > (= I stopped doing something else in order to have a cup of coffee.)
3. I **tried to sleep.**
   > (= I wanted to sleep, but it was difficult.)

   I **tried counting** *sheep and* **drinking** *a glass of warm milk.*
   > (= These were possible ways of getting to sleep.)

Irregular Verbs

Base form	Past Simple	Past participle
be	was/were	been
beat	beat	beaten
become	became	become
begin	began	begun
bend	bent	bent
bite	bit	bitten
blow	blew	blown
break	broke	broken
bring	brought	brought
build	built	built
buy	bought	bought
can	could	been able
catch	caught	caught
choose	chose	chosen
come	came	come
cost	cost	cost
cut	cut	cut
dig	dug	dug
do	did	done
draw	drew	drawn
dream	dreamed	dreamed
drink	drank	drunk
drive	drove	driven
eat	ate	eaten
fall	fell	fallen
feed	fed	fed
feel	felt	felt
fight	fought	fought
find	found	found
fit	fit	fit
fly	flew	flown
forget	forgot	forgotten
forgive	forgave	forgiven
freeze	froze	frozen
get	got	got
give	gave	given
go	went	been/gone
grow	grew	grown
hang	hanged/hung	hanged/hung
have	had	had
hear	heard	heard
hide	hid	hidden
hit	hit	hit
hold	held	held
hurt	hurt	hurt
keep	kept	kept
kneel	knelt	knelt
know	knew	known
lay	laid	laid
lead	led	led
learn	learned	learned

Base form	Past Simple	Past participle
leave	left	left
lend	lent	lent
let	let	let
lie	lay	lain
light	lighted/lit	lighted/lit
lose	lost	lost
make	made	made
mean	meant	meant
meet	met	met
must	had to	had to
pay	paid	paid
put	put	put
read /rid/	read /rɛd/	read /rɛd/
ride	rode	ridden
ring	rang	rung
rise	rose	risen
run	ran	run
say	said	said
see	saw	seen
sell	sold	sold
send	sent	sent
set	set	set
shake	shook	shaken
shine	shone	shone
shoot	shot	shot
show	showed	shown
shut	shut	shut
sing	sang	sung
sink	sank	sunk
sit	sat	sat
sleep	slept	slept
slide	slid	slid
speak	spoke	spoken
spend	spent	spent
spoil	spoiled	spoiled
spread	spread	spread
stand	stood	stood
steal	stole	stolen
stick	stuck	stuck
swim	swam	swum
take	took	taken
teach	taught	taught
tear	tore	torn
tell	told	told
think	thought	thought
throw	threw	thrown
understand	understood	understood
wake	woke	woken
wear	wore	worn
win	won	won
write	wrote	written

Phonetic Symbols

Consonants

1	/p/	as in	**pen**	/pɛn/
2	/b/	as in	**big**	/bɪg/
3	/t/	as in	**tea**	/ti/
4	/d/	as in	**do**	/du/
5	/k/	as in	**cat**	/kæt/
6	/g/	as in	**go**	/goʊ/
7	/f/	as in	**five**	/faɪv/
8	/v/	as in	**very**	/ˈvɛri/
9	/s/	as in	**son**	/sʌn/
10	/z/	as in	**zoo**	/zu/
11	/l/	as in	**live**	/lɪv/
12	/m/	as in	**my**	/maɪ/
13	/n/	as in	**near**	/nɪr/
14	/h/	as in	**happy**	/ˈhæpi/
15	/r/	as in	**red**	/rɛd/
16	/y/	as in	**yes**	/yɛs/
17	/w/	as in	**want**	/wɑnt/
18	/θ/	as in	**thanks**	/θæŋks/
19	/ð/	as in	**the**	/ðə/
20	/ʃ/	as in	**she**	/ʃi/
21	/ʒ/	as in	**television**	/ˈtɛləvɪʒn/
22	/tʃ/	as in	**child**	/tʃaɪld/
23	/dʒ/	as in	**Japan**	/dʒəˈpæn/
24	/ŋ/	as in	**English**	/ˈɪŋglɪʃ/

Vowels

25	/i/	as in	**see**	/si/
26	/ɪ/	as in	**his**	/hɪz/
27	/ɛ/	as in	**ten**	/tɛn/
28	/æ/	as in	**stamp**	/stæmp/
29	/ɑ/	as in	**father**	/ˈfɑðər/
30	/ɔ/	as in	**saw**	/sɔ/
31	/ɒ/	as in	**hot**	/hɒt/
32	/ʊ/	as in	**book**	/bʊk/
33	/u/	as in	**you**	/yu/
34	/ʌ/	as in	**sun**	/sʌn/
35	/ə/	as in	**about**	/əˈbaʊt/
36	/eɪ/	as in	**name**	/neɪm/
37	/aɪ/	as in	**my**	/maɪ/
38	/ɔɪ/	as in	**boy**	/bɔɪ/
39	/aʊ/	as in	**how**	/haʊ/
40	/oʊ/	as in	**go**	/goʊ/
41	/ər/	as in	**bird**	/bərd/
42	/ɪr/	as in	**near**	/nɪr/
43	/ɛr/	as in	**hair**	/hɛr/
44	/ar/	as in	**car**	/kar/
45	/ɔr/	as in	**more**	/mɔr/
46	/ʊr/	as in	**tour**	/tʊr/

OXFORD
UNIVERSITY PRESS

198 Madison Avenue
New York, NY 10016 USA

Great Clarendon Street, Oxford OX2 6DP UK

Oxford University Press is a department of the
University of Oxford. It furthers the University's
objective of excellence in research, scholarship,
and education by publishing worldwide in

Oxford New York

Auckland Cape Town Dar es Salaam
Hong Kong Karachi Kuala Lumpur Madrid
Melbourne Mexico City Nairobi New Delhi
Shanghai Taipei Toronto

With offices in

Argentina Austria Brazil Chile Czech Republic
France Greece Guatemala Hungary Italy Japan
Poland Portugal Singapore South Korea
Switzerland Thailand Turkey Ukraine Vietnam

OXFORD and OXFORD ENGLISH are registered
trade marks of Oxford University Press in the UK
and in certain other countries

© Oxford University Press 2009

The moral rights of the author have been asserted
Database right Oxford University Press (maker)

Editorial Director: Laura Pearson
Publishing Manager: Erik Gundersen
Managing Editor: Louisa van Houten
Development Editor: Tracey Gibbins
Design Director: Susan Sanguily
Design Manager: Maj-Britt Hagsted
Senior Designer: Michael Steinhofer
Production Artist: Elissa Santos
Image Editor: Robin Fadool
Design Production Manager: Stephen White
Manufacturing Coordinator: Eve Wong
Production Coordinator: Elizabeth Matsumoto

ISBN: 978-0-19-472983-3 STUDENT BOOK
WITH MULTI-ROM (PACK)

ISBN: 978-0-19-472984-0 STUDENT BOOK
(PACK COMPONENT)

ISBN: 978-0-19-472997-0 MULTI-ROM
(PACK COMPONENT)

Printed in China

10 9 8 7 6 5

This book is printed on paper from certified and well-
managed sources.

ACKNOWLEDGEMENTS

*The authors and publisher are grateful to those who have given permission
to reproduce the following extracts and adaptations of copyright materials:*

p10 'Welcome to Our World: The Qus: Beijing, China'; *The Guardian*,
21st October 2006. Copyright Guardian News and Media Ltd 2006;
p11 'Welcome to Our World: The Kamaus Ongata Rongai, Kenya';
The Guardian, 21st October 2006. Reproduced by kind permission of
Xan Rice; p12 'A world in one family': interviews reproduced with
kind permission of Ana Reynoso and family; pp19–20 Adapted
extracts from 'The Best of Times'; *Majesty Magazine*, November 2006.
Reproduced by kind permission of Majesty Magazine; p24 'Smash!
Museum visitor trips on lace and destroys priceless vases'; *The

Daily Telegraph*, 30th January 2006. Copyright The Telegraph Media
Group Ltd; pp26–7 Extracts from 'Romeo and Juliet', Oxford World
Classics; © Oxford University Press 2000; pp33 and 150 'I Believe'
Words and Music by Ian Dury and Michael Gallagher © Templemill
Music and Mute Song. All rights on behalf of Templemill Music
administered by Warner/Chappell Music Ltd, London W6 8BS.
Reproduced by permission; p35 'You don't know you are born',
The Sunday Times, 11th February 2007 © NI Syndication, London
(2007) p41 'Rocket Man, Steve Bennett'; BBC-Saturday Live,
10/03/2007. © BBC Radio. Reproduced with kind permission of
Steve Bennett, Starchaser Plc and BBC Radio. pp42–3 'Year 2025:
We'll find aliens, talk to animals and be sprightly at 100'; from *Daily
Mail*, 16/11/2006 © Daily Mail 2006; pp58–9 'How a book of rules
gave the world the beautiful game'; *Sunday Times*, 19/03/02006.
© NI Syndication, London (2007); p65 'Don't panic, Its only a Fish'
by Lucy Elkins, *Daily Mail*, 17/04/2007. © Daily Mail 2007; pp74–5
'I am sorry: How a burglar and his victim became best of friends',
Daily Mirror, 19/03/2007. © Daily Mirror 2007.

*Although every effort has been made to trace and contact copyright holders
before publication, this has not been possible in some cases. We apologize for
any apparent infringement of copyright and if notified, the publisher will be
pleased to rectify any errors or omissions at the earliest opportunity.*

Illustrations by: Tim Branch: p. 24 (yin yang); Gill Button: pp. 21,
32, 40, 58, 72, 76, 88, 97; Mark Duffin: p. 82 (all optical illusions
except duck-rabbit, elephant re-drawn after Roger N. Shepard, the
Ray Lyman Wilbur Professor Emeritus of Social Science, Stanford
University, California); Melvyn Evans: p. 37 (rocket); Leo Hartas:
pp. 101, 106, 107, 146-147; Detmeer Otto: pp. 2, 3, 57; Gavin
Reece: pp. 12, 22-23, 104, 144; Keith Robinson: pp. 86, 87; Martin
Saunders: p. 62; Jason Stavron: p. 61; Lorna Aps Woodland:
pp. 66-67.

Commissioned photography by: Gareth Boden: pp. 5, 10 (Jenny & Mike),
60, 99, 103, 113, 143 (waiter); Paul Freestone: p. 8 (Ana Reynoso and
family); Mark Mason: pp. 81, 147.

*We would also like to thank the following for permission to reproduce the
following photographs:* Alamy Images: p. 5 (dog/Jeremy Pardoe); p. 5
(saxophone/i love images); p. 9 (Jupiterimages/Creatas); p. 10 (Vicky/
Travelshots.com); p. 16 (cooking/A Room with Views); p. 16 (gym/
Buzz Pictures); p. 16 (tennis/moodboard); p. 16 (music/the box
studio); p. 16 (cycling/Ingram Publishing/Superstock Limited); p. 34
(rainforest/Ern Mainka); p. 37 (Space Shuttle Discovery/KPA/Galaxy/
Content Mine International); p. 44 (Mamma Mia jar/Martin Lee/
Mediablitzimages (UK) Ltd); p. 45 (Devon cottage/Elizabeth Whiting
& Associates); p. 48 (watch/Synthetic Alan King); p. 49 (shoppers/Ian
Dagnall); p. 61 (Jodie/Dynamic Graphics/Jupiterimages/Creatas);
p. 61 (Melissa/Leland Bobbe/Photodisc); p. 65 (football ticket/Nick
Cobbing); p. 86 (skyline/Tim Gaine); Lorna Aps Woodland: p. 67
(Billy small photo); Steve Baxter: p. 20 (fallen visitor); Pearl Bevan:
p. 80 (sunglasses); Mahesh Bhat: p. 47 (Lakshmamma); Chris Boon:
p. 54 (modern football and boots); p. 90 (Nissan); The Bridgeman
Art Library: p. 18 (Vincent van Gogh, Self Portrait, 1889, Private
Collection); p. 18 (Vincent van Gogh, Irises, 1889, Private
Collection); p. 18 (Vincent van Gogh, Red Vineyards at Arles, 1888,
Pushkin Museum, Moscow); p. 19 (Vincent van Gogh, Sunflowers,
1888. Neue Pinakothek, Munich, Germany); p. 50 (David Nolan,
The Princess Elizabeth Storms North in All Weathers, Private
Collection); p. 62 Chinese School (20th c.), Revolutionary Ideal is
Supreme: The Long March of 1935, Private Collection, Archives
Charmet); p. 94 (Justus Sustermans (1597–1681); Portrait of Galileo
Galilei, Galleria Palatina, Palazzo Pitti, Florence; Camera Press:
p. 14 (H.R.H. Prince Charles/Photography by Ian Jones/Gamma);
p. 15 (H.R.H. Prince Charles and H.R.H. Camilla, Duchess of
Cornwall/Richard Gillard); Casio Electronics Company Limited:
p. 30 (Casio EXLIM Zoom EX-Z9 digital compact camera); Christie's
Images: p. 59 (old football boots and football); Corbis: p. 9
(canoeing/David Madison); p. 39 (polar bears/epa); p. 37 (Jules Verne
rocket, From the Earth to the Moon, 1872/Bettmann); p. 45 (father
and son/Alexander Scott/zefa); p. 51 (Jack/Andrew Fox); p. 52 (Calvin
Klein/Jesse Frohman); p. 52 (shop front/James Leynse); p. 55 (World
Cup/John Van Hasselt); p. 62 (Mao/Swim Ink); p. 73 (credit card/LWA-
Dann Tardif); p. 77 (Tom/Little Blue Wolf Productions); p. 94 (Freud/
Bettmann); p. 102 (Mother Teresa smiling/Reuters); p. 102 (Mother
Teresa serious/JP Laffont/Sygma); Creative Technology Ltd: p. 30
(Creative Zen Vision MP3 Player); Stephen Daniels/www.danpics.
com: p. 90 (Jack Neal); Dorling Kindersley: p. 45 (Teddy bear);
Reproduction by permission of the Syndics of the Fitzwilliam
Museum, Cambridge: p. 20 (Chinese porcelain vases c. 1680–1720);
Getty Images: p. 14 (Dave/Peter Dazeley/The Image Bank); p. 15
(Sean Davey); p. 18 (The Royal Family on the balcony /Daniel
Berehulak); p. 15 (Prince Charles with Princes William and Harry/
Tim Graham Photo Library); p. 16 (LWA/Photodisc); p. 25 (John
Cumming/Iconica); p. 26 (questions/Jed Share/Photographer's
Choice); p. 29 (Millie/Photographer's Choice); p. 29 (Frank/Marc
Romanelli/Photographer's Choice); p. 39 (galaxy/Ian Mckinnell/
Photographer's Choice); p. 46 (tarts/Heidi Coppock-Beard/Stone);
p. 47 (Elizabeth Anne Hogan/Stephanie Diani); p. 48 (Grant Faint/
The Image Bank); p. 49 (coffee/Sergio Pitamitz/Iconica); p. 49
(escalator with couple/Justin Pumfrey/Iconica); p. 54 (Nicho
Sodling); p. 54 (woodcut mob football 1721/Rischgitz/Hulton
Archive); p. 56 (Julia/Ron Krisel/The Image Bank); p. 56 (James/
Stock4B); p. 56 (Paul/David Lees); p. 57 (couple/Paul Thomas/Taxi);
p. 58 (globe/George Diebold/Stone); p. 59 (group in Amazon/
Ghislain & Marie David de Lossy/Riser); p. 63 (elephant crossing
river/Hulton Archive); p. 68 (Hulton Archive); p. 69 (Taxi); p. 73

(bank/Christopher Bissell/Stone); p. 77 (Daisy/Jerome Tisne); p. 96
(Jamie Seabrook/Paul Bradbury); p. 97 (T-shirts/Roger Wright/
Stone); Robert Harding World Imagery: p. 108 (running/Regine
Mahaux); p. 111 (cityscape/Siegfried Layda/Photographer's Choice);
p. 111 (Panoramic Images); p. 143 (introducing/Somos/Veer); p. 143
(hotel room/Johannes Kroemer); p. 143 (dinner party); Huw Evans/
www.huwevansimages.com: p. 91 (man throws away money);
Courtesy of Gibson Guitars: p. 45 (ES335 guitar); Grazia Neri: p. 47
(Santina Corvaglia/Franco Origlia); p. 102 (young Mother Teresa /
Giovanbattista Brambilla); iStockphoto: p. 5 (paperclip and page/
Christoph Weihs); p. 5 (laptop/muharrem öner) p. 9, 16 (painting/
Thye Aun Ngo); p. 16 (gardening/Alex Hinds); p. 16 (photography/
blackred); p. 26 (mannequin and question/Palto); p. 27 (two
mannequins/emmgunn); p. 27 (sign post/Vasiliy Yakobchuk); p. 28
(paper/Clayton Hansen); p. 28 (lined paper/Bruce Lonngren); p. 47
(camera/fajean); p. 47 (laptop/shapechanger); p. 48 (Kos boat/Alfred
Rijnders); p. 48 (newspaper ad/Bruce Lonngren); p. 44 (Mamma Mia
illustration); p. 45 (pills/Bill Fehr); p. 46 (tablecloth); p. 51 (bats/
Govinda Trazo); p. 51 (wand/Mihail Glushkov); p. 54 (football
knocked back/Ron Sumners); p. 58 (email icon/Can Gürbüz); p. 58
(mountain/Brandon Laufenberg); p. 65 (20:25/Nikada); p. 72 (Taipei/
tcp); p. 77 (computer/Emrah Turudu); p. 80 (handcuffs/Ivan Mateev)
p. 86 (paper/Gaffera); p. 94 (compass/Olga Samoylova); p. 96 (paper/
christine balderas); p. 96 (paper/Trevor Hunt); p. 96 (paper/
Christopher Hudson); p. 110 (Statue of Liberty/Kjell Brynildsen);
p. 110 (taxi/Markanja); p. 145 (Palto); p. 145 (emmgunn); Joseph
Jastrow, Fact and Fable in Psychology, 1901: p. 295, p. 82 (duck-
rabbit); Dave King: p. 31 (The Gregory family); MTV Networks UK &
Ireland: p. 30 (robot I Sobot Robot); Mary Evans Picture Library:
p. 62 (Hannibal); p. 94 (Pankhurst/The Women's Library);
Masterfile: p. 41 (Pierre Tremblay); Ben McMillan: p. 7 (The Qus
family); Mirrorpix: p. 71 (John Ferguson); Courtesy of Molecular
Expressions/Michael W. Davidson, National High Magnetic Field
Laboratory/http://microscopy.fsu.edu: p. 74 (smurf/Photo Karl E.
Deckart); National Motor Museum: p. 31 (camper van); Nixon: p. 30
(Nixon bag); PA Photos: p. 37 (Steve Bennett/Owen Humphreys/PA
Archive); p. 55 (Cristiano Ronaldo/Joe Giddens/Empics Sport); Panos
Pictures: p. 6 (The Kamaus family/Sven Torfin); p. 55 (boys playing/
Chris Stowers); Philips: p. 30 (Philips widescreen TV); p. 30 (Philips
DC200 IPOD dock); Punchstock: p. 7 (map/BLOOMimage); p. 10
(Terry/image100); p. 13 (Stockbyte); p. 16 (camping/Radius Images);
p. 17 (Stockbyte); p. 29 (Richard/Anthony-Masterson/Digital Vision);
p. 34 (BLOOMimage); p. 34 (gorilla/Gerry Ellis/Digital Vision); p. 34
(ice and snow/Eastcott Momatiuk/Digital Vision); p. 39 (running/
Colin Anderson/Blend Images); p. 39 (Chad Baker/Digital Vision);
p. 56 (Andrew/Image Source Pink); p. 56 (Harriet/Noel Hendrickson,
Digital Vision); p. 61 (Gavin/Image Source Pink); p. 73 (hotel/Digital
Vision); p. 74 (microchip/PhotoAlto Agency/Laurent Hamels); p. 77
(Monica/Glow Images); p. 77 (Justin/Photodisc); p. 77 (David/Digital
Vision/Andrew Olney); p. 84 (John Lund/Digital Vision); p. 84
(Rachel/IS307/Image Source Pink); p. 105 (Stockbyte); p. Rex
Features: . p 29 (Ian Dury/Brian Rasic); p. 51 (three fans reading/
James Fraser); p. 94 (Peasey/SNAP); p. 146 (Ian Dury/Brian Rasic);
Anna Rianne: p. 32 (sign); p. 40 (NOAA); p. 41 (Apollo 11/NASA);
p. 68 (Gustoimages); Science & Society Picture Library p 75
(Babbage computer/Science Museum); Seiko Europe Limited: p. 30
(Orange Monster Watch); Sony Computer Entertainment Europe:
p. 30 (Playstation 3); Sony Ericsson UK & Ireland: p. 30 (Sony
Ericsson W910i mobile phone); Sony UK Limited: p. 30 (Sony Vaio
notebook computer); Tomy Corporation: p. 30 (Rock Band Guitar
(based on a Fender Stratocaster used for Rock Band computer game
published by MTV Games WeSC – WeAretheSuperlativeConspiracy
p. 30 (headphones); www.all-the-flags-of-the-world.c.la: p. 8
(Bolivia); (Union Jack); (Basque); BAA Aviation Photolibrary, www.
baa.com/photolibrary: p. 143 (airport information); Tetra Images /
Alamy: p. 5 (Photographer's Choice/Getty Images: Murat Taner: p. 5
(Empire State Building); Graphi-Ogre/oup: p. 8 (Peruvian and
American flags); Goodshoot/Jupiterimages/AGE Fotostock: p. 10
(waiter); Stockbyte/Alamy: George Doyle p. 10 (policeman);
Photodisc/OUP: pp. 13, 143 (money); Asia Pac/Getty Images: Pool
p. 15 (Prince Charles in Asia); Fancy Collection/Superstock: p. 16
(shopping); Radius/Superstock: p. 17 (Chicago); Brand X Pictures/
Jupiter Images: Jack Hollingsworth p24 (woman); Jupiter Images:
Jose Luis Pelaez Inc.: p. 24 (boy); Masterfile: Kevin Dodge: p. 24
(man); Jupiter Images/ Brand X / Alamy: p. 28; Creatas Images/AGE
Fotostock: p. 34 (man and woman reading a newspaper); Alamy:
Frantisek Staud: p. 34 (indegenous people); Reuters: Manuel
Silvestri: p. 34 (Venice piazza flooded); Photographer's Choice/Getty
Images: Georgette Douwma: p. 34 (underwater life); mauritius
images/AGE Fotostock: Peter von Felber: p. 42; Associated Press: Bill
Haber: p. 50; AFP/Getty Images: Vanderlei Almeida: p. 55 (Brazilian
soccer fans); Pano Pictures: p. 55 (boys playing soccer); Radius
Images/Alamy: p. 58 (girl with a bandage); Stockbyte/Getty Images:
p. 58 (hanging out); Photo Edit Inc.: Jeff Greenberg p. 65 (bus sign);
Alamy: Ted Pink p. 65 (gas pump numbers); AGE Fotostock: Ana
Abadía: p. 65 (bananas); Alamy: p. 73 (woman receives a check);
Fancy/Corbis: Beau Lark p. 73 (order coffee); Alamy/Getty
Images: Insy Shah p. 79 (Burj Al Arab); The Image Bank/Getty
Images: John Lamb p. 78 (Burj Dubai); Daryl Visscher: p. 78 (Dubai
nightlife); The Image Bank/Getty Images: Preston Schlebusch: p. 79
(Dubai man made islands); Alamy: Ludger Vorfeld: p. 78 (map of
Dubai); diffused/AGE Fotostock: p. 84 (woman on phone); Hulton
Archive/Getty Images/Rischgitz: p. 94; AGE Fotostock/johnny
Stockshooter: p. 99 (Philadelphia Museum of Art); Corbis: LWA-
Sharie Kennedy p. 109 (boy with books).